Work and Welfare in Europe

Series Editors: **Denis Bouget**, University of Nantes, France, **Jochen Clasen**, University of Edinburgh, UK, **Ana Guillén Rodriguez**, University of Oviedo, Spain, **Jane Lewis**, London School of Economics and Political Science, UK and **Bruno Palier**, Sciences-Po Paris, France

Titles include:

Simone Baglioni and Marco Giugni
CIVIL SOCIETY ORGANIZATIONS, UNEMPLOYMENT, AND PRECARITY IN EUROPE
Between Service and Policy

Sigrid Betzelt and Silke Bothfeld
ACTIVATION AND LABOUR MARKET REFORMS IN EUROPE
Challenges to Social Citizenship

Sonja Drobnic and Ana Guillén Rodriguez
WORK-LIFE BALANCE IN EUROPE
The Role of Job Quality

Colette Fagan, Maria Gonzalez Menendez and Silvia Gomez Anson
WOMEN IN MANAGEMENT
European Employment Policy

Neil Fraser, Rodolfo Gutierrez and Ramon Pena-Casas
WORKING POVERTY IN EUROPE

Paolo Graziano, Sophie Jacquot and Bruno Palier
THE EU AND THE DOMESTIC POLITICS OF WELFARE STATE REFORMS
Europa, Europae

Karl Hinrichs and Matteo Jessoula
LABOUR MARKET FLEXIBILITY AND PENSION REFORMS
Flexible Today, Secure Tomorrow?

Trudie Knijn
WORK, FAMILY POLICIES AND TRANSITIONS TO ADULTHOOD IN EUROPE

Max Koch and Martin Fritz
NON-STANDARD EMPLOYMENT IN EUROPE
Paradigms, Prevalence and Policy Responses

Colin Lindsay and Donald Houston
DISABILITY BENEFITS, WELFARE REFORM AND EMPLOYMENT POLICY

Ive Marx and Kenneth Nelson
MINIMUM INCOME PROTECTION IN FLUX

Livia Sz. Oláh and Ewa Fratczak
CHILDBEARING, WOMEN'S EMPLOYMENT AND WORK-LIFE BALANCE POLICIES IN CONTEMPORARY EUROPE

Emmanuele Pavolini and Ana M. Guillén
HEALTH CARE SYSTEMS IN EUROPE UNDER AUSTERITY
Institutional Reforms and Performance

Birgit Pfau-Effinger and Tine Rostgaard
CARE BETWEEN WORK AND WELFARE IN EUROPEAN SOCIETIES

Martin Schröder
INTEGRATING VARIETIES OF CAPITALISM AND WELFARE STATE RESEARCH
A Unified Typology of Capitalisms

Costanzo Ranci, Taco Brandsen and Stefania Sabatinelli
SOCIAL VULNERABILITY IN EUROPEAN CITIES
The Role of Local Welfare in Times of Crisis

Rik van Berkel, Willibrord de Graaf and Tomáš Sirovátka
THE GOVERNANCE OF ACTIVE WELFARE STATES IN EUROPE

Work and Welfare in Europe
Series Standing Order ISBN 978–0–230–28026–7
(*outside North America only*)

You can receive future titles in this series as they are published by placing a standing order. Please contact your bookseller or, in case of difficulty, write to us at the address below with your name and address, the title of the series and the ISBN quoted above.

Customer Services Department, Macmillan Distribution Ltd, Houndmills, Basingstoke, Hampshire RG21 6XS, England

---

Civil Society Organizations, Unemployment, and Precarity in Europe

Between Service and Policy

Edited by

Simone Baglioni
Glasgow Caledonian University, UK

and

Marco Giugni
University of Geneva, Switzerland

First published 2014 by
PALGRAVE MACMILLAN

Palgrave Macmillan in the UK is an imprint of Macmillan Publishers Limited,
registered in England, company number 785998, of Houndmills, Basingstoke,
Hampshire RG21 6XS.

Palgrave Macmillan in the US is a division of St Martin's Press LLC,
175 Fifth Avenue, New York, NY 10010.

Palgrave Macmillan is the global academic imprint of the above companies
and has companies and representatives throughout the world.

Palgrave® and Macmillan® are registered trademarks in the United States,
the United Kingdom, Europe and other countries.

ISBN 978–0–230–39142–0

This book is printed on paper suitable for recycling and made from fully
managed and sustained forest sources. Logging, pulping and manufacturing
processes are expected to conform to the environmental regulations of the
country of origin.

A catalogue record for this book is available from the British Library.

A catalog record for this book is available from the Library of Congress.

Typeset by MPS limited, Chennai, India.

Contents

v

List of Figures and Tables

Figures

Tables

Acknowledgments

Results presented in this book have been obtained within the project "Youth, Unemployment, and Exclusion in Europe: A Multidimensional Approach to Understanding the Conditions and Prospects for Social and Political Integration of Young Unemployed" (YOUNEX). This project was funded by the European Commission under the 7th Framework Programme (grant agreement no. 216122). The YOUNEX consortium was coordinated by the University of Geneva (Marco Giugni), and was formed, additionally, by the University of Siegen (Christian Lahusen), the Bocconi University (Simone Baglioni), the CEVIPOF-Sciences Po Paris (Manlio Cinalli), the University of Karlstad (Birgitta Eriksson), and the Polish Sociological Society (Slawomir Nowotny). Results on Portugal have been obtained independently from the YOUNEX project by the Technical University of Lisbon (Maria Vitória Mourão). We thank all the members of the YOUNEX research consortium for their contributions to the project. In addition to the authors who contributed to this volume, a number of other people have participated in the project: Tuula Bergqvist, Piotr Binder, Didier Chabanet, Christopher Fay, Amanda Gavilanes, Paolo Graziano, Jerzy Hołub, Eva-Maria Kolb, Lara Monticelli, Anne Muxel, Natalia Schulz, Karolina Sztandar-Sztanderska, and Lara Tavares.

Notes on Contributors

Ewa Bacia is a project expert and researcher at the Educational Research Institute in Warsaw. A graduate of the University of Warsaw Institute of Applied Social Sciences and Social Policy Institute, she obtained her PhD in political and social studies from the Freie Universität in Berlin, with a study on the impact of social capital on the perception of democracy in Podlasie and Brandenburg.

Simone Baglioni is Reader in Politics at Glasgow Caledonian University, Scotland. His research interests focus on unemployment and civil society issues. He has worked across several EU-funded research including YOUNEX. His new projects investigate youth employment policies (Skills and Labour Markets to Raise Youth Employment – SALM, EU DG Education and Culture funding 2013–2015), and social enterprises and social innovation (EFESEISS project, EU FP7 programme 2013–2016).

Matteo Bassoli is Research Fellow at Bocconi University. As a member of the Department of Policy Analysis and Public Management, he undertakes research on the functioning of private–public partnerships and their network structure, as well as on the social inclusion and political participation of deprived people. On these topics he has published extensively in international journals, edited books, and books.

Manlio Cinalli is Research Professor at Sciences Po (CEVIPOF), CNRS. His research focuses on comparative political behavior, the politics of ethnic relations and integration, networks, and multi-level public policies. He has published numerous articles in scholarly journals and volumes and is currently research director of the French project for LIVEWHAT (EU FP 7 programme).

Birgitta Eriksson is Professor of Working Life Science at Karlstad University, Sweden. Her main research fields are people's attitude to work, the organization of work, and its impact on the employees' working conditions, and unemployment. She is the co-author of *Flexible Organizations and the New Working Life. A European Perspective* (2009), *Contingent Work in the UK and Sweden – Evidence from the Construction Industry* (2010), *Commitment to Work and Job Satisfaction: Studies of Work Orientation* (2012), *and Flexibility in Practice* (2013).

Marco Giugni is Professor at the Department of Political Science and International Relations and Director of the Institute of Citizenship Studies (InCite) at the University of Geneva, Switzerland. His research interests include social movements and collective action, immigration and ethnic relations, unemployment and social exclusion.

Bettina Grimmer is a research assistant in Sociology at Siegen University, Germany. Her research interests include political sociology, social policy, unemployment, and civil society. During her doctoral studies she was a researcher on the YOUNEX project.

Jennifer Hobbins is a PhD student in Working Life Sciences whose dissertation focuses on unemployment in a comparative European perspective. Her research interests include social policy, social structures, governance, citizenship, and political participation. She is currently working at the Swedish National Defense College as a lecturer.

Christian Lahusen is Professor of Sociology at Siegen University, Germany. His research interests include political sociology and social movement analysis, social inequalities, unemployment, and the sociology of Europe and European integration.

Jasmine Lorenzini obtained her PhD in political science from the University of Geneva in 2013. She works on youth unemployment and citizenship with a focus on youth participation in social and political life. She is also interested in the effects of unemployment on personal well-being and life satisfaction. During her doctoral studies she worked on the YOUNEX project.

Lorenzo Mosca teaches Sociology of Media & Communication and Sociology of New Media at the University of Roma Tre. He has taught at the American universities in Florence and Parma. His research interests focus on political participation, social movements, political communication, and online politics. On these topics he has published extensively in international journals, edited books, and books.

Luís Mota is a PhD fellow in Public Administration at the School of Social and Political Sciences, University of Lisbon, and a junior researcher at CAPP (Centre for Public Administration and Public Policy). His research interests focus on Policy Implementation, Network Public Governance, Public Sector Reform, and New Models of Welfare Provision. For the past few years, he has participated in a number of national and international projects (e.g., YOUNEX, ANED or COCOPS).

Maria Vitória Mourão is an assistant professor at the University of Lisbon and an integrated researcher at CAPP (Centre for Public Administration and Public Policy). She holds a PhD in Sociology; her thesis was titled "Symbolic Images and Drug Use among Higher Education Students in Portugal." Her research interests are related to health policy, social epidemiology, social policy, and research methods. Since 2009, she has been coordinating a research project under the topic "Health, Risk and Governmentalization."

Maria Theiss is an assistant professor and vice director of the Institute of Social Policy, Warsaw University. Her research focuses on the issues of social citizenship, social capital, civil society, and the local level of social policy. She has authored and edited books on issues of poverty, social exclusion, and governance processes at the local level in Poland.

Civil Society, Unemployment and Precarity in Europe: An Introduction

Simone Baglioni and Marco Giugni

Context of the study

Youth unemployment has become an increasingly salient concern of both policy-makers and societies across Europe. From 2008 onwards, the financial and economic crisis has exacerbated what was already a chronic situation: In December 2012 the youth unemployment rate in the EU-27 rose above 23% with countries such as Spain and Greece at a frightening peak of having one in every two young people unemployed. If we translate such percentages into numbers, we see that 5.5 million young Europeans were unemployed in 2012, a number which increases to 7.5 million if we include those who were not in employment, education, or training, the so-called NEET category (European commission 2013).

However, for young people, work has not only become more difficult to find compared with previous generations, it has also changed: while their parents had been socialized into a life-long position with a single employer, regulated through a standard open-ended contract guaranteeing social benefits and a pension, for current generations of young people, once they find a job, this is likely to be one of a series. Furthermore, such a series of jobs are likely to be non-standard (fixed terms contracts, part-time, job sharing, etc.), sometimes poorly paid and with limited social security and pension contributions. In 2012, according to EU data (European Commission 2013) 42% of young people worked on a fixed-term contract while 32% were on part-time employment (part-time work that was driven by necessity due to the lack of better opportunities rather than the result of a free choice). Such a change in the structure of employment implies that career paths have become fragmented and that young people often find themselves unemployed between one job and another.

1

Thus, high youth unemployment rates and a significant degree of instability in employment paths (an instability which generates "precarious" workers, i.e., workers employed with non-standard forms of employment and with a high risk of unemployment recidivism) have become key characteristics of the post-Fordist industrial and economic organization of European societies.

To counter such a widespread and long-term phenomenon, public action alone has appeared to be ineffective; therefore, various nongovernmental actors, primarily civil society organizations (CSOs), have intervened, with a range of tools, to increase young people's employability through learning and training but also to protect these unemployed and precariously employed young people from destitution and, more generally, from social exclusion. CSOs have become key policy-implementers, especially in employment policies inspired by activation measures (Defourny and Nyssens 2010), or, in the classic "advocacy" tradition of civil society, CSOs have been vocal actors in calling for different policies and for the respect of specific social and economic rights (Baglioni 2010). In its dual role of service or advocacy provider (a binomial feature of civil society that we emphasize in the book by speaking of service versus policy-oriented organizations), civil society has generated a range of opportunities for unemployed and precariously employed young people to improve their employability potential but also to strengthen their social embeddedness or what is more commonly known as social capital, that is, the acquisition of a civic consciousness nurtured by networks and ties of mutual support and trust (Coleman 1988; Putnam 1993).

This book offers the opportunity to map and understand the functioning mechanisms, organizational features, and networks of civil society actors engaged across seven European cities in the vibrant policy field of unemployment and employment precarity. As we reveal throughout the chapters, the organizational field we focus upon is one which is very diversified and includes organizations with different resources, goals, functioning mechanisms, and outputs. In this sense, we work within the large boundaries of a "multi-organizational field." Furthermore, our organizational field, as with many others, is not only delimited by civil society features and actions per se, but occurs within a *specific* political-institutional context (in our case, seven different political institutional contexts: Cologne/Germany, Geneva/Switzerland, Karlstad/Sweden, Kielce/Poland, Lisbon/Portugal, Lyon/France, and Turin/Italy). We believe, that the understanding of civil society, its actions and networks, is stronger if CSOs are not conceived of as being in opposition to the state, politics, and policy as classical, Tocquevillean conceptualizations of civil society would suggest, but rather as phenomena intertwined with the features of the state and politics (Warren 2001; Skocpol, Ganz and Munson 2000). As such, CSOs should always be studied against the specific features of their political-institutional contexts.

Consequently, this book discusses the variety of organizational features and actions we have found across different local and national contexts. Our contexts share patterns of youth (un)employment: The countries of which they are part of are all characterized by unemployment rates that are higher for young people (aged 16–34) than for mature citizens, whereas the occupational rate follows an opposite path: lower for young people and higher for adults or senior citizens (apart from Germany where the gap between younger and senior citizens in employment opportunities has been smaller than elsewhere, which is evidence perhaps of the well-functioning mechanisms that exist to support the transition from school/education to work) (Mingione and Pugliese 2010).

However, the countries and cities utilized in our research also present a variety of youth (un)employment regimes: While Karlstad (Sweden) and Lyon (France) represent similar versions of the so-called flexicurity model (a mixture of flexibility and security in employment allowing young people to develop a "flexible" career without being deprived of social protection), Lisbon (Portugal), Turin (Italy), and Kielce (Poland) combine a strict employment regulation system with a subprotective social security system, with Cologne (Germany) and Geneva (Switzerland) falling in between (Cinalli and Giugni 2013).

While the civil society literature has widely investigated CSOs' features, actions, and networks, an in-depth analysis of civil society organizations active in the field of unemployment and precarity has not yet been offered. This has been possible thanks to the European Union 7th Framework program which has funded the project entitled "Youth, Unemployment and Exclusion in Europe: A Multidimensional Approach to Understanding the Conditions and Prospects for Social and Political Integration of Young Unemployed" (YOUNEX). The project has for three years investigated the policies and practices of (youth) unemployment at three levels: local (in the seven cities mentioned earlier), national (in France, Germany, Italy, Poland, Portugal, Sweden, and Switzerland) and European. Furthermore YOUNEX has also studied young people's perceptions about their jobless or precarious employment status by means of both a survey and in-depth interviews. Finally, stake holders (policy-makers, social partners, and young people) have

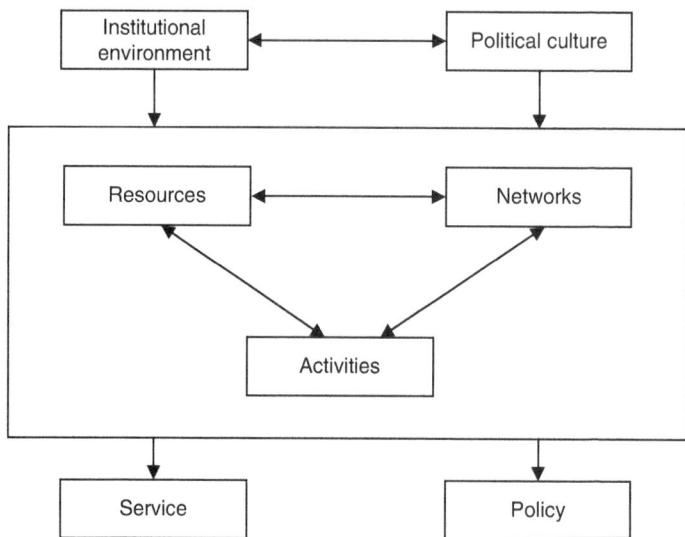

Figure I.1   YOUNEX study of CSOs: an overview

been brought together via discussion groups to express their views and experiences on the matter. Overall the project has analyzed the existing relationship between a problematic employment status and the degree of young people's socio-economic and political inclusion in their respective societies, which differ in terms of constraints and opportunities. As we discuss in this book, YOUNEX has also scrutinized how civil society organizations intervene in the specific policy field of unemployment and precarity (Figure I.1 summarizes our research design for studying civil society organizations in the policy field of unemployment and precarity).

How we have mapped and studied organizations

Following the methodology used by previous research on local organizations (Kriesi and Baglioni 2003; Baglioni 2004; Baglioni et al. 2007; Font et al. 2007), a two-step approach was adopted in the general design of the study. Firstly, in each city we compiled an inventory of all associations active in the field of unemployment, youth unemployment, and related welfare sectors. Secondly, we carried out face-to-face interviews based on a common questionnaire with those associations that agreed to participate.

To be included in our inventory, organizations needed: (1) to not be part of a public agency and not be a branch of the local government (although we included organizations receiving grants and other types of support from public governing bodies provided that their official (legal) status was the one of a civil society actor); (2) to not be profit-oriented or have business as their core activity (however, in some countries, such as Sweden, for-profit organizations play a crucial role in addressing unemployment issues at a local level, hence the Swedish team's decision to include for profit organizations in their survey); and (3) to be visible, that is, having a name and being active and recognized by different sources as active during the period of the research.

We have included both formal and informal organizations because the range of organizations active in our field is highly diversified. Besides formalized and institutionalized organizations such as trade unions or religious organizations, there are also rather small and unorganized groups that play or could play a significant role. In fact, part of the literature on civil society organizations stresses that informal organizations are more adequate settings for people to do things collectively than formal ones (Bang and Soerensen 2001; Torpe and Ferrer-Fons 2007). Restricting our research to fully formalized groups therefore would have resulted in losing important social actors. As a consequence, the absence of a formal statute, of a formal headquarters, and of formalized procedures for decision-making was not considered as a criterion for exclusion. This decision was inspired also by the path-breaking research of Salamon et al. (2003: 7–8) which focused on organizations that "have some structure and regularity to their operations, whether or not they are formally constituted or legally registered. This means that our definition embraces informal, i.e., nonregistered, groups as well as formally registered ones. What is important is not whether the group is legally or formally recognized but that it has some organizational permanence and regularity as reflected in regular meetings, a membership, and some structure of procedures for making decisions that participants recognize as legitimate." In sum, we included organizations existing *de facto* even if they were not formally recognized or legally registered, that is, organizations and groups arranging or taking part in meetings, rallies, marches, etc., or those publishing and disseminating leaflets and similar documents offline and online.

The mapping was carried out using different sources: (1) interviews with key informants (academics, grassroots activists, and local civil servants); (2) document analysis of local authorities and umbrella organizations leaflets, newsletters, and similar information tools;

and (3) detailed searches of official organizations directories, of local governmental offices and of websites. The mapping phase allowed us to identify in each city the associations active in our field. However, we are aware that we cannot claim of having found all associations working on unemployment, youth unemployment, and related welfare domains. We do believe, still, that the organizations we interviewed provide a quite exhaustive picture of the organizational ecology of unemployment in our cities.

At the end of this process, mapped organizations ranged from 13 (Karlstad) to 50 (Turin) (Table I.1 gives an overview of the different organizational universes and the number of interviewed organizations). The relatively large discrepancy between mapped organizations (universe) and interviewed organizations (sample) of some of our cases, like Cologne, Geneva, and Turin, is due to a mixture of reasons including organizations not existing anymore, organizations having refused because of a lack of time available for their personnel to participate or because of "research fatigue" (often reported in Cologne where several social scientists have explored local civil society during previous research, leaving a legacy of "fatigue" among civil society activists; see Grimmer and Lahusen 2009) but also, among the more radical organizations/movements, because of "lack of trust" in the overall aims of the research. Thus, although our research was comprehensively welcomed among organizations in all cities and perceived to be a useful tool to increase knowledge, networking and eventually gain visibility at subsequent research dissemination events, we did meet also with more skeptical interlocutors who preferred to not open their organizations' doors to us.

The organizational universes of our cities differ not only in terms of numbers but also in their degree of heterogeneity. According to our sample criteria and definition, the organizational study could include civil society organizations *stricto sensu* that is volunteering-based organizations outside the direct influence of both the state and the market, but also social movement organizations and religious organizations. We could not, however, neglect trade unions who play a key role in unemployment issues, as well as political parties due to their role

Table I.1 Organizational universes and mapping across selected cities

	Cologne	Geneva	Karlstad	Kielce	Lisbon	Lyon	Turin
Universe	50	36	13	28	30	24	50
Sample	28	21	13	26	30	21	35

Table I.2 Distribution of types of organizations across selected cities (numbers)

	Cologne	Geneva	Karlstad	Kielce	Lisbon	Lyon	Turin
Civil society organization	14	16	3	15	17	17	8
Cooperative		1			2		3
Public institution		1					
Political party	5	3	6	4	2	2	9
Trade union	3			2	6	1	8
Economic association	1		4				
Social movement organization	3				1	1	7
Church-related organization	2			5	2		
N	28	21	13	26	30	21	35

as contributors to policy-making and key-interlocutors in the field. All of these organizations worked either primarily or exclusively on (un)employment issues; accordingly, for the more generalist organizations, including political parties and religious organizations, we have focused interviews with those branches/people working exclusively on (un)employment. Moreover, we also included other organizational types that were identified during the mapping phase as important actors in the unemployment field (social cooperatives, not-for-profit service centres, and for-profit service centres) although only in specific cities, where they were considered as belonging to the general residual category "other."

Table I.2 presents the distribution across the cities of our sample by type of actor. In most of the cities, apart from Karlstad and Turin, more than half of the sample is composed of civil society organizations *stricto sensu* (in Geneva and Lyon this rises to over two-thirds of the sample), although a range of other types of actors such as social cooperatives, social movements as well as economic associations are included, reflecting the complexity of our field.

Organizations have been interviewed face-to-face in all of the cities (usually involving a member of the board or the head of the organization) using a questionnaire which included 57 questions distributed across three main sections: (1) introductory questions about the organization (e.g., date of creation, legal status, place and scope of activity, etc.); (2) mission statement, internal features (e.g., size, decision-making mechanisms), and activities; and (3) networks.

Structure of the book

The book is divided into two parts: The first part discusses the activities and resources of civil society as well as the political opportunities that their respective contexts offer them in terms of both constraints and assets. The second part, by means of network analyses, focuses upon how the various components of civil society, as we have mapped them, interact among themselves as well as with their social-political-economic environment, across multiple levels of government.

Chapter 1 by Baglioni, Lorenzini, and Mosca and Chapter 2 by Hobbins, Eriksson, and Bacia discuss two principal ways that civil society engages with the field of unemployment and precarity: On the one hand by means of advocacy and policy-oriented activities and on the other hand by service provision. In an ideal type situation, policy-oriented organizations strengthen the political and citizenship skills of unemployed and precariously employed young people, whereas the service-oriented organizations work on improving their employability and securing their survival in the absence of an income. Both chapters do point out, however, that some organizations are actually performing both actions, these are "hybrid" organizations and they fall "in the middle" of the ideal policy-service division, a situation which has been identified by previous research on the most effective forms of civil society organizations (Minkoff 2002). Mota and Mourão, in Chapter 3, compare how policy- and service-oriented organizations differ in terms of their internal structure and resources, and also discuss how far the changes in civil society organizations described by previous research (Anheier and Salamon 2006; White 2006; Kriesi 2007; Pestoff 2009; Evers and Zimmer 2010) are consistent with CSOs working on unemployment and precarity across different countries. In Chapter 4, Cinalli and Giugni discuss the impact of specific labour market regulations and employment policies upon the politicization of civil society across the seven cities.

Chapter 5 by Bassoli and Cinalli presents an overall picture of the network composition for each city, as well as discussing how state policies affect the relational nature of civil society. This argument is developed further by Lahusen, Grimmer, and Kolb in Chapter 6, who analyze how civil society organizational structures and activities, in particular whether they opt for a collaborative or for a more confrontational attitude vis-à-vis policy-makers, are affected by specific policy settings and political-institutional features. Bassoli, Cinalli, and Giugni in Chapter 7 focus upon brokerage and gate-keeping, as well as the representation or coordination functions of societal actors, while Bassoli and Theiss explore in Chapter 8 how values and political cleavages contribute toward shaping the networks of cooperation between civil society organizations. Finally, Lahusen in Chapter 9 expands the analysis of civil society networks to the European level, questioning multi-level governance assumptions that consider the European Union and the civil society of member states as being allied actors which support each other in the pursuit of common employment policies.

References

Anheier, H. K. and L. M. Salamon (2006) "The Nonprofit Sector in Comparative Perspective," in Powell, W. W. and R. Steinberg (eds), *The Non-profit Sector: A Research Handbook*, 2nd ed. (New Haven and London: Yale University Press).

Baglioni, S. (2004) *Société civile et capital social en Suisse* (Paris: L'Harmattan).

Baglioni, S. (2010) "The Role of Civil Society Actors in the Contentious Politics of Unemployment," in Giugni, M. (ed.), *The Contentious Politics of Unemployment in Europe* (Houndmills, Basingstoke: Palgrave).

Baglioni, S., B. Denters, A. Vetter, and L. Morales (2007) "City Size and the Nature of Associational Ecologies," in Maloney W. A. and S. Rossteutcher (eds), *Social Capital and Associations in European Democracies* (London: Routledge).

Bang, H. and E. Soerensen (2001) "The Everyday Maker: Building Political Rather Than Social Capital," in Dekker, P. and E. M. Uslaner (eds), *Social Capital and Participation in Everyday Life* (London: Routledge).

Cinalli, M. and M. Giugni (2013) "New Challenges for the Welfare State: The Emergence of Youth Unemployment Regimes in Europe?" *International Journal of Social Welfare*, 22, 290–299.

Coleman, J. (1988) "Social Capital in the Creation of Human Capital," *American Journal of Sociology*, 94, 95–120.

Defourny, J. and M. Nyssens (2010) Conceptions of Social Enterprise and Social Entrepreneurship in Europe and the United States: Convergences and Divergences, *Journal of Social Entrepreneurship*, 1 (1): 32–53.

European Commission (2013) *Youth Unemployment* (Brussels: European Commission).

Evers, A. and A. Zimmer (eds) (2010) *Third Sector Organizations Facing Turbulent Environments* (Frankfurt: Nomos).

Font, J., P. Geurts, W. A. Maloney, and M. Berton (2007) "Organizations in Context. Politics and Culture Shaping Associational Life," in Maloney W. A. and S. Rossteustcher (eds), *Social Capital and Associations in European Democracies* (London: Routledge).

Grimmer, B. and C. Lahusen (2009) "Addressing Work Instability. Organizational Activation on Youth Unemployment and Precariousness in European Cities. National Report Germany," Research report submitted as an official delivery for the European Commission FP7 funded project Younex "Youth, Unemployment and Exclusion in Europe."

Kriesi, H. (2007) "Organizational Resources: Personnel and Finances," in W. Maloney and S. Rossteutcher (eds), *Social Capital and Associations in European Democracies*, (London: Routledge).

Kriesi, H. and S. Baglioni (2003) "Putting Local Associations into Their Context: Preliminary Results from a Swiss Study of Local Associations," *Swiss Political Science Review*, 9, 1–34.

Maloney W. and S. Rossteutcher (eds) (2007) *Social Capital and Associations in European Democracies* (London: Routledge).

Mingione, E. and E. Pugliese (2010) *Il Lavoro* (Roma: Carocci).

Minkoff, D. C. (2002) "The Emergence of Hybrid Organizational Forms: Combining Identity-Based Service Provision and Political Action," *Non-Profit and Voluntary Sector Quarterly*, 31, 377–401.

Pestoff, V. (2009) *A Democratic Architecture for the Welfare State* (London and New York: Routledge).

Putnam, R. D. (1993) *Making Democracy Work: Civic Traditions in Modern Italy* (Princeton, NJ: Princeton University Press).

Salamon, L. M., S. W. Sokolowski, and R. List (2003) *Global Civil Society: An Overview* (Baltimore, MD: The Johns Hopkins University).

Skocpol, T., M. Ganz, and Z. Munson (2000) "A Nation of Organizers: The Institutional Origins of Civic Voluntarism in the United States," *American Political Science Review*, 94, 527–546.

Torpe, L. and M. Ferrer-Fons (2007) "The Internal Structure of Associations," in Maloney W. A. and S. Rossteutcher (eds), *Social Capital and Associations in European Democracies* (London: Routledge).

Warren, M. E. (2001) *Democracy and Association* (Princeton, NJ: Princeton University Press).

White, D. (2006) "State-Third Sector Partnership Frameworks: From Administration to Participation," in Henman, P. and M. Fenger (eds), *Administering Welfare Reform: International Transformations in Welfare Governance* (Bristol: The Policy Process).

Part I
Resources and Activities

1
The Political Role of Civil Society in the Policy Field of Youth Unemployment and Precarious Working Conditions

Simone Baglioni, Jasmine Lorenzini, and Lorenzo Mosca

Introduction

Civil society organizations (CSOs) operating in the field of youth unemployment and precarious working conditions promote a wide offer of political activities that range from providing information and expertise during the process of policy design and implementation to engaging in more confrontational actions such as calling for collective mobilization. The development and use of such a breadth of activities is dependent upon the specific political-institutional setting in which they operate. In particular, different unemployment regimes, namely those contexts within which unemployment and precarious work are tackled with diverse policy tools, provide different incentives to CSOs activity. For example, the use of activation policies, which aim at improving people's employability through engaging them in training, formation, or other skills improvement, have fostered the development of CSOs specializing in service delivery in the field of education and training (Handler 2003; Defourny and Nyssens 2010). Similarly, a change in the configuration of leading actors in labor policy such as trade unions has facilitated the mobilization of CSOs to protest about unemployment (Baglioni et al. 2008). Thus, the action repertoire of societal actors is closely related to the characteristics of the institutional settings in which it develops. Social movements studies have highlighted the importance of political actors' "prevailing strategies" in shaping collective action dynamics (Koopmans and Kriesi 1995). Where an "exclusive strategy" prevails, established authorities will tend to repress potential challenges coming from societal actors, by reaction however the latter will resort to conflict radicalization, while the prevalence of an "inclusive strategy" translates into cooptation of challengers and their demands. However, as della Porta and Diani noted: "while national strategies do have a certain influence on the repertoires of action adopted by social movements, they are not sufficient to explain the strategic choices they make. In the first place, they are not equally long-lived in every country. Second, they do not have the same effects on all movements. Third, they appear to affect some movement strategies and not others" (della Porta and Diani 2006: 210).

In this chapter, we address variations in the political action repertoires of CSOs working in the field of unemployment and precarious employment across six European cities, namely Cologne, Geneva, Karlstad, Kielce, Lyon, and Turin. We investigate the effect of unemployment regulations on the specific political action repertoires proposed by different types of CSOs: what we have described as "policy-oriented" organizations, promoting participation in the civic and political spheres and "service-oriented" organizations mostly providing services. By political action repertoire we refer to all those activities that aim at mobilizing members, raising individuals' political awareness, influencing public opinion or elected bodies through lobbying, protest, or participation in regulation and/or implementation of public policies. We describe the prevalence of certain repertoires according to different unemployment and labor market regulations (Cinalli and Giugni 2013; but see also Cinalli and Giugni in this volume) that generate specific political opportunity structures in the six European cities being studied. To address variation across cities we applied the theoretical framework of prevalent strategies to the field of unemployment regulation. While some cities are more inclusive in offering protection from destitution to the unemployed, others are more exclusive as they leave unemployed people outside the institutional coverage of welfare services or they allow the unemployed only a very limited form of protection. We expect to find differences among organizations in the intensity of their use of politically oriented activities, as well as in their specific activities depending upon the configuration of unemployment regulation. Hence, our hypothesis is that the specific *Political Opportunity Structure* (POS) of unemployment regulation shapes the organizational field. According to evidence produced by the literature on social movements on the role of POS on action repertoire, we expect that more exclusive contexts foster a more radical type of organization, while more inclusive contexts encourage the development of organizations focused upon more cooperative activities such as lobbying or policy implementation.

We first discuss the role of the POS in shaping the field of CSOs, in particular its role with regard to the prevalence of policy-oriented or service-oriented organizations. Then, we discuss how the emphasis on policy and services shapes the political action repertoire of CSOs. We also present the classification of cities according to their specific political opportunity structures. Lastly, we analyze the specific political activities conducted by each type of organization and we discuss the differences between organizations that are mainly devoted to policy or advocacy and those that focus on services and their interaction with their respective specific political opportunity structures.

The political opportunity structure of unemployment regulation

Studies on both civil society and social movements demonstrate how influential the impact of political-institutional specific configurations are upon civil society structure and development. In civil society studies, the neo-institutionalist approach has argued that differences in the type of democracy (participatory versus representative) or forms of the state (federalist versus centralized) have generated diverse patterns of civil society (Baglioni 2007; Birnbaum 1993; Pateman 1970; Skocpol et al. 2002). Similarly, social movements studies have explained variations in the vibrancy of social movements across countries as a consequence of different configurations in these countries' POS (della Porta and Rucht 1995; Eisinger 1973; Tarrow 1983). Political Opportunity Structures can be defined as the different formal and informal degrees of access to the political system and to its elite, the different degrees of cohesion of such elites, and the support elites offer to social movements (McAdam 1982; Kitschelt 1986; Kriesi 1995; Tarrow 1994).

A more recent elaboration of the POS approach has suggested that when studying specific mobilizations such as those made in the name of the unemployed, as well as those made in the name of migrants, one must consider also more *specific political opportunities* (Berclaz and Giugni 2005; Hooghe 2005). In fact, Giugni (2008) has explained that the extent of the unemployed's political mobilization could only be partially understood through the general POS of a specific country. Rather, it was a country specific POS derived from both unemployment and labor market regulations that explained the higher levels of mobilization of the unemployed found in France, Italy, and to some extent Sweden in comparison with other countries. In the field of political mobilization regarding unemployment, other researchers have found similar evidence. Baglioni et al. (2008) have pointed out that in the 1990s in France, Germany, and Italy changes in trade unions, as a component of the specific POS, contributed to explaining the successful mobilization of the unemployed while della Porta (2008) has found that protest is more wide-spread in Italy and France than in countries with neocorporatist industrial relations such as Sweden and Germany. Moreover, Royall (2009) has illustrated how, in Ireland, the State withdrew from the provision of certain services offered to the unemployed by supporting the engagement of CSOs in this field of activity.

Thus, different contexts lead to either political mobilization by the unemployed and by civil society organizations or to the provision of services to complement the welfare state. We therefore assess the differences across our cities in the way that the state regulates unemployment, and the specific POS variations, following Cinalli and Giugni (2013) who have constructed a typology of unemployment regimes on the basis of qualitative indicators to which scores have been assigned comparatively.

We follow this specific POS approach and we explain the "division of labor" within the CSOs as a result of the specific POS emanating from unemployment regulations. In addition, we propose to focus upon a larger repertoire of political activities, an approach exemplified by Cinalli and Füglister (2008) who studied the variations in types of political activities among the unemployed across three countries (Great Britain, Germany, and Switzerland) but did not develop hypotheses related to the specific POS.[1]

Civil society organizations and unemployment regimes

The work of CSOs has for centuries maintained and fixed the thin fabric of social cohesion. Building upon the tradition of political liberalism and Christian charity, Europeans have generated across centuries a plethora of associations and movements aimed at supporting people in need (Edwards 2004; Evers and Zimmer 2010). Providing a welfare state well in advance of the organized recipient regimes of that undertaking, civil society organizations have helped individuals in a wide range of vulnerable situations. With time, associations, in this large field of solidarity and welfare, have also developed specific features leading to a differentiation in dimensions, functioning structures, skills, social "targets" and overall aims. In the specific field of associations working with the unemployed, we found two ways through which CSOs contribute to the inclusion of individuals, such as unemployed young people, who are at risk of marginalization.

On the one hand, there are organizations that foster citizens' participation in the civic and political spheres and where membership enables the sharing of political ideas and values; these organizations provide a range of opportunities for the immediate local engagement of a young person. Following existing research on civil society (Lelieveldt et al. 2007), we describe these first types of organizations as *policy-oriented*. On the other hand, there are organizations whose activity is mainly focused upon service provision, in particular those services which increase young people's skills and thus improve their employability. In this sense, such organizations activate people via training activities, education, internships, and so on. Furthermore they support unemployed young people in their "material" needs such as housing, financial support, and health. We therefore describe these second types of organizations as *service-oriented*.

The resulting division of organizations between policy-oriented and service-oriented corresponds to ideal types in a Weberian sense; in the real world such activities are not mutually exclusive. While policy-oriented groups are more prone to be involved in protest and lobbying activity, they are also likely to provide services to different populations (i.e. migrants or the unemployed). Similarly, although service-oriented organizations are more engaged with offering support and educational activities, they can also employ unconventional forms of political action. When we distinguish between these two types we are therefore considering their *prevailing* activities while keeping in mind that if we were to place our organizations on a continuum defined by "policy" and "service" at the extremes, some of them will fall in the middle.

Although research in this field has highlighted that the unemployed share a low overall level of political participation, explained by either their lack of resources or the stigmatized identity related to unemployment that discourages political participation (Demazière and Pignoni 1998; Giugni 2008; Maurer 2001), policy-oriented organizations will likely foster the political engagement of unemployed young people. These organizations propose political campaigns, rallies, protest events, and other direct actions requiring an active involvement of their constituencies among which there are unemployed and precarious workers. In fact, research analyzing the political mobilization of unemployed people in Europe during the late 1990s and early 2000s reveals the central role of organizations in supporting the collective mobilization of the unemployed (Chabanet 2008; Faniel 2004).

Service-oriented organizations, through their endeavors, will likely foster the socialization of unemployed young people in activities which are directly related to employment and career development. The first type of organizations therefore empower unemployed young people by making their claims heard in the public sphere by undertaking unconventional political action, while the second type of organizations empower them by improving their skills and appeal on the labor market as well as providing basic services.

Our theoretical framework is summarized in Figure 1.1: according to our hypotheses different unemployment regimes provide diverse opportunities for collective action, thus shaping the political action repertoires of CSOs.

We therefore expect to find differences in the political action repertoires of CSOs active in cities with different unemployment regimes. We also expect to find a more policy-oriented community of CSOs in the more "exclusive" contexts, in other words those which are less generous in the protection they offer from unemployment. In such contexts we expect CSOs to use a political action repertoire oriented towards protest and disruptive actions to make their claims visible and to increase their leverage capacity. Moreover, these more exclusive contexts are characterized

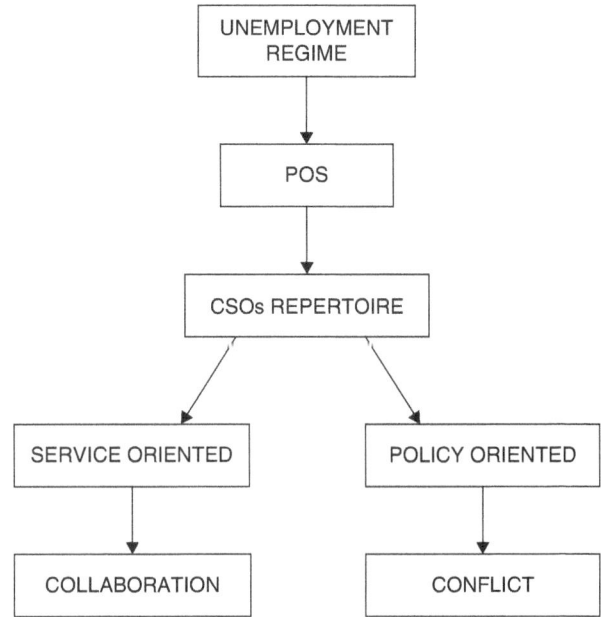

Figure 1.1   Theoretical framework and hypotheses

by the scarcity of welfare state provisions for the unemployed and/or selective and strict general unemployment regulations resulting in a legal and political framework which excludes rather than includes those who are out of the labor market. In a context of absent (or poor) services and regulations which help protect the unemployed, CSOs will likely mobilize for such services and rights to be developed and correctly implemented. This is the "classical" paradigm of the development of advocacy-type CSOs (Baglioni 2001). In contrast, in those contexts where regulations protecting and promoting precarious workers and the unemployed do exist, and where by virtue of such regulations a range of services are usually provided for the unemployed to increase their employability or to support their income and needs, CSOs will primarily focus upon service delivery. In some cases, CSOs will develop professional skills and capacities to deliver specific services by direct request or by an indirect "incitation" by the state (Battaglini et al. 2001). Moreover, in these more inclusive contexts, with regard to their political action repertoire, we expect CSOs to be oriented towards more conventional forms of political participation that include participation in decision-making processes.

The political action repertoire of civil society organizations working on unemployment issues

In what follows we first classify our cities according to an inclusion–exclusion unemployment regime continuum. Then, we focus on presenting the repertoires of action of CSOs across the different cities in light of our hypotheses. Finally, we discuss if and how different settings, that is, different specific political opportunity structures, influence CSOs' relationships with political institutions.

By making use of a combination of eight indicators[2] elaborated in the YOUNEX project (cfr. Cinalli and Giugni 2013), we have designed a continuum along which we have listed the different degrees of protection from unemployment offered by the six cities considered in this chapter. Table 1.1 presents such a continuum. Lyon, Karlstad, and Geneva are all on the "positive" side (right hand side of the figure) of the continuum, and can be considered inclusive in the sense that they offer a thick safety net to unemployed people, whereas Cologne and, in a more marked way, Turin and Kielce, occupy the "exclusive" side in the sense that their safety net in the event of unemployment is thin (Cologne) or even very fragile (Turin and Kielce).

A partial confirmation of our hypotheses is presented in Table 1.2 with the distribution of policy- and service-oriented organizations

Table 1.1   Unemployed inclusion–exclusion continuum

From −1 to −0.5 (Exclusion)	From +0.5 to +1 (Inclusion)
Kielce, Turin, Cologne	Geneva, Karlstad, Lyon

Source: Own elaboration on Giugni and Cinalli 2013.

across the cities: Cologne and Turin are both placed in the "exclusive" side of the previous table and host the highest percentage of policy-oriented organizations (respectively 61.5% and 71.9%). Geneva and Lyon, on the contrary, are part of the "inclusive" side of Table 1.1, for their unemployment regimes are more supportive of unemployed and precarious workers, and as we assumed they both host higher numbers of service-oriented organizations, 72.2% in Geneva and 76.2% in Lyon.

Table 1.2   Types of CSOs in the six cities

	Cologne	Geneva	Karlstad	Kielce	Lyon	Turin	Total
Policy-oriented organizations	61.5	27.8	50.0	29.2	23.8	71.9	46.6%
Adjusted residuals	ns	ns	ns	−1.9	−2.3	3.3	
Service-oriented organizations	38.5	72.2	50.0	70.8	76.2	28.1	53.4%
Adjusted residuals	ns	ns	ns	1.9	2.3	−3.3	
N	26	18	12	24	21	32	133

What may come as a surprise – and in contrast to our expectations – is the result of Kielce, that despite its rather exclusive unemployment regime it hosts a low percentage of policy-oriented CSOs (29.2) and a high number of service-oriented CSOs (70.8). As shown in this volume (Bassoli and Theiss' chapter), Kielce's civil society is mainly the expression of the Catholic church which survived the years of the communist regime and as such is composed of organizations devoted to service delivery more than political mobilization. This result concurs with research on the weakness of civil society in Eastern Europe (Howard 2003). In Karlstad, organizations are equally divided into policy-oriented and service-oriented groups. This could be explained by the peculiar characteristics of the groups sampled in the Swedish city: firstly, the number of groups active on unemployment in Karlstad is very limited (just 12); secondly, compared to other cities included in our study they tend to be less heterogeneous as they are almost equally split between political parties and CSOs. In contrast to CSOs sampled in the other cities, no social movement organizations or religious groups and trade unions were included in the sample. As such the classification on the policy/service divide mirrors the characteristics of the sample. Table 1.3 offers an overall picture of the different activities performed by the organizations in our selected cities. Concerning the political activities conducted by civil society organizations active on issues of unemployment and precarity, we find interesting variations across cities. As we expected, activities that are more policy-oriented like the organization of political events in general and of unconventional political actions such as sit-ins and rallies tend to occur more frequently in cities which have exclusive regulations and where the coverage of benefits for the unemployed is highly selective and limited: this is the case for Turin and Cologne. These cities were therefore placed, albeit with some variation, in the "exclusive" side of Table 1.1.

Accordingly, in those contexts where civil society needs to put pressure upon political elites and public opinion for the development of a more inclusive set of unemployment measures, we find a more vibrant range of policy-oriented activities. Here again Kielce's groups tend to behave like organizations of cities with inclusive regulations while the political activities of Karlstad's groups present forms of action closer to exclusive settings. Karlstad, which is the best representative of the "flexicurity" model, is a clear outlier. On the one hand, this confirms the country's high level of social capital and civic and political

Table 1.3 Political activities conducted by the organizations in the six cities

	Cologne	Geneva	Karlstad	Kielce	Lyon	Turin	Total
Organizing political events (more than once a year)							N=144
	64.3	42.9	61.5	11.5	33.3	40.0	41.0%
Adjusted residuals	2.8	ns	ns	−3.4	ns	ns	
Organizing sit-ins (percentage of yes)							N=134
	21.4	5.0	7.7	7.7	23.8	26.9	16.4%
Adjusted residuals	ns	ns	ns	ns	ns	ns	
Organizing rallies (percentage of yes)							N=134
	53.6	5.0	30.8	11.5	0	34.6	23.9%
Adjusted residuals	4.1	−2.1	ns	ns	−2.8	ns	
Sending letters to local authorities (frequency)							N=105
Once a year or less	36.4	29.4	62.5	50.0	38.9	45.5	41.9%
2–5 times a year	45.5	47.1	25.0	38.9	22.2	36.4	37.1%
Monthly or weekly	18.2	23.5	12.5	11.1	38.9	18.2	21.0%
Adjusted residuals	ns	ns	ns	ns	ns	2.1	

Note: $+p<0.10$, $*p<0.05$, $**p<0.01$, $***p<0.001$.

engagement (Rothstein 2001), but on the other hand, the very small number of organizations mapped and interviewed in the city suggests a cautious approach.

The confirmation of a clear division of tasks among CSOs dealing with unemployment and precarity is demonstrated by Table 1.4, which compares the variation in political activities across types of organizations. There is a sharp difference evident between policy- and service-oriented organizations: the former are far more active than the latter in the full range of the political activities we consider. In fact, while 73.2% of service-oriented organizations declare not organizing political events at all, more than 80% of the policy-oriented ones do so. Similarly, if we consider organizing rallies as political activity, policy-oriented organizations are much more active than their service-oriented counterparts. Organizing sit-ins is also a more frequent activity among policy-oriented than service organizations. The only political activity where the two types do not differ substantially is "writing letters to local authorities": understandably, this is a political action that is ordinarily an activity engaged in by every organization involved in service delivery on behalf of, or in relation with, a local authority.

To better investigate the relationships between organizations and local public authorities, our organizational survey included questions asking CSOs if they had ever been invited to participate in public decision-making processes and, to those who had been invited, we could check whether they finally participated in the policy-making process (Table 1.5).

Table 1.4   Political activities conducted by policy- and service-oriented organizations

	Policy-oriented	Service-oriented	Cramer's v	
Organizing political events (frequency)				
Never	14.5	73.2	.62***	N=133
1–5 times a year	38.7	21.1		
Monthly or weekly	46.8	5.6		
Organizing sit-in (percentage of yes)				
	22.6	12.9	ns	N=123
Organizing rallies (percentage of yes)				
	39.6	11.4	.33***	N=123
Sending letters to local authorities (frequency)				
Seldom	48.4	41.5	ns	N=96
2–5 times a year	32.3	38.5		
Monthly or weekly	19.4	20.0		

Note: +p<0.10, *p<0.05, **p<0.01, ***p<0.001.

Table 1.5   Institutional political participation in the six cities

	Cologne	Geneva	Karlstad	Kielce	Lyon	Turin	Total
Invitation to participate in public decision-making (percentage of yes)							N=113
	54.5	55.6	28.6	85.7	63.2	65.4	71
Adjusted residuals	ns	ns	−1.9	2.4	ns	ns	
Participation in public decision-making at various levels (percentage of yes)							N=71
Permanent member at the district/ neighborhood level	25.0	10.0	–	5.6	8.3	29.4	15.5%
Permanent member at the municipal level	33.3	–	50.0	5.6	8.3	29.4	16.9%
Occasional member at the municipal level	41.7	60.0	–	44.4	16.7	35.3	38.0%
Member of consultation group at the municipal level	83.3	70.0	50.0	66.7	50.0	58.8	64.8%

Table 1.5 reveals that CSOs have been invited to take part in decision-making processes with different degrees of intensity. The lowest value is registered among Swedish CSOs, as in Karlstad less than one third of interviewed CSOs declared having been invited to join a decision-making process, while more than two-thirds of CSOs had been invited in Kielce, Turin, and Lyon, as well as half of them in Cologne and Geneva. If we now consider those that have really participated, we see that in Geneva participation is mainly occasional ("occasional member at the municipal level"), as in Kielce and Lyon. Whereas in Turin and Cologne, organizations have participated at both the district and the municipal levels on a more substantial manner: as permanent members of decision-making fora. Finally, the case of Karlstad is very peculiar for it has a 50% share of organizations who participate as occasional members and another 50% who participate as permanent members, both at the municipal level. In general our hypothesis concerning organizational types and institutional interactions seems not to be confirmed by these findings, as CSOs active in more exclusive settings (Cologne and Kielce) are those which interact more frequently with institutions. This empirical evidence indicates that political action is not detached from institutional dynamics and processes. As other studies have demonstrated (Lipsky 1968), mobilization is a strategy deliberately employed by power-less groups to

obtain political recognition and acquire resources that can be spent in the institutional arena. Cooperation with institutions is therefore not neglected by CSOs employing unconventional forms of action. In the same vein of their strategic use by trade unions, conflict and protest become political resources exploited by CSOs to draw the attention of institutional representatives to the popular support they possess and thus attain more strength in negotiations with public authorities.

Concerning cross-organizational variations in interactions with public authorities (Table 1.6), interesting results emerge from our study. In fact, when we asked organizations to answer a general question about being invited to participate in "public decision-making," we found that service-oriented organizations scored better than policy-oriented ones with 54.8% of the latter saying they had been invited to participate in public decision-making as opposed to 64.8% of the former. However, when analyzing the specific forms and levels of participation in public decision-making, such as permanent membership in decision-making bodies at the local, district, or municipal levels, as well as permanent membership in consultation groups, a larger share of the policy-oriented organizations who have been invited to participate are engaged as permanent members at both the district or neighborhood and the municipal levels (see bottom section of Table 1.6).

While service-oriented organizations may be consulted in matters relating to the direct provision of services, policy-oriented organizations

Table 1.6   Institutional political participation among policy- or service-oriented organizations

	Policy-oriented	Service-oriented	
Invitation to participate in public decision-making (percentage of yes)			
	54.8	64.8	N=102
Participation in public decision-making at various levels (percentage of yes)			
Permanent member at the district/neighborhood level	23.5	10.9	N=63
Permanent member at the municipal level	29.4	10.9	N=63
Occasional member at the municipal level	29.4	37.0	N=63
Member of consultation group at the municipal level	70.6	58.7	N=63

Note: The differences between policy and service oriented organizations are not statistically significant.

could be included more in the development of policies intended to target unemployed and precarious workers. As the latter involves work over a longer period, those policy-oriented organizations who have access to the decision-making processes and who are invited to participate at both levels are more likely to be engaged as permanent members. Finally, we should stress that the two types of organizations are included at different stages of the decision-making processes, but mostly as occasional members.

Considering the motivations for members to join these organizations represents another way for us to understand if an organization is more policy-oriented or is instead one that focuses upon service delivery. The former will most likely call for a more ideological or politically driven membership than the latter. Table 1.7 reveals that our assumption was correct. Members of policy-oriented organizations are more likely to have joined for political reasons, to share political ideas and values, than members of service-oriented organizations, 88.3% compared with 41.2%. Policy-oriented organizations are therefore twice as likely to have members who join for political reasons. Consequently, this is reflected in the types of activities they engage in: organizing political events, rallies, and to some extent sit-ins, actions which they undertake more often than service-oriented organizations whose recruitment of members for political motivations is less frequent.

If we compare the distribution of members joining organizations for political reasons across our six cities, we find further consistencies with our previous assumptions regarding the effect of specific unemployment regimes on types of CSOs. As Table 1.8 illustrates, we find that the highest share of organizations that have members who join on the basis of political motivations are in Cologne (81.5%) and Turin (85.3%). The two cities belonging to the more exclusive unemployment regimes were also the most active with regard to the organization of political events – in general and with regard to unconventional actions such as rallies and sit-ins. Nevertheless, Geneva and Karlstad – which host the more

Table 1.7 Members' political engagement among policy- or service-oriented organizations

	Policy-oriented	Service-oriented	
*Members join to share political ideas/values (percentage of yes)******			
	88.3	41.2	N=128
Adjusted residuals	+5.5	−5.5	

Note: +p < 0.10, *p<0.05, **p<0.01, ***p<0.001.

Table 1.8   Members political engagement in the organizations in the six cities

	Cologne	Geneva	Karlstad	Kielce	Lyon	Turin	Total
Members join to share political ideas/values (percentage of yes)							N=136
	81.5	65.0	61.5	14.3	52.4	85.3	63.2%
Adjusted residuals	2.2	ns	ns	−5.1	ns	3.1	

inclusive unemployment regime models – also have remarkable shares of members who join to exchange political values or ideas. Finally, Kielce has the lowest share of members joining organizations working with unemployed youth and the precariously employed on the basis of political motivations. This corresponds to the low amount of political activities conducted by the organizations we interviewed in Kielce and, as mentioned above, may be due to the specific pattern of civic and political participation in the city, which has been relying mainly upon Catholic organizations devoted to charitable activities.

Conclusion

In this chapter, we have discussed the role CSOs fulfill as political actors within different contexts of political opportunities. Building upon previous research, which has demonstrated how specific political opportunity structures help us to understand the actions of civil society and social movements in a given context, this chapter has compared six cities where unemployment regulations (our specific political opportunity structure) vary in terms of their capacity to safeguard unemployed young people from destitution. In other words, we have analyzed the political activities of civil society among cities that are more or less inclusive in terms of the protection they offer to unemployed young people.

Our first hypothesis claims that differences in the inclusiveness (or exclusiveness) in terms of unemployment protection policies among cities can contribute towards explaining the different composition of civil society organizations active in the field of unemployment in these cities. In the more exclusive contexts, where unemployment regulations were still poorly developed, a range of organizations advocating a sharp development of such regulations and protection could be imagined, we have named this type of organization as policy-oriented. In contrast, a context offering an already developed set of measures to protect the young unemployed from destitution may have paved the way for the creation of organizations dealing with the implementation of such measures, which we have named service-oriented organizations. In a nutshell, we hypothesized a functional differentiation of civil society organizations. On one side, in the more exclusive settings, the prevalence of policy-oriented organizations, in other words groups more devoted to advocacy or political mobilization-type activities. On the other side, the prevalence of service-oriented organizations in the more inclusive contexts, that is, organizations delivering services more than advocating for young unemployed people.

Our results, based upon an organizational survey conducted among CSOs in six European cities (Cologne, Geneva, Karlstad, Kielce, Lyon, and Turin), have corroborated the hypotheses. In cities such as Cologne and Turin, which our findings revealed to be more "exclusive" with regard to young unemployed people, civil society associations active in this field appeared to be "more politicized" and prone to advocacy than in cities offering stronger levels of protection to the jobless. The analysis has also revealed however that some cases tend to deviate from the overall trend because of historical motivations (Kielce) and sampling reasons (Karlstad).

Thus, we have contributed to the literature focusing upon the impact of POS by demonstrating that, in addition to influencing the patterns of civil society (Baglioni 2007; Birnbaum 1993; Pateman 1970; Skopol et al. 2002) and the vibrancy of social movements across countries (della Porta and Rucht 1995; Eisinger 1973; Tarrow 1983), POS also contributes towards the shaping of the political action repertoires of CSOs active in the field of unemployment and precarious employment in European cities. In this chapter, however, following the path opened by Giugni (2008) we have also argued that scholars should consider the impact of specific political opportunities structures which have been deemed to affect the specific field and population under study, not only the general POS. The specific POS we adopted is a measure of unemployment regulations which enables us to understand the diverse repertoires of the political actions of policy- and service-oriented organizations in the six cities.

The policy lesson we can derive from this first set of findings pertains to the intimate relationship which exists between policy development, particularly policy related to the welfare state and unemployment issues, and civil society actors: either when these actors are acting as partners in policy development or when they are challenging political institutions for policy innovation (to meet unmet needs), policy making would not be the same in a given context without the punctual intervention of CSOs.

Our chapter has also shown that functional diversification among civil society associations working in this field still exists when we consider the type of interaction they establish with political actors. While both service-oriented and policy-oriented organizations do engage in political collaboration or create political ties with local political institutions, they appear to be different in the breadth of such collaborations. A larger share of service-oriented rather than policy-oriented organizations have ties with political institutions, but the latter appear to be more deeply integrated in political activities. Our second hypothesis, which assumed that policy-oriented organizations would have established more contentious relations with policy makers than their service-oriented counterparts – and that such a contentiousness would have prevented them from becoming policy partners – has not been clearly confirmed by the data. This suggests that while mobilization dynamics can be explained by the degree of openness of local institutional settings towards specific issues, institutional cooperation at the local level concerns both service-oriented and policy-oriented groups. Protest can be used by resource-poor groups as a way to gain access to institutional settings, while cooperation with institutions is unsurprising for service-oriented groups who form a significant part of the local welfare system.

Here as well, the policy lesson we derive points to the need for policy makers and political institutions to further stimulate the development of cooperative ties between themselves and CSOs as a means for strengthening the inclusiveness of their policy processes and, as such, their democratic legitimacy.

Lastly, our chapter finds that members join CSOs for political reasons when CSOs are policy-oriented and less so when they are service-oriented. Consequently, there is a relationship between the repertoires of political actions and the individuals' motivations for joining the organizations. Future research should analyze the links between the political action repertoires of CSOs, within the different specific POS, and their capacity to mobilize unemployed and precariously employed young people.

Notes

The article was a collaborative work, but each author contributed specifically to a section; Simone Baglioni wrote the section "The political action repertoire of civil society organizations working on unemployment issues," Jasmine Lorenzini the section "Civil society organizations and unemployment regimes," and Lorenzo Mosca the section "The political opportunity structure of unemployment regulation." All authors contributed to the introductory and concluding sections.

1. Cinalli and Füglister (2008) found that the unemployed in the three countries use different forms of political action – more specifically they describe the prevalence of protest (social movements and public demonstrations) in Germany – while in Switzerland the political participation of the unemployed is more conventional with access to the pre-parliamentary phases of decision-making and in Great Britain it is more hidden with lobbying being the prevalent form of political participation for the unemployed.
2. The index of 8 indicators includes: (a) Formal pre-requisites for obtaining social provisions; (b) Level of coverage of unemployment insurance; (c) Extension of coverage; (d) Shifting to social aid; (e) Role played by private and public employment agencies; (f) Counter-provisions and sanctions; (g) Percentage receiving unemployment benefits; and (h) Percentage receiving sanctions for abusing the benefit system.

References

Baglioni, S. (2001) "Solidarity Movement Organizations: Towards an Active Global Consciousness?" in Giugni, M. and Passy, F. (eds), *Political Altruism? Solidarity Movements in International Perspective* (Lanham: Rowman and Littlefield).

Baglioni, S. (2007) "The Effects of Direct Democracy and City Size on Political Participation: The Swiss Case," in Zittel, T. and Fuchs, D. (eds), *Participatory Democracy and Political Participation: Can Participatory Engineering Bring Citizens Back In?* (London: Routledge).

Baglioni, S., B. Baumgarten, D. Chabanet and C. Lahusen (2008) "Transcending Marginalization: The Mobilization of the Unemployed in France, Germany, and Italy in a Comparative Perspective," *Mobilization*, 13, 323–335.

Battaglini, M., S. Cattacin and V. Tattini (2001) "Reconnaissance et coopération: Quelle institutionnalisation de l'associationnisme? Première partie," *Associations transnationales/Transnational Associations*, 1, 60–73.

Berclaz, J. and M. Giugni (2005) "Specifying the Concept of Political Opportunity Structures," in Kousis, M. and C. Tilly (eds), *Economic and Political Contention in Comparative Perspective* (Colorado: Paradigm).

Birnbaum, P. (1993) "Mouvements sociaux et type d'Etats: vers une approche comparative," in Chazel, F. (ed.), *Action Collective et mouvements sociaux* (Paris: Presses Universitaires de France).

Chabanet, D. (2008) "When the Unemployed Challenge the European Union: The European Marches as a Mode of Externalization of Protest," *Mobilization*, 13, 311–322.

Cinalli, M. and K. Füglister (2008) "Networks and Political Contention over Unemployment: A Comparison of Britain, Germany, and Switzerland," *Mobilization*, 13, 259–276.

Cinalli, M. and M. Giugni (2013) "New Challenges for the Welfare State: The Emergence of Youth Unemployment Regimes in Europe?" *International Journal of Social Welfare*, 22, 290–299.

Defourny, J., Nyssens, M. (2010) Conceptions of Social Enterprise and Social Entrepreneurship in Europe and the United States: Convergences and Divergences, *Journal of Social Entrepreneurship*, 1: 1, 32–53.

della Porta, D. (2008) "Protest on Unemployment: Forms and Opportunities," *Mobilization*, 13, 277–295.

della Porta, D. and M. Diani (2006) *Social Movements: An Introduction* (Malden/Oxford/Victoria: Blackwell).

della Porta, D. and D. Rucht (1995) "Left-Libertarian Movements in Context: Comparing Italy and West Germany, 1965–1990," in Jenkins, J. C. and B. Klandermans (eds), *The Politics of Social Protest: Comparative Perspectives on States and Social Movements* (Minneapolis: University of Minnesota Press).

Demazière, D. and M. T. Pignoni (1998) *Chômeurs: Du silence à la révolte. Sociologie d'une action collective* (Paris: Hachette).

Edwards, M. (2004) *Civil Society* (Cambridge: Polity Press).

Eisinger, P. K. (1973) "The Conditions of Protest Behavior in American Cities," *American Political Science Review*, 67, 11–28.

Evers, A. and A. Zimmer (eds) (2010) *Third Sector Organizations Facing Turbulent Environments* (Frankfurt: Nomos).

Faniel, J. (2004) "Chômeurs en Belgique et en France: Des mobilisations différentes," *Revue internationale de politique comparée*, 11, 493–506.

Giugni, M. (2008) "Welfare States, Political Opportunities, and the Mobilization of the Unemployed: A Cross-National Analysis," *Mobilization*, 13, 297–310.

Handler, J. F. (2003) "Social Citizenship and Workfare in the US and Western Europe: From Status to Contract," *Journal of European Social Policy*, 13, 229–243.

Hooghe, M. (2005) "Ethnic Organisations and Social Movement Theory: The Political Opportunity Structure for Ethnic Mobilisation in Flanders," *Journal of Ethnic and Migration Studies*, 31, 975–990.

Howard, M. M. (2003) *The Weakness of Civil Society in Post-Communist Europe* (Cambridge: Cambridge University Press).

Kitschelt, H. (1986) "Political Opportunity Structures and Political Protest: Anti-Nuclear Movements in Four Democracies," *British Journal of Political Science*, 16, 57–85.

Koopmans, R. and H. Kriesi (1995) "Institutional Structures and Prevailing Strategies," in Kriesi, H., R. Koopmans, J. W. Duyvendak and M. Giugni (eds), *New Social Movementsin Western Europe: A Comparative Analysis* (Minneapolis: University of Minnesota Press).

Kriesi, H. (1995) "The Political Opportunity Structure of New Social Movements: Its Impact on Their Mobilization," in Jenkins, J. C. and B. Klandermans (eds), *The Politics of Social Protest: Comparative Perspectives on States and Social Movements* (Minneapolis: University of Minnesota Press).

Lelieveldt, H., J. Astudillo and L. Stevenson (2007) "The Spectrum of Associational Activities: From Self-Help to Lobbying," in Maloney, W. and S. Rossteutcher (eds), *Social Capital and Associations in European Democracies* (London: Routledge).

Lipsky, M. (1968) "Protest as a Political Resource," *American Political Science Review*, 62, 1144–1158.

Maurer, S. (2001) *Les chômeurs en action (décembre 1997 – mars 1998): Mobilisation collective et ressources compensatoires* (Paris: L'Harmattan).

McAdam, D. (1982) *The Political Process and the Development of Black Insurgency 1930–1970* (Chicago: University of Chicago Press).

Pateman, C. (1970) *Participation and Democratic Theory* (Cambridge: Cambridge University Press).

Rothstein, B. (2001) "Social Capital in the Social Democratic Welfare State," *Politics and Society*, 29, 207–241.

Royall, F. (2009) "Political Challengers, Service Providers or Service Recipients? Participants in Irish Pro-unemployed Organizations," in Giugni, M. (ed.), *The Politics of Unemployment in Europe: Policy Responses and Collective Action* (Farnham: Ashgate).

Skocpol, T., M. Ganz and Z. Munson (2002) "A Nation of Organizers: The Institutional Origins of Civic Voluntarism in the United States," *American Political Science Review*, 94, 527–546.

Tarrow, S. (1983) *Struggling to Reform: Social Movements and Policy Change during Cycles of Protest* (Ithaca: Center for International Studies, Cornell University).

Tarrow, S. (1994) *Power in Movement: Social Movements, Collective Action and Politics*, (Cambridge: Cambridge University Press).

2

Addressing Unemployment in Different Welfare Regimes: Civil Society Organizations and Their Strategies

Jennifer Hobbins, Birgitta Eriksson, and Ewa Bacia

Introduction

The dramatic increase in unemployment in Europe since the 1990s has garnered the attention of policy-makers in particular and society in general. Youth unemployment particularly has serious consequences in terms of economic life conditions, shame, and health (Starrin et al. 1996; Starrin et al. 1999). Youth unemployment also has a critical effect on future career opportunities (Nordström Skans 2004). The European Union (EU) has reacted to this problem through the European Social Fund and addressed unemployment directly through the European Employment Strategy (EES). In terms of policy responses and collective action on a national level, there are three types of reactions to high unemployment rates (Giugni 2009). Governments respond by redistributing collective resources, by adjusting labor market policies toward activation and a certain degree of conditionality for social rights (e.g., Gilbert 2002; Handler 2003), and further, in terms of collective action via the civil society.

Since classical antiquity, civil society has been a part of the civilized culture representing free citizens who strive for common interests out of free will (Schmidt 2007). Civil society also constitutes a scene for argument, deliberation, and associational and institutional collaboration. Representing all viewpoints, civil society is a vital element in establishing and maintaining democracy (Edwards 2009). Thus, nonprofit organizations are engaged in all forms of interest, value, and belief representation and also in providing services such as education, housing, and health (Salamon et al. 2003). Consequently, civil society organizations delivering direct services are often active in fields that overlap with what is regarded as the responsibility of the welfare state. Unemployment, which is the focus of this chapter, is one example that targets a specific complex of problems.

In this chapter, we investigate similarities and differences in the strategies and goals of service-oriented civil society organizations engaged in services for the unemployed in four European countries. We also discuss if these strategies and goals can be explained by the ideology and function of welfare regime types. Drawing on qualitative data, we argue that the welfare regime type is important to understand organizations' paths in various countries. However, common trends concerning the direction of EU-level policies are also indicated in the field of (un)employment. The chapter begins with a theoretical discussion of civil society and the institutional framework within which it acts: the welfare regime model. After presenting the methodological aspects of this study, we describe the analysis and results. We begin by focusing on the goals and move on to each of the four types of strategies addressing unemployment found in the data. Finally, we summarize and discuss the results of our research in the concluding section of this chapter.

Theoretical considerations

This section reviews the role of civil society in society at large and its relationship to the state. These patterns comprise the whole spectrum of civil society organizations, from religious movements and trade unions to sports organizations and environmental associations. However, this chapter is only interested in a small part of civil society, and the patterns of the particular field of unemployment may differ from the patterns of civil society in general. We will then describe welfare regime types, which constitute a framework for civil society organizations and the roles they play in relation to the state. The welfare state strongly influences the development of civil society and the path it follows, as described in the literature. Nevertheless, civil society organizations working with unemployment issues may follow other paths, crossing the boundaries of welfare regime types. For this reason, this theoretical background forms a basis for understanding similarities and differences in the strategies and goals of the organizations participating in this study.

Civil society research involves a wide range of aspects. Some scholars focus on different outcomes of civil society, such as social capital (e.g., Putnam 1993) or the economic role of nonprofit organizations (Hansmann 1980). Other studies focus on the nature and role of the nonprofit sector, as well as its relationship with the state (Baglioni et al. 2011; Stryjan and Wijkström 1996). Research in this field has typically drawn on classical economic theory focusing on public goods, trust, or supply-side approaches, with the underlying assumption of institutional choice and utility-maximizing individuals (Salamon and Anheier 1998). The terms used for describing these associations vary and are often linked to their connotation. For instance, *third sector* assumes that civil society is a sector in addition to the public and the private sectors, while the term *nonprofit organizations* indicates that the aims differ from those of the market and *nongovernmental organizations* stresses that they are not part of the state. In this article, the terms *nonprofit organization* and *nongovernmental organization* are used synonymously with the term *civil society organization*.

The main welfare providers are the family, the market, and the welfare state (Esping-Andersen 1990). However, not all families can provide sufficient support for needy members, and the nature of the market lies in its aim for profit rather than providing charitable free services. When the state also fails to provide high-quality services and goods, consumers then turn toward nonprofit organizations for the supply of public goods that neither the market nor the state will provide. In this view, nonprofit organizations complement the welfare state. However, the choice of upon whom to rely for social welfare services (state, market, or civil society associations) is strongly linked not only to available options but also to the context of historical development (Salamon and Anheier 1998).

The perception of civil society's role is related to normative understandings of democracy (Cohen and Arato 1992). An even more comprehensive picture emerges when integrating political theory, and contributes to a broader understanding of the relationship between state and civil society. Accordingly, liberalism, communitarianism, and the social or expansive democracy approach have characteristic features of certain regime types that illustrate the principles surrounding civil society (Janoski 1998).

Nonprofit associations play an important role within the public sphere, which is where civil society intermediates between political institutions and the wider public (Steffek and Nanz 2008). The public sphere varies with the regime type in three ways. First, the public sphere makes different assumptions regarding the forms of political organization, such as corporatism, social democracy, and liberalism. These three forms of political organization correspond to Esping-Andersen's (1990) classification of three welfare regime models, which are described more thoroughly in the following section. Second, the public sphere differs in how it overlaps with the market sphere (which comprises private firms) the state sphere, and the private sphere. The nature of the overlap illustrates the relationship between the state and civil society in the various regime types. Finally, the public sphere differs in size in each country (Janoski 1998). Thus, in practice, the state, market, public, and private spheres are neither separate from, nor independent of, each other (Edwards 2009).

In corporatist regimes, three different institutions provide social welfare: the family, the state, and federations consisting of organizations representing different interests. The cooperation between the welfare state and federations is well established, and the latter strongly influence political processes and decision-making. Accordingly, the state sphere overlaps largely with the market and public spheres. In terms of voluntary participation and participatory structures in nongovernmental organizations, the public sphere is smaller in corporatist regimes than in social democracies and liberal regimes. This is due to the principle of subsidiarity and the importance of the family as a welfare provider. Contrary to the corporatist model, social democratic regimes recognize social cleavages as a problem that can only be solved through the intervention of both state and civil society. Subsequently, overlapping areas exist between all spheres, and most nonprofit associations rely partly or fully on governmental subsidies. Due to the assumption that social inequality is counterbalanced relatively effortlessly, the state has no significant engagement in liberal regimes. Although contributing to some extent, the state does not support permanently nonprofit organizations. For that reason, the public sphere is much larger than in corporatist regimes, and the areas overlapping with the market and the state spheres are small.

These classifications of welfare regimes only apply to Western European countries, which makes it important to describe Eastern Europe, and Poland in particular. During the communist era, the Eastern European countries possessed small, strongly regulated public spheres that developed quite differently. The case of Poland is particularly interesting, where the solidarity movement contributed to a relatively large public sphere in the 1980s. After a period of restrictions during the Communist regime, the number of nongovernmental organizations increased. These organizations offered welfare services no longer provided by the Communist regime, but not yet provided by the democratic regime (Les et al. 2000). However, commercialization of social services has led to an auxiliary role for these voluntary associations. Despite legal possibilities for cooperation with voluntary associations, public institutions at the local level only offer limited support and cooperation (Les et al. 2000; see also Rymsza 2007; Makowski 2007; Golinowska 2008).

The existence, role, and development of civil society are framed by the welfare state (see Powell and DiMaggio 1991). One of the most famous welfare state regime typologies is that of Esping-Andersen (1990), in which welfare regimes were defined through the relationship between state, market, and family. The welfare state regimes differ with regard to the degree of decommodification and the outcome of social stratification. The concept of decommodification concerns the disconnection of social insurance from the labor market. This means that the reduction of the "goods" character of work decreases workers' dependency on the market. In other words, the higher the degree of decommodification, the less power employers have over their employees. This lays the foundation for workers' movements and solidarity within social classes. Esping-Andersen's approach examines the historical development of both social and political forces. Based on the social security systems, he distinguished three types of welfare regimes: Liberal, conservative or corporatist, and social democratic. In this analysis, the social security model also represents the politics of social classes (Esping-Andersen 1989).

In the corporatist regime, comprising most central and southern European countries, the family, federations, and the state are the main welfare providers. Welfare state intervention follows either through the social security system based on previous contributions, resulting in a modest decommodification, or via a minimum of means-tested social assistance for those who are neither entitled to these funds nor can rely on families to support them. The principle of subsidiarity is due to the Catholic Church's strong influence, which supported and strengthened the traditional family model. The social security system is extensive, complex, and aims to maintain the social status of the individual. The social security system, as introduced in Germany by Bismarck in the 19th century, had two goals. First, the system aimed to prevent the working class from uniting in protest by giving different privileges to different social classes and groups, thus splitting worker interests. Second, the system tied individual loyalties to the state through, for instance, public contributions to old-age pensions. Therefore, the social hierarchy was maintained and reproduced.

A universal insurance model characterizes the social democratic welfare regime. It is associated with the Nordic countries, where the welfare state carries the responsibility for all individuals. This system is based on the Beveridge model. The state provides social services financed via taxes and redistributing social resources to promote social equality. Because the market does not play a significant role regarding providing welfare services, this regime type harbors the highest degree of decommodification. In addition to universal basic insurance, this model features voluntary health and unemployment insurance based on previous contributions.

The liberal regime model is mainly found in the Anglo-Saxon world. Here, corporations are the main providers of welfare through private insurance because the state's responsibility is limited to low-level, means-tested, welfare provision. The degree of decommodification is low because the state promotes the market via low compensations in the social security system and subvention of private insurances. As a result, this system contributes to a society divided into an underclass relying on state-financed assistance and a middle class with private insurances.

However, Esping-Andersen's "three worlds" do not exist in the pure states described above. Furthermore, the country clusters are not coherent unities but are interrelated with different forms of welfare arrangements and cultures (Pfau-Effinger 2005). Esping-Andersen's typology does not sufficiently explain these intracluster differences (Serrano Pascual 2007). Consequently, (sub)regimes of social protection must be differentiated (Barbier 2004). This differentiation is particularly true for the corporatist regime. An additional regime comprising the southern European democracies was added due to their strong orientation toward the principle of subsidiarity and their comparatively recent development of a relatively weak social insurance system (e.g., Ferrera 1996; Bonoli 1997; Rhodes 1996; Ebbinghaus 1998). Other studies focus on labor market regulations and social protection (Cinalli and Giugni 2010) or integrating active labor market policies (Powell and Barrientos 2004; Janoski 1994; Gallie and Paugam 2000; Lødemel and Trickey 2000) into the welfare regime approach.

Esping-Andersen's classification (1990) was based on the relationship between state, market, and family. Due to the absence of market, the Eastern European countries were not included in his analysis. Consequently, the particular case of Poland is instructive. The country has maintained a strong orientation toward the EU countries since beginning membership negotiations in 1993, and ultimate EU entry in 2004 (Plomien 2004). Similar to the Southern European (corporatist) countries, the family and the Catholic Church are important elements in the welfare state. Social protection is weak, and the access to benefits is linked to professional status. Thus, following the classification of Esping-Andersen (1990), Poland could belong to the group of corporatist Bismarckian countries (Zukowski 2009). However, due to the Polish social security system that orients toward a larger extent of market solutions (Rymsza 2007; Makowski 2007), the low degree of decommodification, and significant social inequalities (Zukowski 2009), the Polish welfare model currently seems closer to the residual or liberal welfare regime. This development has led to a mixed structure and, consequently, Poland has been described as a "paternalistic-market hybrid" (Księzopolski 2004).

Against this theoretical background, we formulated the following research questions: What similarities and differences can be observed between countries with regard to their patterns of services and activities offered to unemployed clients? Can welfare regime theory explain these similarities and differences?

Methodology

Data in this study was collected during 2009 in one city per country in four EU member states: Germany (Cologne), Italy (Turin), Poland (Kielce), and Sweden (Karlstad). The cities, although varying in size and structure, are regarded as representatives for each country and, in turn, for each regime type. Germany and Italy represent the corporatist regime, Poland the liberal, and Sweden the social democratic. Therefore, the cities are not further mentioned. Instead, the civil society organizations are described by the country within which they exist. To be included in the sample, the organizations must exhibit a nonprofit orientation and status as nongovernmental actors, and be active in the field of unemployment. This highly inclusive approach allowed for a sample comprising civil society organizations, social movement organizations, church-related organizations, trade unions, political parties and other types of organizations, such as cooperatives and service centers.

The strategies and actions the organizations undertake in the form of offered services and activities mirror two things: their understanding of the negative implications of unemployment and which gaps in the welfare state's provision of welfare they can fill. For that reason, we only selected service-oriented organizations that focused on offering services and activities, rather than political involvement. Although the two categories are not mutually exclusive, policy-oriented organizations are characterized by activities expressing values, interests, and beliefs, while service-oriented organizations focus on the direct delivery of services

(Salamon et al. 2003). In Cologne, 23 service-oriented organizations participated in the study, along with 28 in Turin, 24 in Kielce, and 7 in Karlstad that all met our criteria for inclusion. The heterogeneity, both in terms of sample size and composition, and the cities in which they are active may limit the prerequisites for generalizations. However, although our results should be treated carefully, they still provide interesting insights into how civil society partly or entirely addresses unemployment and thereby how they complement the welfare state in which they are active.

Data was collected through face-to-face interviews with one representative of each organization (typically the formal contact person) by means of a semistructured questionnaire. Our results are based on three open-ended questions regarding the organizations' main goals, perceived usefulness of their work, and wishes concerning future activities: how does your organization relate to its main goals to help unemployed people; how do you consider your work to be useful for the unemployed; and what would your organization like to do about unemployment that it is not able to do? Open-ended questions allow the respondents to answer freely with their own thoughts and wording, emphasizing issues they perceive as important. In this respect, this is a study of 82 interviews based on qualitative data, which allowed an inductive approach to the analysis. Inspired by grounded theory (see Corbin and Strauss, 2008), the analytic process began with coding of the data, while simultaneously allowing for us to write memos of our thoughts and reflections. We then moved to the second step, which is described as axial coding or categorizing the codes. The categories we found allowed us to identify country-specific patterns.

Goals and strategies

The overarching goal of the civil society organizations active in this field is the social integration of their clients, which permits these individuals to participate in society. In the views of the organizations, important prerequisites for the social integration of the individual include the following: awareness of social rights, learning the language, having full citizenship status, and better living conditions. Thus, participation in society involves a wide spectrum of factors and, depending on the target groups of the various organizations, different aspects are emphasized.

The organizations understand unemployment as but one element within an entire life situation. Unemployment is not necessarily regarded as the source of all problems in other spheres of life but seen as a problem affecting all other life spheres in a negative way. Some associations address only unemployment by offering training, education, and job searching activities, while others primarily support clients suffering from poverty or homelessness, offering (them) also unemployment-related activities. This view on unemployment becomes evident when studying the organizations' services and activities, which mirror the strategies for reaching the two overarching goals of social integration and fighting poverty.

These strategies differ in two respects. Firstly, the organization's target groups vary. In Germany, Italy, and Poland, most associations are open to broader-defined groups of clients who are in a highly vulnerable situation. Many of these clients are in a complex, difficult situation, some of whom are homeless or suffering from long-term unemployment, which shows that these problematic aspects often overlap. In contrast, the Swedish associations are often highly specialized, targeting long-term unemployment with additional difficulties, such as being an immigrant not speaking the language, lacking social contacts, or having a history of imprisonment. In addition to working under rather tight financial constraints, which the organizations in all four countries have in common, the choice of target groups influences the strategies chosen to reach their goals.

Secondly, differences are evident in the organizations' provided services and activities. Our analysis shows that the organizations provide

Table 2.1 Typology of services and activities

	Germany	Italy	Poland	Sweden
Labor market integrating activities				
Training/education (no/yes)	Yes	Yes	Yes	Yes
Trainee jobs/subsidized jobs (no/yes)	Yes	Yes	Yes	Yes
Job searching activities (no/yes)	Yes	Yes	Yes	Yes
Benefit system-related activities				
Poverty (no/yes)	Yes	Yes	Yes	No
In-kind support (no/yes)	Yes	No	No	No
Access to social rights (no/yes)	Yes	Yes	No	Yes
Activities related to political structure				
Awareness of political structures (no/yes)	Yes	Yes	No	Yes
Awareness of own rights (no/yes)	Yes	Yes	No	No
Solidarity (no/yes)	Yes	Yes	No	Yes
Psychosocial activities				
Moral support, counseling (no/yes)	Yes	Yes	No	Yes
Self-esteem (no/yes)	Yes	Yes	No	Yes

four different types of services. In all countries, the services provided directly target labor market integration of the unemployed via training, education, or job-searching support. Complementary areas of services and activities are undertaken simultaneously: benefit systems, policies, or empowerment. Table 2.1 shows the typology of activity fields covered by the organizations in the various countries.

Integration through work and the labor market

The first identified strategy for pursuing the overarching goal of social integration concerns work. The predominant position of work as a socially integrating element becomes evident when considering that civil society organizations in all countries not only offer employability-increasing activities but also would like to extend these activities. Training, education, trainee jobs, subsidized jobs, and job searching activities are forms of support directly targeting unemployment and are offered in all four countries, to various extents.

When addressing the labor market, the organizations in Germany, Italy, and Poland focus on activities such as training, education, and internships. Activities such as application training are also provided. Workshops, internships, and placements are considered useful, and also help the unemployed gain new competencies by offering various educational programs such as those to "retrain the unemployed farmers so that they can begin a new job" (director, Poland). In these three countries, interviewees expressed the desire to extend the offer of employment measures.

For the young unemployed, other forms of support are also provided, such as helping them "find their way. Current youth need orientation about where to find a job, how to apply, and which job is the best, considering their skills and expectations" (responsible for help desk for unemployed, Italy). This lack of direction is not necessarily an indication of current trends in youth cultures, but may demonstrate that many of the young, long-term unemployed "do not have assistance at home to find a job, so the organization tries to fill those gaps" (administrative leader, Germany).

The Swedish associations offer training and education to a more modest extent. Instead, they support the social integration of their clients primarily by providing an occupation within the organization, as in the case of social cooperatives, or by giving assistance in job seeking. These activities are adjusted to the organizations' specific target groups, many of whom have problems other than the lack of employment: not speaking the language, mental illness, or previous drug abuse. The clients have little or no work experience. In one organization, the "participants work themselves well and healthy together" (instructor). In another organization "it is a good start for the participants to learn to be punctual and the like to be able to move on to society" (chairman). A strong belief persists that work in an environment of understanding will support the way (back) into the labor market. In Sweden, the conviction that social integration will follow through (re)entrance into the labor market is widespread, which demonstrates the importance of employment in this society (Esping-Andersen 1990).

The nonprofit organizations in this study are trying to adapt their activities to the demands of their countries' labor markets. In Sweden, the need for education among the civil society organizations' clients is relatively small. This condition may reflect that active labor market policies, which include training, constitute only one of two pillars of Swedish labor market policies. Knowledge and education characterize the second pillar. The Adult Education Initiative, called *Komvux*, allows adults with incomplete or no upper secondary-school education to complete their compulsory education or to graduate. Furthermore, regional colleges partly function as active labor market policies (Salonen 2001). The extent to which German, Italian, and Polish associations provide employability-increasing activities indicates a need for these services that are not sufficiently offered by the state.

Since the 1990s, employability has been a core element of the EES, as well as in the national social and labor market policies of many European countries. Employability is often depicted as central to the transition from job to job and from unemployment to employment (Keune and Jepsen 2007). The concept has a distinct focus on individual characteristics, explaining unemployment through a lack of employability (Garsten and Jacobsson 2004; Serrano Pascual 2001; Lindsay and Serrano Pascual 2009). Thus, a supply-side orientation is implied (Jacobsson 2004). European social policy also had a strong impact on Polish social policy and labor market regulations, such as the unemployment benefit system (Portet and Sztandar-Sztanderska 2010) and active labor market policies influenced by the notion of flexicurity (Golinowska 2009).

In Poland, the main problem concerns the financial constraints limiting the amount of assistance programs for the unemployed, especially for active measures. The associations would like to expand their activities. Although promoting social economy via social cooperatives has been mentioned, increasing clients' qualifications and activating more of the unemployed are central. The Polish welfare state regime has systematically followed a trend toward liberalization and privatization in its social and unemployment policies by introducing workfare and explicitly following the liberal welfare regime scheme (Standing 1996). The interest in increasing employability in many Polish organizations could be interpreted as a reaction in line with the logic of workfare or as a consequence of the low level of unemployment benefits that the long-term unemployed receive (Portet and Sztandar-Sztanderska 2010).

The organizations in the four countries all would like to establish or expand cooperation with organizations in other spheres. However, there are distinctive patterns. Our results show that the desire for stronger ties to the state is predominant in all countries, but collaboration with other spheres is also mentioned, although in different combinations. The Italian and German associations believe that better cooperation between civil society organizations and public bodies, such as the Public Employment Service (PES) and the municipality, would help them achieve their goals of social and possibly also labor market integration. Although the economic situation of the associations is often described as harsh, their strongest desire is not for direct financial support but for cooperation, primarily with the PES. In Germany, many organizations state that their clients are not being heard or respected in their contact with authorities and do not understand the information they are given. Consequently, the organizations offer specific types of assistance to support the unemployed by, for instance, accompanying them to the PES and other offices. Several other organizations also wish to offer this service. In the Southern European democracies, cooperation between different spheres is generally weak (Ebbinghaus 1998). In Italy, this results in the demand for cooperation in wider circles, including the social partners (mainly state and market), to establish a direct link between training and employment.

One important area of difficulties expressed among the Polish organizations concerns the surrounding network of authorities. The organizations face negative attitudes from officials at the lower levels of public administration. Thus, despite annually renewed programs of cooperation between public authorities and civil society organizations (Sztandar-Sztanderska 2009), the cooperation of the labor market and social policy public institutions with nonpublic actors remains insufficient (Rymsza 2007; Makowski 2007). However, the voluntary organizations express not only a wish for more cooperation with public institutions. Due to a weak network among nonprofit organizations targeting similar groups of clients, they also wish for extended collaboration with other nonprofit organizations in the field as well as the private sector. This desire implies a trend toward market orientation within civil society.

The social security system in the social democratic regime is, in literature, often described as universalistic and generous. However, the clients of the Swedish organizations often have complex personal situations and need support from various authorities, which is not always met. This leads to an explicit wish for better cooperation with the state sphere in a slightly broader sense to ensure their clients' need for long-term security. These authorities include the PES, the social insurance office, the municipality, and the county council. One of the organizations' desires for improvement of activities is the space of action, which is perceived to be limited through rigid regulations. For instance, despite positive results, a successful project for migrant women was cancelled due to surrounding legislation. Although the system supports voluntary associations to a large extent because the state sphere largely overlaps with the public one (Janoski 1998), this situation indicates that the highly regulated Swedish system also hampers the activities of the civil society organizations.

Integration through the benefit system

The second category of strategies concerns access to the benefit system. Although work is considered central to social integration, the financial situation of the unemployed is another important element. In Germany, Italy, and Poland, the long-term unemployed who cannot rely on their families' resources depend on social assistance. However, acquiring access to the social security system is a difficult task, especially for immigrants and people with minimal education, for whom the formal bureaucratic language is often an insurmountable undertaking. The welfare system may be unfamiliar, there is a long list of information the applicants must provide, and the bureaucratic language is often difficult to understand, even for native speakers.

Consequently, nonprofit organizations in all countries offer support in obtaining access to the welfare system. The main task is to direct clients where to turn, translate documents, and educate them about the social security system and their rights. In some of the German organizations, volunteers also accompany the clients to the PES because those visits are linked to unemployment benefits. The demand for these services is so great that many organizations would like to expand their staff in order to provide these activities to a larger extent. In Sweden, the reason for helping clients access the welfare system is somewhat different. Despite a universal social security system, many clients have difficulties with authorities not cooperating with each other. This leaves clients caught between the responsibilities of two different authorities, which results in less support than that to which they feel entitled. This situation could be an indication of the increasing conditionality for social benefits, with demands that the weaker groups in society have difficulty fulfilling.

Poverty is addressed as a major problem among German, Italian, and Polish organizations, which can be directly linked to the rather modest benefit levels in corporatist social security systems (Zukowski 2009). This situation leads to an explicit wish for a higher level of financial support for the unemployed. Thus the voluntary organizations are active in areas characterized with poverty and unemployment but work also with many homeless people, most of whom are also unemployed. Access to the social security system is often accompanied by in-kind support such as providing food and clothing. In Germany, one highly specialized service involves organizations selling furniture at a significantly reduced rate. The provision of in-kind support, such as housing, financial support, and food, has been of historical importance in Poland (Les et al. 2000). These services are often combined with activities to increase the clients' job-searching skills. However, despite the long tradition of charity organizations, the intense focus on homelessness and poverty-related issues is unsurprising, given the low number of registered unemployed receiving benefits. Additionally, the levels of unemployment benefits are low, and the financial situation of those not entitled to unemployment benefits is extremely limited (Sztandar-Sztanderska 2009; Portet and Sztandar-Sztanderska 2010).

Targeting unemployment policies

The third strategy is directed toward policies related to unemployment. The service-oriented civil society organizations in this study are not limited to practical, labor-market-related services. Working with weak and vulnerable groups in society, associations in Germany, Italy, and to some extent also Sweden perceive their role to be a mouthpiece for their clients. Although collective protests of post-Communist civil society organizations have been a sign of a strong civil society (see e.g. Ekiert and Kubik 1999; Kopecky and Mudde 2003), the Polish associations participating in this study are the exception and do not address the political structure as a particular problem on a noteworthy level.

Two possible explanations are either that this form of advocacy is only performed by policy-oriented organizations or, considering that the main goal of Polish organizations is alleviating the consequences of poverty, the organizations primarily focus on practical matters rather than structural issues.

As a contrast, German organizations demand more publicity to "give a real picture of unemployment and poverty without pretending the unemployed are responsible for their situation" (managing director). This approach is strongly linked to efforts to abolish the Hartz IV reform and the 1-Euro jobs, due to their severe impact on clients' financial and psychological situations. Most German organizations are palpably aware of politics and speak of societal solidarity, convinced that unemployment is a structural problem. Political awareness in Italy is equally strong, although the focus is slightly different. A significant number of organizations perceive their activities as a way to achieve political and democratic goals, which are described as "providing individuals a full citizenship status through their work" (president of cooperative, Italy). Italian unemployment policies are changing toward more active labor market policies, but also to increase the role of the public sector regarding financial compensation of the unemployed. This approach results from the weak social security system in southern European democracies (Ebbinghaus 1998). In both countries, the associations take advocacy roles, drawing public attention to the complex problems of unemployment and defending social rights (Salamon et al. 2003).

As mentioned previously, many clients of the Swedish associations have a history of perceiving that they do not belong to any authority's area of responsibility and are left without support. In these specific cases, health issues have made them unable to work, yet their health problems and the reasons for them are disregarded. The interpretation of unemployment as an "illness" that can be treated and cured has been described as the medicalization of welfare (Schram 2000; Holmqvist 2009). In this perspective, the fundamental problems leading to unemployment are ignored. Contrary to that view, the organizations do not regard their members' low employability or lack of contact with the labor market as the primary problem. Rather, they focus on and problematize the lack of respect for the main problems of their clients, such as mental illness, need for re-socialization, and complicated financial or housing situations, that need to be solved before a (re-)entrance on the open labor market is possible.

Solidarity is a key concept among the voluntary associations in Germany, Italy, and Sweden, which share a common understanding of unemployment as a structural problem. Data shows that this position is clearly a reaction against the public discourse on unemployment as a problem of the individual. The associations communicate understanding and acceptance for their clients' unemployment without judging them and work to better their clients' lives or at least, as one German organization put it, make it acceptable. Giving advice about citizenship, social rights, and where to turn for other services is an essential service in Germany that is intertwined with assistance in accessing the welfare system. "Showing solidarity" (former chairman) is important, as well as "making clear that unemployment is not their own fault" (managing director, Germany).

The Italian organizations emphasize the role of the individual as a citizen in the welfare state. Aiming at supporting the unemployed to become aware of their situation, the organizations also help defend their clients' legal and social rights. This approach is important because "very often, young people do not know the mechanisms behind their realities, the mechanisms that strongly affect their life" (spokesperson). By helping clients claim benefits to which they are entitled, these associations mediate between state and citizen (Kohler-Koch and Quittkat 2011; see also Salamon et al. 2003) and function as platforms for the interests of the target groups (European Commission 2011). Consequently, the organizations serve as a means for maintaining self-government (Kohler-Koch and Quittkat 2011).

In Sweden, the influence of labor and social movement organizations has contributed to a state-financed, generous, extensive social security system. Because the social democratic welfare state delivers welfare services, the need for involvement by nonprofit organizations in this field has traditionally been limited. Instead, these organizations have been more engaged in advocacy and related fields (Salamon et al. 2003). However, the activities offered by service-oriented associations working with the unemployed reflect an immense need for services complementary to those of the welfare state and more suited to clients' needs, which indicates that the need for tailor-made solutions respecting the individual is increasing, for instance through involving nonprofit organizations. Furthermore, the organizations express the need to support and protect their clients against regulations forcing them into a labor market for which they are not ready. This demonstrates the perceived importance of advocating for the interests of the unemployed.

A market-oriented vision dominates the Polish nonprofit associations not focused on charity issues, who regard unemployment as a problem that the individual must personally address in order to change their situation. Consequently, the activities usually concern the "improvement of the unemployeds' qualifications so that they meet labor market needs" (leader), teaching the unemployed "how to be an active citizen and how to cooperate" (spokesperson), and "changing people's mentality so they can better organize themselves and be punctual" (spokesperson). This view point is an expression of, or adaption to, an increasingly individualized society with a liberal approach to activation, where the unemployed are expected to rely on themselves and their own capabilities in the labor market (see Sztandar-Sztanderska 2009).

Integration via psychosocial counseling of the individual

As we have seen, most nonprofit organizations in this study focus on the so-called weaker groups in the labor market, such as the long-term unemployed, immigrants, homeless people, former convicts, and people with mental illness. Consequently, the need for individual counseling is immense among these clients, who often have difficulty or cannot claim their social rights and individually adjusted placements of education, training, and jobs. Engaging in the clients' personal situation, as well as encouraging, understanding, and empowering clients, is highly valued in Germany, Italy, and Sweden. In these countries, almost all organizations emphasize and practice this form of psychosocial counseling, which is an important example of services that complement those of a government that fails to provide the public goods required (Salamon and Anheier 1998).

The German associations depict a huge need for the provision of counseling adapted to individual situations, particularly for young people who do not get the support they need from their parents, non-German speaking immigrants, the homeless, former convicts, and the mentally ill. However, psychosocial counseling is also offered for the "future perspectives of the unemployed to give their lives a meaning" (chairwoman). The organizations' work on enhancing clients' low self-esteem, for instance, through "making them able to speak for themselves" (managing director), is perceived as an important step toward independence as a citizen.

With an emphasis on the psychological aspect, the Italian organizations empower their young clients to become "more aware about their possibilities and their potential" (president), but also to help them "find their way" (responsible for unemployment help desk), "improve their self-perception" (president of association), and "allow them a better understanding of the world they live in" (spokesperson). Understanding the surrounding world may also include information about where to find a job and how to apply.

Similar to the Italian associations, Swedish organizations emphasize the importance of recognizing the individuals' factual capabilities. By helping their clients discover their qualities and strengths and by providing "shelter and stability" (tutor), the organizations try to give these individuals a chance to build their self-confidence. Giving "constant acknowledgement and the feeling of being needed" (supervisor) is crucial because a healthy self-esteem is the "be all and end all for those who have been away from the labor market for a long time" (instructor). Among the Polish associations, psychosocial counseling as it is understood in this study, was not mentioned. As shown previously, the strategies of the Polish organizations are divided into two main paths: employability-increasing or fighting poverty. It is possible that the harsh financial situation of most organizations' clients makes charity for the most needy and employability-increasing activities or (subsidized or trainee) job placements for clients with a greater ability to work prioritized. Additionally, the organizations' sources of funding may influence which services to offer. Nonprofit organizations offering employability-increasing activities are partially supported by European funds. Further, the viewpoint that unemployment is an individual problem may also explain the absence of psychosocial counseling among the Polish organizations.

Conclusions

The objectives of this chapter were to explore similarities and differences in the strategies of service-oriented, civil society organizations and to discuss if the welfare state regime to which they belong can help explain these similarities and dissimilarities. Against the theoretical conceptualization of civil society in the context of political theory on the one hand, and welfare state regime types on the other, large dissimilarities could be expected. However, the empirical data shows that despite varieties in patterns and country clusters, similarities dominate regarding goals, strategies, and activities and services offered.

We classified the strategies of the civil society organizations in this study into four categories according to the kinds of services and activities they provide. Our research shows that the overarching goals of social integration or relieving the consequences of poverty are achieved via four channels: work or work-related activities, services addressing the welfare-system, individual psychosocial counseling, and activities directed toward the political structure. The fourth category is an example of the dual nature of many civil society organizations, primarily engaged in services, but also in political involvement and advocacy that relate to the political system.

The prominent position of work-related and employability-increasing activities among organizations in all four countries is striking. In part, the high value of work, training, and education is a consequence of the severe competition for available jobs that follows high unemployment rates of a long duration. When competition is high, weaker groups in the labor market, such as the long-term unemployed, young people, immigrants, and the disabled, will have even more difficulty (re)entering the labor market.

Another interesting result is that organizations in all four countries are engaged in different forms of activities related to the financial situation of their clients and the benefit system. This finding is particularly surprising in the case of Sweden, a country with a social democratic welfare regime, where the social security system has traditionally been universal and considered generous. Access to the Swedish welfare system is difficult for many clients, which supports the signs of change toward a higher level of conditionality when claiming social benefits.

The German, Italian, and Swedish organizations pursue similar strategies with respect to addressing the political structures and thematizing solidarity, but also with regard to psychosocial counseling. The emphasis on solidarity with the unemployed is an important element. In contrast, the Polish civil society organizations do not claim to be involved in either psychosocial counseling or advocacy of the unemployed. Another difference is that, contrary to the German, Italian, and Swedish, the Polish nonprofit organizations tend to regard unemployment as an individual problem, rather than a structural one. This approach may be explained by the strong orientation toward liberalism in Poland during the past decade, which differs from both the conservative tradition in Germany and Italy, and the social democratic tradition in Sweden.

Thus, welfare models seem to be a significant variable when explaining path dependencies and patterns of civil society. On the other hand, the similarities in our empirical data can be seen as examples of the interrelation between countries, despite different historically and culturally established welfare traditions (see Pfau-Effinger 2005). The strong focus on the labor market and employability increasing, and benefit-system activities could also be interpreted as a trend toward a convergence in the traces of European employment policies. However, the recommendations of the EES and the guidelines on employability are not homogeneously translated into national debates (Lahusen 2009). In other words, cultural context has a significant influence on the implementation of the EES.

A final remark concerns an important aspect of the role of civil society organizations for the unemployed within the welfare state. The similarities in goals, strategies, and activities of civil society organizations working with the unemployed imply that the patterns break with the schemes of civil society's role within different welfare regime types. More importantly, these similarities indicate that none of the welfare regime models sufficiently support the needs of the weakest groups in society. Noteworthy in this context is the organizations' perception of unemployment, which reaches far beyond a mere lack of employment, implying a need for support in job searching and acquiring work experience and competencies. Reflected in the spectrum of activities offered by civil society organizations in corporatist Germany and Italy, social democratic Sweden and liberal Poland (see Zukowski 2009), their perception of unemployment comprises and emphasizes also the individual consequences of unemployment, including the often vulnerable situation of the unemployed that requires different forms of support related to harsh financial conditions. In Germany, Italy, and Sweden, this holistic approach to unemployment and thus the organizations' own role also includes relieving the pressure of the unemployed to feel responsible for their own situation, mainly by showing moral support and increasing the self-esteem of the unemployed, but also by advocacy of their clients. These may be the most important steps toward an improved life situation of the unemployed.

References

Baglioni, S., B. Denters, L. Morales, and A. Vetter (2011) "City Size and the Nature of Associational Ecologies," in Maloney, W. A. and S. Rossteutscher (eds), *Social Capital and Associations in European Democracies: A Comparative Analysis* (London and New York: Routledge).

Barbier, J. C. (2004) "Systems of Social Protection in Europe: Two Contrasted Paths to Activation, and Maybe a Third," in Lind, J., H. Knudsen, and H. Joergensen (eds), *Labour and Employment Regulation in Europe* (Bruxelles: PIE Lang).

Bonoli, G. (1997) "Classifying Welfare States: A Two-Dimension Approach," *Journal of Social Policy*, 26, 351–372.

Cinalli, M. and M. Giugni (2010) "Welfare States, Political Opportunities, and the Claim-Making in the Field of Unemployment Politics," in Giugni M. (ed.), *The Contentious Politics of Unemployment in Europe: Welfare States and Political Opportunities* (Basingstoke, Hampshire, UK: Palgrave Macmillan).

Cohen, J. L. and A. Arato (1992) *Civil Society and Political Theory: Studies in Contemporary German Social Thought* (Cambridge, MA: MIT Press).

Corbin, J. M. and A. L. Strauss (2008) *Basics of Qualitative Research: Techniques and Procedures for Developing Grounded Theory* (3rd ed.) (Thousand Oaks: Sage).

Ebbinghaus, B. (1998) "European Labor Relations and Welfare-State Regimes: A Comparative Analysis of Their 'Elective Affinities'," Paper presented at the International Conference of Europeanists, Baltimore, 26 February–1 March.

Edwards, M. (2009) *Civil Society* (2nd ed.) (Cambridge: Polity Press).

Ekiert, G. and J. Kubik (1999) *Rebellious Civil Society: Popular Protest and Democratic Consolidation in Poland, 1989–1993* (Ann Arbor: University of Michigan Press).

Esping-Andersen, G. (1990) *The Three Worlds of Welfare Capitalism* (Oxford: Polity Press).

Esping-Andersen, G. (1989) "The Three Political Economies of the Welfare State," *Canadian Review of Sociology*, 26, 10–36.

European Commission (2011) European Governance: A White Paper. COM, 2001 428 Final, Brussels, http://eurlex.europa.eu/LexUriServ/site/en/com/2001/com2001_0428en01.pdf, accessed 23 October 2011.

Ferrera, M. (1996) "The 'Southern Model' of Welfare in Social Europe," *Journal of European Social Policy*, 6, 17–37.

Gallie, D. and Paugam, S. (2000) "The Experience of Unemployment in Europe: The Debate," in Gallie, D. and S. Paugam (eds), *Welfare Regimes and the Experience of Unemployment in Europe* (Oxford/New York: Oxford University Press).

Garsten, C. and K. Jacobsson (2004) "Learning to Be Employable: An Introduction," in Garsten, C. and K. Jacobsson (eds), *Learning to Be Employable: New Agendas on Work, Responsibility and Learning in a Globalizing World* (New York: Palgrave Macmillan).

Gilbert, N. (2002) *Transformation of the Welfare State: The Silent Surrender of Public Responsibility* (Oxford: Oxford University Press).

Giugni, M. (2009) "State and Civil Society Responses to Unemployment: Welfare, Conditionality and Collective Action," in Giugni, M. (ed.), *The Politics of Unemployment in Europe: Policy Responses and Collective Action* (Aldershot: Ashgate).

Golinowska, S. (2009) "The National Model of the Welfare State in Poland: Tradition and Changes," in Golinowska, S., P. Hengstenberg, and M. Zukowski (eds), *Diversity and Commonality in European Social Policies: The Forging of a European Social Model* (Warszawa: Scholar).

Golinowska, S. (2008) "A Case Study of the European Welfare System Model in the Postcommunist Countries – Poland," in *State-based Welfare Prospects of Social Security and Harmony in Asia and Europe* (Beijing: FES and China Social Insurance Association).

Handler, J. F. (2003) "Social Citizenship and Workfare in the US and Western Europe: From Status to Contract," *Journal of European Social Policy*, 13, 229–243.

Hansmann, H. B. (1980) "The Role of Nonprofit Enterprise," *The Yale Law Journal*, 89(5), 835–902.

Holmqvist, M. (2009) "Medicalization of Unemployment: Individualizing Social Issues as Personal Problems in the Swedish Welfare State," *Work Employment & Society*, 23, 405–421.

Jacobsson, K. (2004) "A European Politics for Employability: The Political Discourse on Employability of the EU and the OECD," in Garsten, C. and K. Jacobsson (eds), *Learning to Be Employable: New Agendas on Work, Responsibility and Learning in a Globalizing World* (Houndmills, Basingstoke: Palgrave Macmillan).

Janoski, T. (1998) *Citizenship and Civil Society: A Framework of Rights and Obligations in Liberal Traditional and Social Democratic Regimes* (Cambridge: Cambridge University Press).

Janoski, T. (1994) "Direct State Intervention in the Labor Market: The Explanation of Active Labour Market Policy from 1950 to 1988 in Social Democratic, Conservative and Liberal Regimes," in Janoski, T. and A. M. Hicks (eds), *The Comparative Political Economy of the Welfare State* (Cambridge: Cambridge University Press).

Keune, M. and M. Jepsen (2007) "Not Balanced and Hardly New: The European Commission's Quest for Flexicurity," in Jörgensen, H. P. and P. K. Madsen (eds), *Flexicurity and Beyond* (Copenhagen: DJØF).

Kohler-Koch, B. and C. Quittkat (2011) "What Is 'Civil Society' and Who Represents it in the European Union?" in Liebert, U. and H. -J. Trenz (eds), *The New Politics of European Civil Society* (London: Routledge).

Kopecky, P. and Mudde, C. (2003) "Rethinking Civil Society," *Democratization*, 10, 1–14.

Księżopolski, M. (2004) "Co dalej z polityką społeczną w Polsce? Od socjalistycznych gwarancji do paternalistyczno-rynkowej hybrydy," in Rymsza, M. (ed.), *Reformy społeczne. Bilans dekady* (Warsaw: Institute of Public Affairs).

Lahusen, C. (2009) "The Hidden Hand of the European Union and the Silent Europeanization of Public Debates on Unemployment: The Case of the European Employment Strategy," in Giugni, M. (ed.), *The Politics of Unemployment in Europe: Policy Responses and Collective Action* (Aldershot: Ashgate).

Les, E., S. Nalecz, and J. Wygnanski (2000) Defining the Nonprofit Sector: Poland. Working Papers of the Johns Hopkins Comparative Nonprofit Sector Project, no. 36. (Baltimore: The Johns Hopkins Center for Civil Society Studies).

Lindsay, C. and A. Serrano Pascual (2009) "New Perspectives on Employability and Labour Market Policy: Reflecting on Key Issues," *Environment and Planning C: Government and Policy*, 27, 951–957.

Lødemel, I. and H. Trickey (eds) (2000) *An Offer You Can't Refuse: Workfare in an International Perspective* (Bristol: Policy Press).

Makowski, G. (2007) "Polityka rządu wobec organizacji," in Kolarska-Bobińska, L. (ed.), *Demokracja w Polsce w latach 2005–2007* (Warsaw: Institute of Public Affairs).

Nordström Skans, O. (2004) Scarring Effects of the First Labour Market Experience: A Sibling Based Analysis. Working paper 2004: 14 (Uppsala: IFAU).

Pfau-Effinger, B. (2005) "Culture and Welfare State Policies: Reflections on a Complex Interrelation," *Journal of Social Policy*, 34, 3–20.

Plomien, A. (2004) From Socialism to Capitalism: Women and Their Changed Relationship with the Labour Market in Poland. Working paper No. 68. (Bamberg: Globalife).

Portet, S. and K. Sztandar-Sztanderska (2010) "Poland. Unemployment Benefit: Haunted by a Lack of Legitimacy," in Lefresne, F. (ed.), *Unemployment Benefit*

Systems in Europe and North America: Reforms and Crisis (Brussels: European Trade Union Institute).

Powell, M. and A. Barrientos (2004) "Welfare Regimes and the Welfare Mix," *European Journal of Political Research*, 43, 83–105.

Powell, W. W. and P. J. DiMaggio (eds) (1991) *The New Institutionalism in Organizational Analysis* (Chicago: The University of Chicago Press).

Putnam, R. D. (1993) *Making Democracy Work: Civic Traditions in Modern Italy* (Princeton, NJ: Princeton University Press).

Rhodes, M. (1996) "Southern European Welfare States: Identity, Problems and Prospects for Reform," *South European Society and Politics*, 1, 1–22.

Rymsza, M. (2007) "Polityka państwa wobec sektora obywatelskiego w Polsce w latach 1989–2007," in Rymsza, M. (ed.), *Państwo a trzeci sector* (Warsaw: Institute of Public Affairs).

Salamon, L. M. and H. K. Anheier (1998) "Social Origins of Civil Society: Explaining the Nonprofit Sector Cross-Nationally," *Voluntas: International Journal of Voluntary and Nonprofit Organizations*, 9, 213–247.

Salamon, L. M, S. W., Sokolowski, and R. List (2003) *Global Civil Society: An Overview* (Baltimore: Center for Civil Society Studies, The John Hopkins University).

Salonen, T. (2001) "Sweden: Between Model and Reality," in Alcock, P. and G. Craig (eds), *International Social Police: Welfare Regimes in the Developed World* (Basingstoke: Palgrave Macmillan).

Schmidt, J. (2007) *Zivilgesellschaft: Bürgerschaftliches Engagement von der Antike bis zur Gegenwart* (Reinbek, Germany: Rowohlt).

Schram, S. F. (2000) "In the Clinic: The Medicalization of Welfare," *Social Text* 62, 18, 81–107.

Serrano Pascual, A. (2001) "The Role of Social and Civil Partnership Networks in Combating Youth Unemployment," in Serrano Pascual, A. (ed.), *Enhancing Youth Employability through Social and Civil Partnerships* (Brussels: European Trade Union Institute).

Serrano Pascual, A. (2007) "Reshaping Welfare States: Activation Regimes in Europe," in Serrano Pascual, A. and Magnusson, L. (eds), *Reshaping Welfare States and Activation Regimes in Europe* (Brussels: Peter Lang).

Standing, G. (1996) "Social Protection in Central and Eastern Europe: A Tale of Slipping Anchors and Torn Safety Nets," in Esping-Andersen, G. (ed.), *Welfare States in Transition: National Adaptations in Global Economies* (London: Sage).

Starrin, B., U. Rantakeisu, and E. Forsberg (1999) "I arbetslöshetens spår: ekonomisk stress, skam och ohälsa," in Bustos Castro, P. and A. Härenstam (eds), *I vanmaktens spår: om sociala villkor, utsatthet och ohälsa* (Umeå: Boréa).

Starrin, B., Rantakeisu, U. and C. Hagquist (1996) "Om arbetslöshetens ekonomi och skam" *Socialvetenskaplig tidskrift*, 1–2, 91–114.

Steffek, J. and P. Nanz (2008) "Emergent Patterns of Civil Society Participation in Global and European Governance," in Steffek, J., C. Kissling, and P. Nanz (eds), *Civil Society Participation in European and Global Governance: A Cure for the Democratic Deficit?* (Basingstoke: Palgrave Macmillan).

Stryjan, Y. and F. Wijkström (1996) "Cooperatives and Nonprofit Organizations in Swedish Social Welfare," *Annals of Public and Cooperative Economics*, 67, 5–27.

Sztandar-Sztanderska, K. (2009) "Activation of the Unemployed in Poland: From Policy Design to Policy Implementation," *International Journal of Sociology and Social Policy*, 29: 624–636.

Zukowski, M. (2009) "Social Policy Regimes in the European Countries," in Golinowska, S., P. Hengstenberg, and M. Zukowski (eds), *Diversity and Commonality in European Social Policies: The Forging of a European Social Model* (Warszaw: Scholar).

3

Between Passion and Money: Human and Financial Resources and Patterns of Professionalization of Civil Society Organizations

Luís Mota and Maria Vitória Mourão

Introduction: the shifting role of civil society organizations in the policy-making process

There is a long history of relationships between the Public and the Civil Society sectors (Pestoff and Brandsen 2010: 223). Their number and scope have nevertheless increased since the early 1980s, particularly due to the "collapse of a consensus concerning the central and dominant role of the State in all areas of welfare provision" (Scott 2007: 308). As a consequence of the increasing development of partnerships between these two sectors that has taken place under the so-called managerial public sector reforms, civil society organizations have taken a significant position within the discourse and the practices of welfare policies (Scott 2007: 308).

Therefore, in addition to the traditional role of civil society organizations in the input side of the policy-making process, by being a "buffer between the rulers and ruled" (Pestoff 2009: 183) and a pressure group within the agenda-setting and decision-making processes (Rathgeb Smith and Grønbjerg 2006: 222), they also often play a role in the output side[1] of the policy-making process (Pestoff 2009: 199). That is, they may be contracted to perform policy delivery tasks or to monitor other players' deliveries (Rathgeb Smith and Grønbjerg 2006: 221).

Regardless of the lack of consensus about their main features and roles, there is general agreement about the processes of transformation and increasing differentiation of civil society organizations (Anheier and Salamon 2006: 90; White 2006: 45). In this context, several popular perceptions about the Civil Society sector have been questioned recently, including the idea that civil society organizations are all small and dependent primarily on the work of volunteers and on membership fees (Scott 2007: 309, 319). Recent research has demonstrated that, despite the co-existence of several typologies of civil society organizations, they are generically becoming larger, more professionalized, and less dependent upon their members (Barnes 2006: 105, Kriesi 2007: 118). These patterns are reportedly dependent upon factors such as the main organizational function and specific national contexts (Anheier and Salamon 2006: 97–98).

In this chapter we intend to analyze the patterns of resource distribution and professionalization that are applicable to the objects of the study, 174 civil society organizations that are active on the policy fields of youth unemployment and precariousness in seven cities from different European countries. Moreover, we will also analyze if the variance among civil society organizations regarding these organizational features is related to (a) the main organizational function; (b) the country in which the organizations are located and the corresponding national civil society regime.

Having these goals in mind, this chapter begins with a literature review concerning the amounts and sources of human and financial resources and the patterns of professionalization that civil society organizations are expected to have, depending on their main function and the civil society regime. The following section presents a description of methodological remarks. The chapter continues with the presentation of the results regarding the overall distribution of financial and human resources and the patterns of professionalization as well as results according to the main organizational function, and the country of origin and related national civil society regime. The chapter concludes with brief remarks about the findings and their contribution to theory.

The transformation of civil society organizations and their differentiation according to the main organizational function and civil society regime

The aforementioned policy's prominence of the Civil Society sector has led not only to its increasing transformation but also to the awareness that there is no such thing as a unique concept of civil society organizations. The differences from popular perceptions are primarily related to the civil society organizations' resources and patterns of professionalization, which, according to Rathgeb Smith and Grønbjerg (2006: 221), vary across several dimensions, including the main organizational function and space.

Focusing attention on the main organizational function, it has been suggested that there are considerable differences between policy-oriented and service-oriented civil society organizations with regard to the amount and sources of human and financial resources and the patterns of professionalization. As Kriesi (2007: 128) and Scott (2007: 321) argue, the provision of services requires more human resources than policy advocacy tasks, considering the activities that service-oriented organizations develop are more labour-intensive and have a more regular and continuing nature, thus requiring a workforce structure with more paid staff members. This reliance on paid staff members then leads to the need for more funds and to a greater dependence on contract-related government grants and/or on the organization's own resources resulting from "user fees" (Scott 2007: 321). On the contrary, the development of mobilization and activation tasks usually involves organizational members on a volunteer basis, particularly because there is no need for a large and continuous workforce structure (Kriesi 2007: 128–129). Therefore, policy-oriented organizations tend to rely financially primarily on membership fees and fundraising (Kriesi 2007: 128–129).

In this context, our first hypothesis is that service-oriented civil society organizations are expected to have a smaller percentage of volunteers within their workforce structures than policy-oriented organizations. Likewise, the second hypothesis is that service-oriented civil society organizations are expected to have a revenue structure that is more dependent upon state funds than policy-oriented organizations.

In addition to the influence on the amount and sources of human and financial resources, it is also believed that the increasing size and contractual requirements that service-oriented civil society organizations have to deal with have led them to improve their administrative and technical skills (Scott 2007: 330), to develop new organizational techniques, and to have a governance structure that is less dependent upon the organization's associates (Kriesi 2007: 118). According to Vernis et al. (2006: 112, 115), this need for increasing professionalization of service-oriented civil society organizations has led them to hire qualified staff members to perform management and technical support tasks, usually from outside the organization, so to avoid organizational entropy. Policy-oriented civil society organizations have, on their turn, more sporadic activities and fewer financial and, more importantly, human resources to manage, thus requiring a less professionalized structure in which the management and technical support roles are performed by a reduced number of senior and volunteer members (Vernis et al. 2006: 114–115).

As a result, our third hypothesis is that service-oriented civil society organizations are expected to have more management and technical support positions within their structures. Similarly, our fourth hypothesis is that service-oriented organizations use external recruitment techniques to hire these professionals more frequently than policy-oriented organizations.

With regard to the "space" dimension, there is general agreement about the existence of variance between civil society organizations from different countries or groups of countries clustered around what one may call "civil society regimes" (Evers and Laville 2004; Anheier and Salamon 2006; Matthies 2006). In this regard, Salamon and his associates formulated the "Social Origins Theory," which holds that civil society sectors are deeply embedded in their national current and past contexts (Anheier and Salamon, 2006: 106). Observing some common features among countries and inspired by the logic of Esping-Andersen's welfare regimes, Salamon and his team (cfr. among other, Salamon and Sokolowski 2010) have suggested the existence of the following ideal-types of civil society regimes:

- Liberal: characterized by a civil society sector that tends to assume a service-provision orientation as a consequence of the government's decreased involvement, thus requiring a large workforce but depending largely upon volunteers and private philanthropy;
- Welfare partnership (also known as Corporatist): typical of countries with relatively high public social welfare spending but where service provision is largely devoted to civil society organizations which are, therefore, highly dependent upon paid staff members and revenues from government contracts;
- Social democrat: typical of countries categorized by high levels of public welfare spending and public direct provision and by civil society organizations that play majorly an active and strong expressive role and that depend largely upon volunteers and private sources of revenue;
- Statist (also known as Deferred Democratization): typical of countries characterized by low public welfare spending and limited involvement of the civil society sector as a consequence of past repressive political regimes that discouraged volunteering as they tended to see the civil society sector as a menace;
- Traditional: typical of less developed countries in which the government welfare support is low and the civil society sector is generically composed of small organizations that are primarily devoted to poverty relief and development assistance and depend largely upon funds from foreign or religious institutions.[2]

Given the characteristics of each ideal-type, civil society organizations from "social democrat" regimes are expected to have a higher share of volunteers than civil society organizations from "liberal," "welfare partnership," and "statist" regimes. This is our fifth hypothesis. Similarly, our sixth hypothesis is that civil society organizations from "welfare partnership" regimes are expected to have greater dependence upon public funds than civil society organizations from "liberal," "social democrat," and "statist" regimes.

It is also expected that civil society organizations from "welfare partnership" and "liberal" regimes will have a more professionalized management board, as they tend to have larger workforce structures and more financial resources. Considering this professionalization pattern and their smaller share of volunteers, civil society organizations from these two regimes are also expected to use external recruitment techniques to hire management and technical support professionals more frequently than civil society organizations from "social democrat" and "statist" regimes. On the contrary, "social democrat" civil society sectors are expected to have a smaller number of management and technical support professionals, given their orientation toward expressive tasks and their subsequently smaller workforces and budgets. It is important to mention that these generic propositions, which are primarily based on the number of paid staff members and amount of financial resources, may fail in some national contexts, such as Nordic countries, that have a long history of many and dedicated volunteers who usually take on some of those positions in a quite professionalized way (Vernis et al. 2006: 114). Either way, there will be a predisposition for organizations from the "social democrat" civil society regimes to use internal recruitment processes more frequently. Finally, it is expected that organizations from "statist" civil society regimes will be less professionalized due to their smaller size, lack of public legitimacy, and less mature development processes.

Hence, our seventh hypothesis is that civil society organizations from "welfare partnership" and "liberal" regimes are expected to have more management and technical support positions than civil society organizations from "social democrat" or "statist" regimes. The civil society organizations from the two former regimes are also expected to use external recruitment techniques to hire these professionals more frequently than civil society organizations from "social democrat" and "statist" regimes, which is our eighth hypothesis.

In sum, the Civil Society sector is nowadays characterized by increasing diversity on several dimensions, particularly regarding the financial and human resources that each organization from this sector has at its disposal and its level of professionalization. Among other potential explanatory factors, it is believed that this diversity is related to determinants, such as the main organizational function or the civil society regime in which the organization is framed. These generic assumptions and the presented operational hypotheses will be tested using the data collected in the below mentioned survey. The following section presents the main data-collection and data-analysis strategies.

Methodological remarks

The source of this chapter's empirical data is the "organizational survey" of the Younex Project, particularly the questions related to the amount and sources of financial and human resources that the examined organizations have at their disposal and to their patterns of professionalization.

Regarding financial resources, respondents were first asked about the exact figures of their organizations' 2009 budget. As some respondents could not know or refused to divulge the exact figures, they were also given the option to answer on a pre-given scale (see the survey and Table 3.3), which is the variable to be used in this chapter. In addition to these more general figures, respondents from the organizations were also asked about the sources of the budgets using a list of budget lines, including returns from fundraising; membership fees; donations from individuals; sponsoring from companies/firms; finance from federation or umbrella organization; grants or financing of specific projects from governments; and a residual category to account for other sources. Although the survey solicited approximate figures in Euros, respondents were also given the option to provide an estimate of the share of each category on their overall budget. Given that respondents demonstrated a tendency not to provide the precise figures in Euros, the analysis in this chapter will be based on the share of each category, particularly on the share of public funding.

Concerning human resources, respondents were asked about the number of volunteers and full-time and part-time staff members that the organization had at its disposal. Considering the enormous variety, these figures were grouped into categories based on the human resources dimension of the European classification of enterprises (Commission Recommendation 2003/361/EC): ≤ 9 persons (micro), which was sub-divided into the categories "0 persons" and "1–9 persons"; 10–49 persons (small); 50–249 persons (medium); and ≥ 250 persons (large). In addition to these three "raw" variables, our analysis was based on three other calculated variables: the "staff," which was the sum of the figures of full-time and part-time staff; the "human resources," which was an aggregate of the number of full-time and part-time staff members and the number of volunteers; and the "percentage of volunteers within the workforce structure," which was the number of volunteers divided by the total number of human resources.

This chapter is also founded upon questions that provided a better understanding of the levels of organizational professionalization. Among them is the question in which the respondents were asked if their organization had the following professional positions: board, president, chairperson, secretary, spokesperson, and treasurer. Based on this information, the level of professionalization was assessed according to the number of management positions (board, president, and chairperson) and the number of technical support positions (secretary, spokesperson, and treasurer) that existed in each organization. Moreover, the level of professionalization was assessed by evaluating the main type of recruitment (internal, external, or mixed) used for management positions.

All three dimensions (financial resources, human resources, and professionalization patterns) are analyzed according to the main organizational function and the country of origin/civil society regime.

As regards the main organizational function, the analysis was based on the data gathered through the question in which the respondents were asked to report if their organization developed each of the following activities and to identify which one was the most important: (1) mobilization of members through protest, demonstrations, and direct actions; (2) political education of citizens by raising their awareness for policy issues; (3) interest representation; (4) provision of services to members; (5) provision of services to clients; (6) social integration; (7) fundraising; and (8) other activities. Based on their answer to the question about the most important activity, each analyzed organizations was then categorized as being predominantly policy oriented (if the most important activity was expressive in nature, namely mobilization, political education, or interest representation) or service oriented (if the provision of services to members or clients was considered to be the most important organizational activity). When the most important activity was "social integration," "fundraising," or "any other," the data-collection team analyzed whether there was a predominance of policy-oriented or service-oriented activities and categorized the organization accordingly. There were 18 cases for which this exercise was impossible, leading the team to categorise the main organizational function neither as "policy-oriented" or "service-oriented," but as "other." It is important to highlight that these 18 organizations were not included in the analysis according to the main organizational function.

Regarding the civil society regimes, we opted not to straightforwardly label each country according to what the theory suggests as the characteristics that led to those previous labelling processes could have changed in the meantime. Instead, we opted to first analyze the available empirical data about the workforce, revenue structure, and share of public welfare spending (namely, the percentage of GDP devoted to unemployment issues) from the seven countries being examined (see Table 3.1).

Starting the analysis with Sweden, this country has a civil society sector that is largely dependent upon volunteers, has a quite modest share of paid staff, a relatively low dependence on public funds (see Table 3.1) and tends to play mainly expressive roles, as some scholars mention (Pestoff 2004: 79–80; Evers 2006: 376). These characteristics combined with a high proportion of the GDP devoted to welfare protection and a medium-high percentage of the GDP dedicated to

Table 3.1 Data about workforce, revenue structure and percentage of GDP devoted to welfare from the analyzed countries

	Workforce size[a]		Revenue structure[b]			% of GDP devoted to welfare[c]		
	% of volunt.	% of paid staff	% of public funding	% of philanth. funds	% of fees funding	ALPM	Unemp. protection	Generic welfare spending
SW	7.0	2.5	28.7	9.1	62.3	1.0	0.5	27.5
FR	3.1	5.9	57.8	7.5	34.6	0.8	1.3	29.8
CH[d]	2.6	4.3	35.0	8.0	58.0	0.3	0.5	18.4
DE	3.0	3.7	64.3	3.4	32.3	0.8	1.3	25.2
IT	1.8	2.4	36.6	2.8	60.6	0.5	0.5	25.8
PT[e]	1.3	3.0	40.0	12.0	48.0	0.6	0.9	23.1
PO	0.2	0.7	24.1	15.5	60.4	0.2	0.2	20.3

[a] The data of workforce size regarding the total of economic active population (except for Switzerland and Portugal) are from Global Civil Society, Volume III, Johns Hopkins Center for Civil Society Studies *apud* (Johns Hopkins Center for Civil Society Studies 2010).
[b] The data of revenue structure are from Comparative Data Tables (2004) (data from 1995–2002). Available at http://ccss.jhu.edu/wp-content/uploads/downloads/2013/02/Comparative-data-Tables_2004_FORMATTED_2.2013.pdf (data from 1995–2002).
[c] The data from % of GDP devoted to welfare are from OECD Social and Welfare Statistics. Available at http://stats.oecd.org/BrandedView.aspx?oecd_bv_id=socwel-data-en&doi=els-socx-data-en (data from 2008).
[d] The data from Switzerland regarding revenue structure are from (Helmig et al. 2011) (data from 2005).
[e] The data from Portugal regarding revenue structure are from (Franco et al. 2005) (data from 2005).

(un)employment issues influenced us to consider Sweden has a "social democrat" civil society regime.

Data from Table 3.1 also reveal that the French civil society sector is largely dependent upon paid staff, despite a considerable share of volunteers, and upon public funds. Furthermore, France has a quite protective welfare system, particularly regarding (un)employment issues, which is consistent with the analysis from the Younex project (see Cinalli and Giugni 2013). The conjugation of both contexts led us to consider France has a "welfare partnership" civil society regime, given that it is commonly seen as a state partner (Archambault et al. 1999; Chanial and Laville 2004).

The Swiss civil society sector is characterized by a medium-high dependence on paid staff, despite its considerable share of volunteers, and by a medium-low dependence on public funds. The combination of these characteristics with a low share of the GDP devoted to the welfare system, even though the country is becoming more concerned with social security and has an employee-friendly labour law (Helmig et al. 2011, 10; Cinalli and Giugni 2013), influenced us to consider Switzerland has a "liberal" civil society regime.

Data from Table 3.1 about the German context reveal that the national civil society sector is characterized by a medium-high dependence on paid staff (despite the considerable share of volunteers) and very high dependence on government funds. Also, the country has a reasonably protective welfare system, both generically and regarding unemployment. These data influenced us to consider Germany has a "welfare partnership" civil society regime. Despite the fact that the country has a civil society regime often labelled as "welfare partnership" or "corporatist," some scholars (Priller et al. 1999: 115–117; Bode and Evers 2004) stress that there is substantial diversity that should be taken into account.

Unlike what happens with most of the other cases under analysis, the Italian civil society sector cannot be categorized straightforwardly, given its pronounced hybrid nature. On the one hand, the low dependence upon public funding of civil society organizations and an above-average percentage of the GDP devoted to the welfare system (despite the low attention to unemployment issues) may indicate the "social democrat" nature of the Italian civil society sector. On the other hand, a low share of volunteers working in the civil society sector, which is even lower than the share of paid staff, led us to consider the "welfare partnership" label could be more appropriate. This idea of hybridity is also expressed by Borzaga (2004: 60), who states that the Italian civil society sector has been characterized by a "constant endeavour to combine the production of social services with advocacy" for the past decades. Given this impasse, we opted to follow previous categorizations (Anheier and Salamon 2006: 108) and to consider the Italian civil society sector as "social democrat," although we did not ignore its hybrid nature.

Portugal has a civil society sector that clearly relies more on paid staff than on volunteers. In addition, it is fairly dependent upon public funds, even though it has a much lower dependence than the French and German civil society sectors. These two characteristics and the reasonably low percentage of public spending on welfare issues led us to consider Portugal has a "welfare partnership" civil society regime. It is important to highlight that, despite this "welfare partnership" label, the Portuguese civil society sector has some features of a "statist" civil society regime, primarily due to the paternalist state action and the dictatorship regime that lasted until 1974 and generically suppressed public participation and civic movements (Franco et al. 2005: 31; Ferreira 2006: 220).

Finishing our analysis with Poland, data from Table 3.1 indicate that its civil society sector is generically rather small and that it depends more on paid staff than on volunteers. Further, its dependence on public funding is relatively low. The national welfare system is less protective, particularly regarding unemployment issues, which is consistent with the Younex project's analysis (see Cinalli and Giugni 2013). These contexts, in combination with a recent past of a repressive political system and low levels of civic participation, led us to conclude that Poland has a "statist" civil society regime, despite some scholars (Zimmer 2006; Leś, Nałęcz and Wygnański 2000) report that it is moving toward a "welfare partnership" civil society regime.

To summarize, for the purposes of this chapter, we consider Sweden and Italy have "social democrat" civil society regimes, Poland has a "statist" civil society regime, Switzerland has a "liberal" civil society regime, and France, Portugal and Germany have "welfare partnership" civil society regimes.

Keeping in mind the hypotheses presented in the theoretical framework section, the variables mentioned in this section will be used to analyze if the levels of financial and human resources and the patterns of professionalization of the examined civil society organizations are dependent upon the main organizational function and the national civil society regime. In the next section the main empirical results are described and discussed.

The distribution of human and financial resources and patterns of professionalization

This section includes an analysis of the level of influence that the main organizational function and the national civil society regimes (independent variables) have on the distribution and the structure of human and financial resources and the level of professionalization (the dependent variables). In the second and third parts of this section, we will provide an overview of resource distribution and levels of professionalization according to the two determinants. But before, we take an overall look at resource distribution and the levels of professionalization.

An overall look at resource distribution and levels of professionalization

As previously discussed, recent research has questioned the traditional views which claim that most civil society organizations are small and dependent on the work of volunteers and on membership fees. However, it has also recognized that those traditional views cannot be ignored and that empirical analysis is required to determine whether a specific context follows traditional patterns or not.

Starting the analysis with the levels of human resources that the examined organizations have at their disposal, data from the third column of Table 3.2 reveal that there was a predominance of organizations with a relatively small number of staff members. Specifically, 19.1% did not have a single employee, whereas 41.4% had between 1 and 9 employees. Moreover, only a small fraction (10.8%) of these organizations had more than 50 employees.

These figures changed significantly when volunteers were considered within the workforce structure. Taking into account the last column of Table 3.2, the proportion of organizations with fewer than 10 people within their workforce structure decreased to 17.6%, whereas the share of organizations with more than 50 people increased to almost one-third (33.1%) of the examined organizations. Therefore, it is no surprise that the data revealed that volunteering was the most important source of human resources for more than half (55.8%) of the analyzed organizations. This volunteering predominance was, however, smaller than what "traditional assumptions" would suggest, since almost half (44.2%) of the examined organizations had more employees than

Table 3.2 Workforce structure (%)

Number of persons	Full-time Staff	Part-time Staff	Staff (part+full)	Volunteers	Human Resources (staff + volunteers)
0	33.7	39.5	19.1	16.5	0
1–9	35.0	47.1	41.4	24.0	17.6
10–49	22.1	9.6	28.7	35.4	49.3
50–249	6.7	3.8	7.6	13.3	20.9
≥250	2.5	0	3.2	10.8	12.2
Total	100% (N=163)	100% (N=157)	100% (N=157)	100% (N=158)	100% (N=148)

Table 3.3 Distribution of organizations according to budget classes (%)

Total Budget	
under €2,500	7.8
€2,500–€9,999	9.2
€10,000–€99,999	27.0
€100,000–€199,999	9.2
over €200,000	46.8
Total	100% (N=141)

volunteers. Further, 16.5% of them did not have a single volunteer (see Table 3.2, column 4).

Shifting the focus to financial resources, the results from Table 3.3 reveal that the analysed organisations generically have medium-high budgets, since only a small percentage (7.8%) of organizations had a budget under €2,500. In addition, less than one-fifth (18.0%) of the organizations had a budget lower than €10,000. Moreover, more than half (56.0%) of these organizations had an annual budget in 2009 of over €100,000 and almost all of these had a budget higher than €200,000.

Regarding the revenue structure, data from Figure 3.1 reveal that "grants or financing of specific projects from governments" was the most important funding source for approximately one-third (33.6%) of the organizations. Also, only 18.0% of the examined organizations had "membership fees" as the most important funding source – figures which also challenge the traditional assumptions we mentioned before.

Concerning the overall level of professionalization, data in Figure 3.2 reveal that the majority of the examined organizations had a

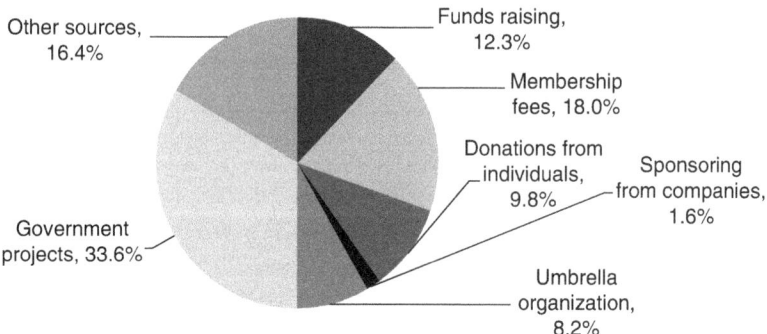

Figure 3.1   Distribution of organizations according to the most important source of funding (%)

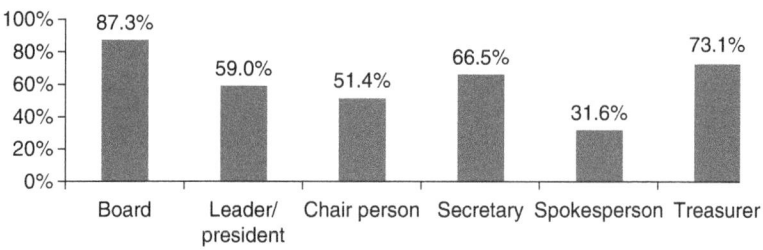

Figure 3.2   Share of organizations with certain management and technical support positions (%)

management board (87.3%), but only slightly more than half of the organizations had a president (59.0%) or a chairperson (51.4%). Further analysis showed that these latter two management positions were often alternatives to one another. As also revealed in the Figure 3.2, technical support positions of secretary and treasurer were relatively common among the analyzed organizations, unlike the spokesperson position.

As observed in the presented data, the universe of the examined civil society organizations was characterized by huge diversity. According to what was presented in the theoretical framework section, this diversity may be related to, among other factors, the main organizational function and the national civil society regime. The following subsections include an analysis of the main features of resource distribution and the patterns of professionalization according to these two variables: the main organizational function (policy-oriented or service-oriented) and the national civil society regime (liberal, welfare partnership, social democrat, or statist).

Distribution of resources according to the main organizational function

As previously explained, it is believed that one of the determinants of unequal amounts and sources of human and financial resources among civil society organizations is their main organizational function. According to the theory presented in the literature review, service-oriented civil society organizations are expected to have more resources than those that are policy-oriented because their activity is more labour intensive, which requires the hiring of staff members and, consequently, more financial resources to pay them.

The gathered empirical data revealed that the examined service-oriented organizations were actually the ones with more paid staff members within their workforce structure, even though more than a half (53.9%) of them had fewer than 10 employees. However, the percentage of policy-oriented organizations in the same situation was much higher (79.3%). Furthermore, 14.8% of the examined service-oriented organizations had more than 50 employees, whereas only about 4.8% of the policy-oriented organizations were in the same situation.

Similarly, the number of volunteers tended to be higher among policy-oriented organizations. As shown in Table 3.4, almost one-fourth

Table 3.4 Level of dependence on volunteers according to the main organizational function (%)

% of volunteers/workforce	Policy-oriented	Service-oriented
0%	8.6	22.8
[0%–25%]	6.9	17.7
[25%–50%]	5.2	14.5
[50%–75%]	12.1	15.8
[75%–100%]	67.2	31.6
Total	100%	100%
	(N=58)	(N=76)

Note: Number of cases with no information about the number of volunteers = 22. Number of cases with "other" main organizational function = 18.

(22.8%) of the service-oriented organizations had no volunteers in their workforce structure, whereas more than two-thirds (67.2%) of policy-oriented organizations reported a very high dependence on volunteers.

Regarding financial resources, the enquired service-oriented organizations were more resourceful than policy-oriented organizations. Data revealed that more than half (52.6%) of service-oriented organizations had a budget over €200,000, whereas only 29.4% of policy-oriented organizations had a budget that fell into that category. Moreover, approximately 29.4% of the examined policy-oriented organizations had a budget under €10,000, whereas only 10.6% of the service-oriented organizations were in an equivalent situation.

Concerning the revenue structure, Figure 3.3 shows that the majority (66.7%) of policy-oriented organizations did not receive any funds from the public sector. Further, only 19.6% of these organizations depended on the public sector to obtain more than half of their budgets. Conversely, more than one-third (35.8%) of service-oriented organizations depended upon the public sector to acquire more than half of their budgets. Only 34.3% of this typology of organizations did not depend on state funding at all.

Regarding the number of management and technical support positions according to the main organizational function, Figure 3.4 reveals that there were some differences between policy-oriented and service-oriented organizations concerning the number of management positions. As revealed by this figure, the percentage of service-oriented organizations with two or three management positions was significantly higher than the percentage of policy-oriented organizations in a similar situation. An opposite situation was revealed with regard to technical support positions, as there were more policy-oriented organizations with two or three technical support positions than service-oriented organizations, although the difference was minimal (4.9%).

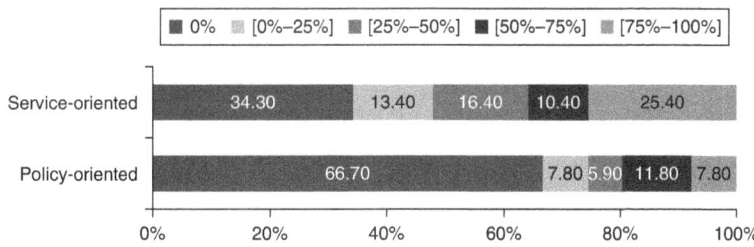

Figure 3.3 Level of dependence on public funding according to the main organizational function (%)

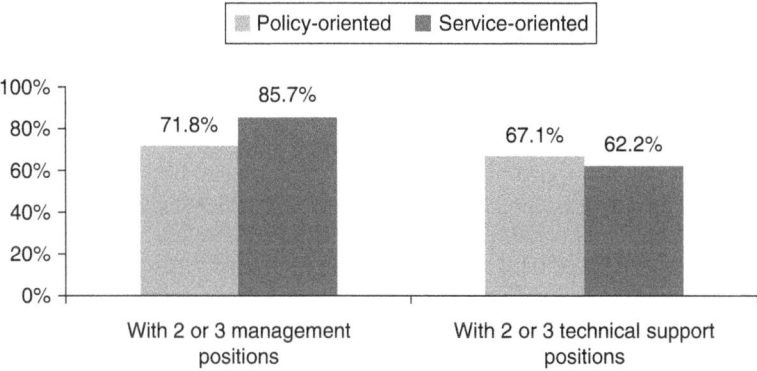

Figure 3.4 Organizations with two or three management and technical support positions, according to the main organizational function (%)

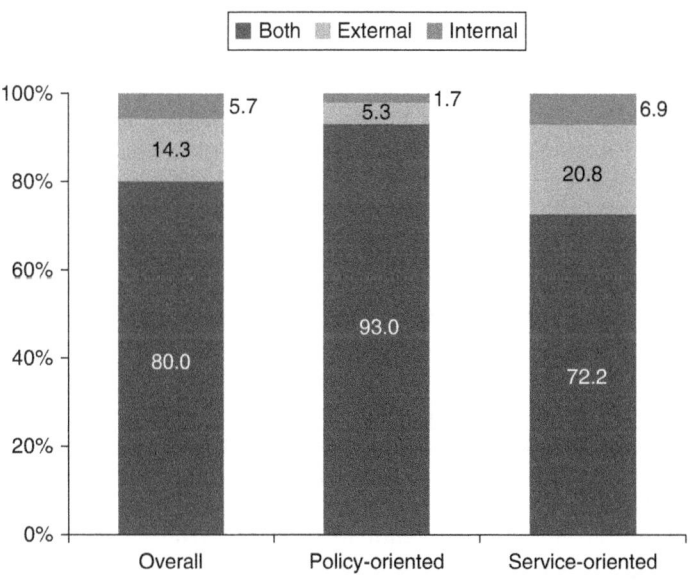

Figure 3.5 Type of recruitment to hire management professionals, according to the main organizational function (%)

Concerning the type of recruitment for management roles, the other element considered to be relevant to measure the level of professionalization, Figure 3.5 reveals that the majority of the analyzed organizations (80.0%) recruited their managers among their own associates. This tendency was even more relevant for policy-oriented organizations, as 93% of them recruited managers internally, whereas the share of service-oriented organizations in the same situation was considerably smaller (72.2%).

In sum, data revealed that service-oriented civil society organizations had larger shares of paid staff, higher budgets, and greater dependence upon state funds than policy-oriented organizations. Consequently, they also tended to be more professionalized organizations, as they had more management positions and used external recruitment techniques to hire their managers more frequently.

Distribution of resources according to the country of origin and corresponding civil society regime

As explained in the introductory section, it is believed that the uneven distribution of resources among civil society organizations is also related to the so-called civil society regimes, which are typically associated with national borders. Therefore, we also analyzed the distribution of human and financial resources and patterns of professionalization according to the country in which each organization was located. For the following analysis, it is important to recall that we considered that Sweden and Italy have "social democrat" civil society regimes, France, Germany, and Portugal have "welfare partnership" civil society regimes, Switzerland has a "liberal" civil society regime, and Poland has a "statist" civil society regime.

According to the formulated hypotheses, it was expected that the examined Swedish and Italian civil society organizations would have a higher share of volunteers, a lower dependence upon public funds, and, consequently, a smaller degree of professionalization. On the contrary, the examined civil society organizations in France, Switzerland, Germany, and Portugal (and, in a certain way, in Poland, given its proximity to the "welfare partnership" regime) were expected to have more paid staff members, a greater dependence upon public funds and higher levels of professionalization.

Starting our analysis with human resources, data revealed that the two countries that had civil society organizations with a higher median number of paid staff members, Portugal ($\bar{x} = 21$) and Switzerland ($\bar{x} = 7$), were actually countries with "welfare partnership" and "liberal" civil society regimes. On the opposite side, the countries whose analyzed organizations had the lowest median number of paid staff members were Sweden ($\tilde{x}=1$) and Italy ($\tilde{x}=2$), both with "social democrat" civil society regimes. With in-between figures, we had the French civil society organizations ($\tilde{x}=6$), followed by the organizations from Poland ($\tilde{x}=5.5$) and Germany ($\tilde{x}=4$).

On the contrary, data from Table 3.5 reveal that the countries whose civil society organizations had greater dependence upon volunteers were Italy ($\tilde{x}=94.1\%$) and Sweden ($\tilde{x}=91.2\%$), both countries with a "social democrat" civil society regime. After these two countries, the greatest dependence upon volunteers is from the organizations located in Germany ($\tilde{x}=86.9\%$), France ($\tilde{x}=80.0\%$), and Switzerland ($\tilde{x}=62.5\%$). The countries with organizations with the lowest median percentage of volunteers within their workforce were Portugal ($\tilde{x}=21.3\%$) and Poland ($\tilde{x}=26.1\%$), a feature that may be related to both countries' past repressive political systems, which discouraged civic participation.

Regarding the budget that the examined civil society organizations had at their disposal, data revealed that the countries whose analyzed organizations had the lowest mean budgets were Sweden ($\bar{x}=$ €103,913), Germany ($\bar{x}=$ €214,938), and Italy ($\bar{x}=$ €242,951). On the opposite extreme, the organizations with the highest mean budgets were the ones from Switzerland ($\bar{x}=$ €501,065) and Portugal ($\bar{x}=$ €432,575), the former having a "liberal" civil society regime, whereas the latter having a "welfare partnership" civil society regime. Occupying an intermediate position right after the Swiss and Portuguese organizations were the French ($\bar{x}=$ €281,915) and Polish ($\bar{x}=$ €271,438) civil society organizations.

Concerning the level of dependence upon public funding, data from Table 3.6 demonstrate that the organizations that were less dependent

Table 3.5 Level of dependence on volunteers according to the country of origin (%)

% of volunteers/ workforce	FR	SW	CH	DE	IT	PT	PO
0%	9.5	30.0	23.8	4.0	10.0	17.2	31.3
[0%–25%]	14.3	.0	14.3	.0	13.3	37.9	12.5
[25%–50%]	4.8	10.0	4.8	24.0	10.0	3.4	25.0
[50%–75%]	19.0	.0	23.8	8.0	3.3	24.1	6.3
[75%–100%]	52.4	60.0	33.3	64.0	63.3	17.2	25.0
Total	100%	100%	100%	100%	100%	100%	100%
	(N=21)	(N=10)	(N=21)	(N=25)	(N=30)	(N=29)	(N=16)
Median percentage	80.0	91.2	62.5	86.9	94.1	21.3	26.1

upon this source of revenue were the ones from Sweden ($\bar{x}$=16.2%) and Italy ($\bar{x}$=22.5%), two countries which have "social democrat" civil society regimes. On the opposite side, greater dependence upon public funding was observed in organizations located in Switzerland ($\bar{x}$=48.0%) and France ($\bar{x}$=40.8%), countries with "liberal" and "welfare partnership" civil society regimes, respectively. Polish ($\bar{x}$=31.4%), German ($\bar{x}$=24.8%), and Portuguese ($\bar{x}$=22.9%) civil society organizations had an intermediate dependence upon public funding.

Moving our attention to the patterns of professionalization, data from Figure 3.6 revealed that the countries in which all organizations had at least two management positions were Switzerland ("liberal" civil society regime), Portugal ("welfare partnership" civil society regime), and Sweden ("social democrat" regime). On the other hand, only a few more than half of the civil society organizations from Italy (51.4%) and Germany (64.3%) had at least two management positions. Finally, data also showed that more than three-quarters of the examined organizations from France (85.7%) and Poland (80.8%) had at least two management positions.

Regarding the existence of at least two technical support positions, the countries that had a higher share of organizations in that situation were France (85.7%), Sweden (83.3%), Portugal (82.8%), and Switzerland (70.0%) – with the exception of Sweden, countries with "welfare partnership" or "liberal" civil society regimes. The countries with the lower percentage of organizations with at least two technical support positions were Germany (42.9%), Italy (55.9%), and Poland (57.7%).

Finally, data from Figure 3.7 revealed that the countries whose examined organizations use external, or at least mixed, recruitment techniques

Table 3.6 Level of dependence on public funding according to the country of origin (%)

% of public funding/ revenue structure	FR	SW	CH	DE	IT	PT	PO
0%	28.6	80.0	10.5	54.5	57.7	45.0	52.9
[0%–25%]	7.1	.0	15.8	13.6	11.5	20.	11.8
[25%–50%]	28.6	.0	31.6	4.5	7.7	15.0	.0
[50%–75%]	14.3	.0	15.8	18.2	7.7	10.0	11.8
[75%–100%]	21.4	20.0	26.3	9.1	15.4	10.0	23.5
Total	100%	100%	100%	100%	100%	100%	100%
	(N=14)	(N=10)	(N=19)	(N=22)	(N=26)	(N=20)	(N=17)
Mean percentage	40.8	16.2	48.0	24.8	22.5	22.9	31.4

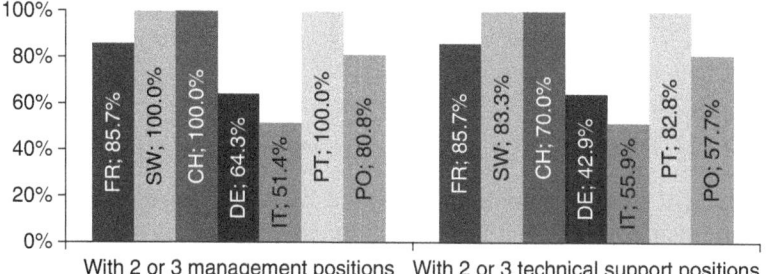

Figure 3.6 Organizations with two or three management and technical support positions, according to the country of origin (%)

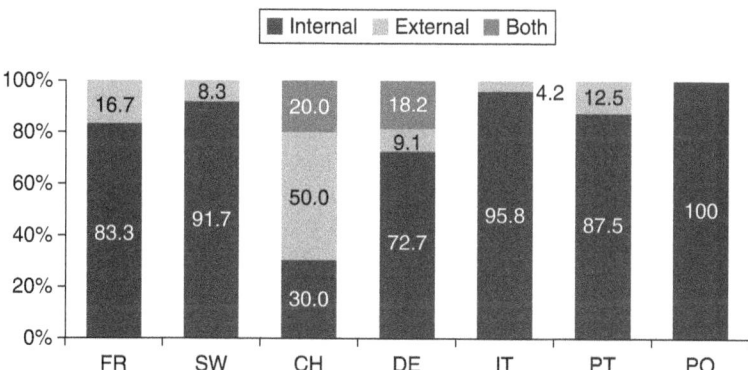

Figure 3.7 Type of recruitment to hire management professionals, according to the country of origin (%)

to hire their managers more frequently were Switzerland (70.0%), Germany (27.3%), France (16.7%), and Portugal (12.5%), all countries with "liberal" or "welfare partnership" civil society regimes. On the contrary, the examined organizations that used external sources for recruiting managers less frequently were the ones from Poland (0%), Italy (4.2%), and Sweden (8.3%), that is, organizations from countries with "social democrat" and "statist" civil society regimes (Figure 3.7).

Despite the existence of exceptions that will be further explored in the following section, the examined organizations from countries with a "welfare partnership" or "liberal" civil society regimes (France, Portugal, and Switzerland) generally had greater dependence on paid staff and state funds and presented higher levels of professionalization than the organizations from countries with "social democrat" or "statist" civil society regimes (Sweden, Italy, and Poland).

Results discussion

Given the results that were presented in previous sections, the examined civil society organizations showed considerable variation in the amount and sources of financial and human resources as well as in their patterns of professionalization. These findings confirmed the proposition presented in the introduction that advocated that the Civil Society sector was far from being a unique and consistent concept. In contrast, the other general idea, which stated that civil society organizations were becoming larger and less dependent upon volunteers, was only partially confirmed. Data revealed that the traditional idea that civil society organizations were small and had a workforce that was majorly dependent upon volunteers has still some basis in reality. On the one hand, we were able to observe that over 66% of the examined organizations had fewer than 50 human resources (paid staff or volunteers) (Table 3.2) and that more than half of them (55.8%) had more volunteers than paid staff members in their workforce. On the other hand, almost half of the examined organizations had more paid staff members than volunteers and 12% of them had more than 250 human resources (Table 3.2).

Given these data about the human resources, one could easily assume that the majority of the examined organizations were actually relatively small, proving that the "traditional assumption" previously highlighted is not as obsolete as one may presume.

However, accounting for only the element of "human resources" to measure organizational size was insufficient and it was also necessary to consider the financial resources that the civil society organizations had at their disposal. By analysing this variable, we concluded that the examined organizations were not as small as popular perceptions could lead us to believe, as over 46% of them had a 2009 budget over €200,000 (Table 3.3). Moreover, the traditional assumption that civil society organizations are majorly dependent upon membership fees was also disconfirmed, as public funding was the "most important source of income" for over 33% of the examined organizations (Figure 3.1).

In this context, it comes as no surprise that a great share of the examined organizations showed considerable levels of professionalization, as the majority of them had several differentiated management and technical support positions (Figure 3.2). Considering the diverse setting that was just described, the purpose of the previous two subsections was to analyze whether this diversity was somehow related to two theoretically suggested determinants: the main organizational function and the country of origin, which was associated with the national civil society regime.

Focusing attention first on the "main organizational function," data revealed that policy-oriented organizations had fewer paid staff members than service-oriented organizations and, consequently, greater dependence upon volunteers (Table 3.4). This finding supported our first hypothesis. Regarding financial resources, data demonstrated that the percentage of service-oriented organizations with budgets over €200,000 was much higher than the share of policy-oriented organizations in a similar situation. This difference was believed to be related to their contracting to perform tasks that required more paid staff members. Therefore, it is no surprise that state funding was found to be much more important for service-oriented organizations than for policy-oriented ones (Figure 3.3). This finding supported our second hypothesis.

Given that organizational professionalization tends to be related to a necessary organizational adjustment to more financial and human resources, it is also no surprise that service-oriented organizations have more management positions than policy-oriented ones (Figure 3.4). However, unlike what happens in management positions, the main organizational function seems to have no influence on the number of technical support positions, as there is no significant difference between the percentage of service-oriented organizations with at least two technical support positions and the percentage of policy-oriented organizations in the same situation. Under these circumstances, our third hypothesis was only partially confirmed. Service-oriented organizations had actually more management positions than policy-oriented ones, but they did not have more technical support positions. We believe that this finding is related to the fact that policy-oriented organizations generally require more technical support positions, such as a secretary or treasurer, as these professionals may eventually be the only ones who are permanent employees. Moreover, these professionals generally complete organization and mobilization tasks, which are essentially the bases for policy-oriented organizations.

Finally, data also revealed that service-oriented organizations had a higher level of professionalization in relation to their recruitment techniques because they used external sources to recruit their managers more frequently than policy-oriented organizations (Figure 3.5). This finding confirmed our fourth hypothesis.

Under these circumstances, it is possible to conclude that the examined service-oriented civil society organizations had at their disposal more paid staff members, more financial resources related with public funding, more management positions and used external recruitment more frequently than policy-oriented civil society organizations. Policy-oriented civil society organizations were, on their turn, more dependent upon volunteers and funding from membership fees and fundraising. These findings revealed that the main organizational function clearly influenced the amount and sources of human and financial resources and, consequently, the patterns of professionalization.

With regard to the other determinant, the figures reveal that the patterns of resource distribution and professionalization from the examined civil society organizations were generically consistent with the assumptions presented in the literature review on civil society regimes.

Starting with the analysis of human resources, data showed that the countries whose examined organizations have less paid staff members were Sweden and Italy, that is, countries with "social democrat" civil society regimes. The countries whose analyzed organizations have more paid staff members are Portugal and Switzerland, countries with "welfare partnership" and "liberal" civil society regimes. The high median number of employees from the Portuguese organizations is notable. This finding may be explained by the fact that the analyzed organizations were located in Lisbon, where larger organizations tend to be placed due to the highly centralized Portuguese political and organizational system. Also worth noting is the relatively low median number of employees that German organizations had at their disposal. We believe that this finding can be explained by the fact that the majority of analysed organizations were more policy oriented than service oriented, unlike what theory suggests to occur in Germany.

On the contrary, the countries whose organizations revealed greater dependence on volunteers were Italy and Sweden, which have "social democrat" civil society regimes (Table 3.5). The countries whose organizations revealed a fewer dependence on volunteers were Poland and Portugal, whose civil society regime have "statist" features regarding this issue. This finding confirmed our fifth hypothesis. It is important to highlight the significantly high percentage of dependence upon volunteers among German organizations, a finding that may be explained by their predominant policy orientation. The relatively low dependence upon volunteers among the examined organizations in Portugal and Poland is also notable. This finding may be explained by both countries' "statist" orientation and low levels of civic participation that still characterizes the Polish and Portuguese civil society sectors. This context is believed to be related to both countries' recent history of political dictatorship.

Regarding financial resources, the countries whose organizations had the lower budgets and a fewer dependence upon public funds were Sweden and Italy, that is, two countries with a "social democrat" civil society sector (Table 3.6). On the contrary, the countries whose organizations had higher mean budgets were from national contexts with "welfare partnership" and "liberal" civil society regimes (Switzerland and Portugal). A similar trend occurred with regard to the dependence upon public funds, as the countries with higher figures were Switzerland and France (Table 3.6). These findings confirmed our sixth hypothesis.

The relatively low budgets and low dependence upon public funding among German organizations are worth noting. Again, these findings are possibly due to their predominant policy-orientation. Further, the high budgets among Portuguese organizations (which are eventually explained by their location in Lisbon) and their low dependence upon public funding (which is potentially related to the "statist" features of the civil society sector) are also notable.

Regarding the levels of professionalization, data revealed that the countries whose organizations have a higher number of management and technical support positions are the ones from France, Switzerland, Portugal ("welfare partnership" and "liberal" civil society regimes), and Sweden ("social democrat" civil society regime) (Figure 3.6). On the other hand, the countries that had a lower number of organizations with these standards of professionalization were Italy ("social democrat" civil society regime), Poland ("statist" civil society regime), and Germany ("welfare partnership" civil society regime). One of the exceptions to the expected trend was Sweden, whose organizations had an unexpectedly high level of professionalization. This finding may be explained by their long history of structured civil society activation. The other exception was Germany, whose organizations had a lower level of professionalization than expected. This finding may be explained by their predominant policy-orientation. Despite these exceptions, data reveal that the organizations from countries with "welfare partnership" or "liberal" civil society sectors generally had more management and technical support positions than organizations from countries with "social democrat" or "statist" sectors. This finding confirmed our seventh hypothesis.

Similarly, the analysis of the most common kind of recruitment for management roles indicated that the organizations that had lower levels of professionalization were from Sweden and Italy ("social democrat" civil society regimes) as well as from Poland ("statist" civil society regime) (Figure 3.7). On the other hand, organizations from countries with "welfare partnership" and "liberal" civil society sectors recruited managers from outside of the organization more often. This pattern was particularly relevant for Swiss organizations. This finding confirmed our eighth hypothesis.

Conclusion

As suggested by recent research, the Civil Society sector has achieved increasing policy prominence over the last few decades. Further, civil society organizations have undergone significant transformations in what is related to the functions they play and regarding their structure and management practices. In this context of change, the traditional assumptions that civil society organizations are small and dependent primarily on the work of volunteers and on the fees paid by their members have been questioned by several scholars. However, these researchers have also argued that there is significant diversity among civil society organizations and that the resources that they have at their disposal and their patterns of professionalization may be dependent upon factors, such as their main organizational function or the national context of the civil society sector.

The collected data enabled us to conclude that the majority of the examined organizations had a reduced number of employees at their disposal and depended upon volunteers. Nevertheless, the share of organizations which depended more upon paid staff members than on volunteers was also substantial, a finding which points to an actual change regarding traditional features.

Another shift from traditional features is the fact that a majority of the examined civil society organizations had medium-high budgets. In addition, state funds were the most important source of revenues for approximately one-third of the sample. Again, these figures represent a shift from the traditional features.

Moreover, it was also possible to determine that a significant share of organizations had a considerable number of management and technical support professionals, even though they were primarily recruited internally. This finding demonstrated a significant degree of professionalization.

Throughout this chapter, it was also possible to conclude that the main organizational function was a useful predictor of the amount and sources of human and financial resources and professionalization patterns. As suggested by theory, the examined civil society organizations more oriented towards service provision were more dependent upon paid staff and state funds and had higher levels of professionalization.

Similarly, the broad national "civil society regime" also appeared to be a helpful predictor of human and financial resources and patterns of professionalization in the examined organizations. The civil society organizations from Sweden and Italy (countries with "social democrat" civil society regimes) have fewer paid staff members, lower budgets, and less dependence on state funding than the analyzed organizations from countries with "welfare partnership," "liberal," and "statist" civil society regimes. On the contrary, the examined organizations from Switzerland, France, and Portugal (countries with "liberal" or "welfare partnership" civil society regimes) had more paid staff members, higher budgets, and greater dependence on state funds as well as higher levels of professionalization. Also, it was shown that real national civil society sectors reveal a hybrid nature, as almost all of them include features from different "ideal-types."

Despite the generic confirmation of the formulated hypotheses regarding civil society regimes, there was one major exception: the organizations from Germany. The German civil society sector tends to be theoretically labelled as a "welfare partnership" regime, but the analyzed organizations more closely resembled a "social democrat" civil society regime. It seems that this situation is related to the fact that most of the examined organizations had a policy orientation, unlike what theory suggests would happen in this country. This exception led us to conclude that the main organizational function is clearly the best of both predictors.

In this context, data clearly reveal that there were generally two kinds of civil society organizations in our sample: (1) those that were primarily service oriented and required more paid staff members and higher budgets that were mostly assured by state funds and tended to present higher patterns of professionalization and (2) those that primarily performed advocacy tasks and were more dependent on volunteers and membership fees and did not become so professionalized.

Although this context of diversity may lead to some difficulties in trying to create common frameworks for the study and understanding of this sector, this duplicity of roles may also indicate a certain complementarity that may be the secret ingredient for this sector's increasing prominence. As the title of this chapter indicates, the civil society sector has to find a balance "between passion and money."

Notes

1. When we mention the "input" and the "output" side of the policy-making process, we are using David Easton's "Political Systems Model" (1965) as a reference. According to the author, the political decision-making process may be viewed as a system that receives inputs (namely, the demands and support expressed by public opinion, elected officials or public managers, the media, or interest groups) and produces outputs, such as decisions and actions that are expressed through laws, regulations, or other kinds of "statutes" (Easton 1965).
2. We will not analyze this typology in detail in the following sections, as all of the examined organizations are from European countries and, therefore, would hardly fall into that category.

References

Anheier, H. K. and L. M. Salamon (2006) "The Nonprofit Sector in Comparative Perspective," in Powell, W. W. and R. Steinberg (eds), *The Non-profit Sector: A Research Handbook* (2nd ed.) (New Haven and London: Yale University Press).

Archambault, E., M. Gariazzo, H. K. Anheier, and L. M. Salamon (1999) "France: From Jacobin Tradition to Decentralization," in Salamon, L. M., H. K. Anheier, R. List, S. Toepler, S. W. Sokolowski and Associates (eds), *Global Civil Society: Dimensions of the Nonprofit Sector* (Baltimore: The Johns Hopkins Center for Civil Society Studies).

Barnes, J. (2006) "From Charity to 'Not-for-profit': Changes in the Role and Structure of Voluntary Social Service Agencies," in Henman, P. and M. Fenger (eds), *Administering Welfare Reform: International Transformations in Welfare Governance* (Bristol: The Policy Press).

Bode, I. and A. Evers (2004) "From Institutional Fixation to Entrepreneurial Mobility? The German Third Sector and Its Contemporary Challenges," in Evers, A. and J.-L. Laville (eds), *The Third Sector in Europe* (Cheltenham: Edward Elgar).

Borzaga, C. (2004) "From Suffocation to Re-emergence: The Evolution of the Italian Third Sector," in Evers, A. and J.-L. Laville (eds), *The Third Sector in Europe* (Cheltenham: Edward Elgar).

Chanial, P. and J.-L. Laville (2004) "French Civil Society Experiences: Attempts to Bridge the Gap between Political and Economic Dimensions," in Evers, A. and J.-L. Laville (eds), *The Third Sector in Europe* (Cheltenham: Edward Elgar).

Cinalli, M. and M. Giugni (2013) "New Challenges for the Welfare State: The Emergence of Youth Unemployment Regimes in Europe?" *International Journal of Social Welfare*, 22: 290–299.

Comparative Data Tables (2004) http://ccss.jhu.edu/wp-content/uploads/down loads/2013/02/Comparative-data-Tables_2004_FORMATTED_2.2013.pdf, date accessed 10 May 2013.

Easton, D. (1965) *A Systems Analysis of Political Life* (New York: Wiley).

Evers, A. (2006) "Third Sector Organizations and Welfare Services: How Helpful Are the Debates on Welfare Regimes and a European Social Model?," in Matthies, A.-L. (ed.), *Nordic Civic Society Organisations and the Future of Welfare Services: A Model for Europe?* (Copenhagen: Nordic Council of Ministers).

Evers, A. and J.-L. Laville (in collaboration with C. Borzaga, J. Defourny, J. Lewis, M. Nyssens, and V. Pestoff) (2004) "Defining the Third Sector in Europe," in Evers, A. and J-L. Laville (eds), *The Third Sector in Europe* (Cheltenham: Edward Elgar).

Ferreira, S. (2006) "The South European and the Nordic Welfare and Third Sector Regimes – How Far Were We from Each Other?" In Matthies, A.-L. (ed.), *Nordic Civic Society Organisations and the Future of Welfare Services: A Model for Europe?* (Copenhagen: Nordic Council of Ministers).

Franco, R. C., S. W. Sokolowski, E. M. H. Hairel, and L. M. Salamon (2005) *O Sector Não Lucrativo Português numa Perspectiva Comparada* (Portugal: Universidade Católica Portuguesa and Johns Hopkins University).

Helmig, B., M. Gmür, C. Bärlocher, G. von Schnurbein, B. Degen, M. Nollert, M. Budowski, S. W. Sokolowski, and L. M. Salamon (2011) *The Swiss Civil Society Sector in a Comparative Perspective* (Fribourg: Institute for Research on Management of Associations, Foundations and Cooperatives).

Johns Hopkins Center for Civil Society Studies (in cooperation with the Brazilian Institute of Geography and Statistics and United Nations Volunteers) (2010) *Nonprofit Organizations in Brazil: A Pilot Satellite Account with International Comparisons* (Brazil: CCSS, IBGE, and UNV).

Kriesi, H. (2007) "Organizational Resources: Personnel and Finances," in Maloney, W. A. and S. Roßteutscher (eds), *Social Capital and Associations in European Democracies: A Comparative Analysis* (New York: Routledge).

Leś, E., S. Nałęcz, and J. Wygnański (2000) "Defining the Nonprofit Sector: Poland," *Working Paper of the Johns Hopkins Comparative Nonprofit Sector Project* no. 36 (Baltimore: The Johns Hopkins Centre for Civil Society Studies).

Matthies, A.-L. (ed.) (2006) *Nordic Civic Society Organisations and the Future of Welfare Services: A Model for Europe?* (Copenhagen: Nordic Council of Ministers).

OECD Social and Welfare Statistics, http://www.oecd-ilibrary.org/social-issues-migration-health/data/oecd-social-and-welfare-statistics_socwel-data-en;jsessionid=g3rrgaj8961s.x-oecd-live-01, data accessed 10 May 2013.

Pestoff, V. (2004) "The Development and Future of the Social Economy in Sweden," in Evers, A. and J.-L. Laville (eds), *The Third Sector in Europe* (Cheltenham: Edward Elgar).

Pestoff, V. (2009) *A Democratic Architecture for the Welfare State* (London and New York: Routledge).

Pestoff, V. and T. Brandsen (2010) "Public Governance and the Third Sector: Opportunities for Co-production and Innovation?" in Osborne, S. (ed.) *The New Public Governance? Emerging Perspectives on the Theory and Practice of Public Governance* (London and New York: Routledge).

Priller, E., A. Zimmer, H. K. Anheier, S. Toepler, and L. M. Salamon (1999) "Germany: Unification and Change," in Salamon, L. M., H. K. Anheier, R. List, S. Toepler, S. W. Sokolowski and Associates (eds), *Global Civil Society: Dimensions of the Nonprofit Sector* (Baltimore: The Johns Hopkins Center for Civil Society Studies).

Rathgeb Smith, S. and K. A. Grønbjerg (2006) "Scope and Theory of Government-Nonprofit Relations," in Powell, W. W. and R. Steinberg (eds), *The Non-profit Sector: A Research Handbook* (2nd ed.) (New Haven and London: Yale University Press).

Salamon, L. and W. Sokolowski (2010) "Explaining Patterns of Civil Society: The Social Origins Approach," Paper prepared for delivery at the 9th International Conference of the International Society for Third Sector Research. Istanbul, July 2010.

Scott, D. (2007) "The Role of the Voluntary and Community Sectors," in Baldock, J., N. Manning and S. Vickerstaff (eds), *Social Policy* (3rd ed.) (New York: Oxford University Press).

Vernis, A., M. Iglesias, B. Sanz, and À. Saz-Carranza (2006) *Nonprofit Organizations: Challenges and Collaboration* (New York: Palgrave Macmillan).

White, D. (2006) "State-Third Sector Partnership Frameworks: From Administration to Participation," in Henman, P. and M. Fenger (eds), *Administering Welfare Reform: International Transformations in Welfare Governance* (Bristol: The Policy Process).

Zimmer, A. (2006) "Comparing Nonprofit Embeddedness in the Nordic and East European Countries," in Matthies, A.-L. (ed.), *Nordic Civic Society Organisations and the Future of Welfare Services: A Model for Europe?* (Copenhagen: Nordic Council of Ministers).

4
The Impact of Political Opportunity Structures on the Politicization of Civil Society Organizations in the Field of Unemployment and Precarity

Manlio Cinalli and Marco Giugni

Introduction

Civil society organizations carry out a number of different actions: they may provide services, such as advisory or counseling activities, to their members or to a larger constituency; invest in educational and awareness-raising activities; organize social and cultural events; raise funds to ensure their survival; and so on. However, they can also engage in political activities. By "politicization", here, we refer to the variable recourse of organizations to political activities: the more an organization engages in them, the more it becomes politicized. At the same time, political activities can take various forms, ranging from moderate and "hidden" forms, such as lobbying and representing interests, to more radical and disruptive forms, such as protest and direct action. Most crucially for this chapter, the political activities of civil society organizations do not occur in a vacuum; rather, they are likely to be strongly influenced by certain features of the context in which they are active.

In what follows, we focus on a number of characteristics of the political context within which civil society organizations that deal with unemployment and precarity mobilize. By comparing the seven cities of this study, we aim to ascertain whether political opportunities specific to the unemployment political field, alongside more general opportunities that stem from certain features of the institutionalized system, influence the degree of politicization for civil society organizations. To what extent do institutional approaches to unemployment politics account for variations in political activities by civil society organizations in the field of unemployment and precarity? How crucial is the impact of specific opportunities that stem from the contexts of the seven cities of this study on their politicization? What about the role of more general opportunities that are available to any civil society organization in a given context, regardless of the fact that the selected organizations of this study specifically deal with unemployment and precarity? Of course, in answering these questions, one has to keep the impact of the main endogenous characteristics of organizations under control, such as by evaluating the structural conditions of the choices that organizations make on the basis of their focus on policy or service provisions, respectively.

We single out two main dimensions of politicization: general engagement in political activities (henceforth, political activities) and specific involvement in protest activities (henceforth, protest). As the first step, we assess the extent to which organizations engage in political events, including all types or forms of these events. We then focus specifically on protest and appraise the degree to which civil society organizations mobilize their members through demonstrations, direct action, and other forms of protest. In our framework, these two dimensions are considered to be at the core of the concept of politicization, thus following recent work that has stressed the need to go beyond the simple dichotomy between participation and non-participation (van Deth et al. 2007). The decision to select political activities and protest may also clarify the relationship between these two forms of action vis-à-vis variations in political opportunity structures. The literature is hardly consensual on this point, with some scholars being more flexible than others in their decision to include the most disruptive forms of protest within the same repertoire of contention (Tilly 1978). In fact, many works that have dealt specifically with political participation and mobilization of the unemployed themselves (Bagguley 1991; Demazière and Pignoni 1998; Piven and Cloward 1979; Richards 2002) seem to pinpoint a divergence between more structured forms of political activism, on the one hand, and the recourse to unbalanced mixtures of apathy and radical direct action, on the other (Bay and Blekesaune 2002). Along this distinction, we can also assess the extent to which involvement in political activities and protest follow distinct patterns under the impact of the same variations in political opportunity structures.

We deal in particular with the potential impact of four main aspects of the political context: the degree of inclusiveness or exclusiveness of unemployment regulations, the degree of rigidity or flexibility of labor market regulations, the unemployment-specific political opportunity structure, and the general political opportunity structure. The first three dimensions are relevant for the field within which the selected organizations intervene. The fourth dimension has been added because previous works on mobilization and contentious politics have considered the general political opportunity structure to be a crucial factor that influences the political behavior of organizations (Kriesi 1996).

Our analysis is based on a sample of civil society organizations that are active in the field of unemployment and precarity in the seven cities under study.[1] Some questions in the questionnaire dealt with the activities and, more specifically, the political activities carried out by the organizations. These questions have been used to capture their variable degrees of politicization. Information deriving from a systematic analysis of the existing legislation on unemployment and precarity, as well as the institutional features of the local political system, has been used to grasp the different political opportunity structures available to the organizations in the seven cities, according to a methodological procedure that will be described in more detail below.

In the next section, we discuss the literature on political opportunity structures, which today forms a major strand of research on mobilization and contentious politics, including recent developments that stress the opportunities that stem from the institutional approaches of the welfare state and represent the main focus of our analysis. We then show our operationalization of the various dimensions of political opportunity that we focus upon and of the other variables considered in the analysis, including the two measures of the politicization of civil society organizations. Afterwards, we present the descriptive results of our analysis and stress variations across cities, in terms of political contexts and politicization of civil society. Lastly, in a more explanatory tone, we show the results of regression analyses aimed at studying the impact of the four dimensions of political opportunity structures on the two aspects of the politicization of civil society organizations that are active in the field of unemployment and precarity in the seven cities.

Political opportunities in the field of unemployment politics

Unemployment has become the core of the political agenda in many European states; it has fostered key reforms, or at least extensive discussions about them, in terms of labor market provisions and broader social policies. Following this Europe-wide trend (Eurofund 2008; European Commission 2009), one can notice increasing interventions over the promotion of flexible and short-term contracts, the necessity of pushing the unemployed into available jobs, and consequent provisions to adapt the roles of the main pillars of welfare. It is sufficient to mention that the Employment Guidelines 2005–2008 have also been designed to instigate and coordinate states' employment policies, that the EU finances relevant measures through European Structural Funds, and again that the Commission itself has become committed to building employment pathways to improve the matching to labor market needs, expand investment in human capital, and adapt education and training systems to new competence requirements. This also provides further opportunities for a common European social policy based on widening consultation with non-state actions, for example, with regard to social and civil dialogue between capital and labor, as well as a greater participation of civil society organizations that represent the unemployed and other excluded groups.

Yet, it should also be emphasized that welfare in general, as well as labor market mechanisms, social protection systems, and social services, is still at the core of traditional prerogatives of the state, having in fact shaped the formation of specific national approaches built into well-defined regimes (Esping-Andersen 1990; Ferrera 1996; Taylor-Gooby 1991). Hence, groups of unemployed people, pro-unemployed organizations, and more broadly, civil society actors that engage in the field of unemployment and precarity have found themselves at the intersection of a complex articulation that is made of common transnational pressures and the influence of distinct national contexts (Cinalli 2010). As said, we focus here on the relationship between these complex exogenous articulations, on the one hand, and variations in the politicization of civil society organizations in the unemployment and precarity field, on the other. We thus draw upon a long-standing scholarship tradition that has singled out the role of political opportunities (Eisinger 1973; Kitschelt 1986; Kriesi et al. 1995; Tilly 1978; Tarrow 2010; see Kriesi 2004 and Meyer 2004 for an overview), while acknowledging the importance of looking at the different nature and modes of intervention of the welfare state (Gallie and Paugam 2000; Paugam and Gallie 2004; see Green-Pedersen and Haverland 2002 and van Kersbergen 2002 for an overview).

Complex articulations of labor market, welfare, and social policies do not stop at the level of distinct national contexts of policy-making and legislation. Our comparison of cities follows the fact that policies with more direct impacts on the daily lives of the unemployed (and other groups at risk of exclusion) are often designed and implemented at the local level. Local governments, particularly when in charge of urban areas with dense populations, have been the first to experience the policy challenges brought about by the dynamics of unemployment and broader processes of exclusion, and provide responses that do not necessarily align with national policies (Bassoli and Cinalli, forthcoming). Also, activation measures have been explicitly designed in many European countries to improve the situation of the unemployed at the local level (Warner Weil et al. 2005). Our analysis thus benefits from a number of studies that, since the seminal work of Eisinger (1973), have emphasized the explanatory role of local policies and institutions in the specific field of unemployment (Bagguley 1991, 1992). In addition, civil society organizations have more opportunities to become involved in political life at the local level, where more possibilities exist to forge links with other actors in the field – for example, unions and political parties – and hence engage in different forms of political action. By focusing on the local level, we place the study of civil society organizations at the core of a detailed analysis that looks at their inclusion within the policy domain of institutions and decision-makers, while at the same time complementing previous studies that have already advanced similar analyses of the field of unemployment and precarity at the national level (Cinalli and Giugni 2010; Giugni et al. 2009).

As said earlier, we argue that variations in the politicization of civil society organizations depend upon variations in four main dimensions of political opportunities. Firstly, an analysis of the field of unemployment and precarity needs to refer to state welfare approaches to unemployment, thus following the teachings of the seminal scholarship on exclusion by Gallie and Paugam (2000). These authors have focused on the relationship between unemployment-providence regimes and the experience of unemployment, and have based their models on indicators of policies aimed at fighting unemployment, such as the degree of coverage, the level of financial compensation, and the importance of active measures for employment. Here, we examine the role of unemployment regulations as a crucial dimension of political opportunities for civil society organizations in the field.

Secondly, references to welfare approaches to unemployment and precarity need to be combined with an analysis of the labor market (Giugni et al. 2009), as institutional approaches to unemployment and precarity include both state measures directed at the target population of the unemployed and the precarious (as a part of the welfare state) and those addressing the labor market. Labor market regulations are central to the functioning of the modern welfare state (Esping-Andersen 1990, 1999) and interact with unemployment policies (Bonoli 2003). For example, the precise formulation of active measures and the ongoing debate about flexibility are at the crossroads between unemployment legislation and labor market regulations. We thus consider labor market regulations as a crucial dimension of opportunities that has to be considered in our analysis. In this context, it is also important to assess the existence of a clear distinction between protected workers, precarious workers, and unemployed as a consequence of the type of labor market regulations.

Thirdly, we need to consider the structure of specific opportunities. Here, we refer to aspects of the legal–institutional context specifically relating to unemployment and precarity that may facilitate or constrain the activities of civil society organizations in the field, such as local spending in passive and active measures for the unemployed and the precarious, or the inclusion of civil society organizations in the formulation and/or implementation of unemployment policies. This dimension should not be confused with the unemployment regulations dimension. While the latter concerns the ways in which the state regulates unemployment, the former deals with institutional access and participatory mechanisms for actors in the field. They are often found at the local level.

Finally, the general political opportunity structure stands out as a necessary dimension of analysis, due to the explanatory role that general opportunities play in many studies about repertoires of contention (see Kriesi 2004 and Meyer 2004 for an overview). As in the case of the structure of specific opportunities, we refer here to the degree of institutional access, as well as the participatory mechanisms, but on the general level, not only in the specific field of unemployment and precarity.

Beyond this assessment of the main dimensions of political opportunities, we are interested in learning more about their impact on variations of politicization. A number of scholars in the political opportunity research tradition have long stressed the existence of a curvilinear relationship when focusing more specifically on social movements and contentious politics (Eisinger 1973; Kitschelt 1986; Tilly 1978). According to these scholars, an increasing availability of opportunities is matched by increasing levels of mobilization up until a certain point, after which mobilization starts to shrink back. Our framework enables us to check for linear or curvilinear relationships between political opportunities and both indicators of politicization, in order to look for relevant distinctions across different dimensions of political opportunities, on the one hand, and the two main aspects of politicization on the other, as curvilinear and linear relationships may well coexist in more articulated dynamics when dealing with political activities and protest, respectively.

Of course, the role that complex articulations of political opportunities take cannot be grasped in full unless we control the likely impact of endogenous characteristics of civil society organizations. Some scholars have addressed the importance of resources (McCarthy and Zald 1977; Oberschall 1973; Zald and McCarthy 1987), for example, by focusing on the importance of budgets and organizational assets, and more generally on the dependence of weak groups – such as the unemployed and the precarious – upon more resourceful pro-beneficiary groups (Giugni and Passy 2001). In what follows, we aim to keep at least a number of these endogenous characteristics under control, including the organizational structuring of different actors, the duration of their presence in the field of unemployment and precarity, and the scope of their actions.

Data and operationalization

Having argued that institutions and policy-making combine into a multi-level structure that can be assessed by disentangling each of the four main dimensions of political opportunities, we can now show how we methodologically approach the measurement of political opportunities. We consider this step to be an essential part of our research, since previous studies of political context have rarely paid full attention to empirical measures of political opportunities themselves, often relying on abstract and anecdotic operationalizations. In particular, the four dimensions have been translated into a systematic series of indicators that can be appraised in a continuum between +1 and −1. The first dimension of unemployment regulations refers to the continuum of inclusion/exclusion (with +1 being inclusion and −1 being exclusion). In this case, we refer not only to conditions of access to rights and welfare provisions for the unemployed and the precarious but also to the obligations attached to full enjoyment of rights and provisions. The average score for this first dimension is based on eight indicators: formal pre-requisites for obtaining social provisions, level of coverage, extension of coverage, shifts to social aid, the role played by private and public employment agencies, counter-provisions and sanctions, number of people receiving unemployment benefits, and number of people receiving sanctions for abusing the benefit system.[2]

The second dimension refers to the flexibility/rigidity continuum as a consequence of state intervention in the labor market (with +1 being flexibility and −1 being rigidity). In this case, we acknowledge that rights and obligations deriving from unemployment legislation, and more generally from state welfare, can go hand in hand with labor market arrangements. The average score for this second dimension is based on eight indicators: protection of permanent workers against dismissal, regulations on temporary forms of employment, specific requirements for collective dismissals, temporary work, role of unions in the benefit system, union protection for workers, number of flexible workers, and number of participants in activation measures.[3]

The third dimension refers to the openness/closeness continuum of the unemployment-specific opportunity structures (with +1 being openness and −1 being closeness). The average score for this third dimension is based on five indicators: power of the city, in terms of unemployment policy; local spending on passive and active measures for the unemployed and the precarious; public information and support services for the unemployed and the precarious; inclusion of organizations of the unemployed in the elaboration of unemployment policies; and inclusion of other civil society organizations in the elaboration of unemployment policies.

The fourth dimension refers to the openness/closeness continuum of the general political opportunity structure (with +1 being openness and −1 being closeness). The average score for this fourth dimension is based on five indicators: presence of referenda at the local level, number of referenda held over the past five years at the local level, presence of citizens' assemblies, degree of state decentralization, and degree of decentralization at the local level. By including this last dimension of political opportunities, we can assess situations where unemployment-specific opportunities depart from the broader shape of general opportunities.[4]

There were two main steps in the data collection: (1) collecting information to describe each city's context across the selected indicators and (2) standardizing information along the continuum from −1 to +1 for comparative purposes. The first step has provided qualitative information on which the quantitative treatment of the second step is grounded. The indicators could thus be translated into an interval measure along a 3-point scale. The normative dimension that is built into such an operationalization of indicators can be translated into empirically testable hypotheses. Take, for example, the second dimension of labor market regulations: reforms that foster flexibility have been viewed by many neo-liberals as an effective means of improving the position of the unemployed and the precarious (based on the idea that the interests of the outsider-unemployed conflict with the interests of insider-workers). Yet, in the socialist camp, the same type of reforms have often been seen as leading to the marginalization of the unemployed and to the weakening of their voice in the public domain (based on the idea that working-class unity should not be broken). Here, we want to establish whether a relationship exists, and in which direction it goes, between labor market regulations, on the one hand, and the degree and forms of politicization of civil society organizations, on the other. In other words, we do not necessarily expect that more flexibility opens up further space for the political intervention of unemployment organizations, but we are theoretically prepared to discover empirical evidence that might even go in the opposite direction. A similar reasoning applies to the other three dimensions.

Our dependent variable focuses on two main indicators. The first refers to a comprehensive measure of political activities. The interviewed organizations were asked whether they engaged in any political events over the course of the previous two years.[5] In this case, we wanted to assess their general degree of politicization through involvement in a wide range of potential events. The second indicator of politicization included the specific measure of protests, so as to have a more complete understanding of political contention over unemployment. In this case, organizations in the field were asked whether they took part in protest events over the course of the previous two years.[6]

In the regression analyses below, we also include four dummy variables that refer to the internal characteristics of civil society organizations: year of foundation, presence of paid staff, availability of office space, and scope of action. The year of foundation allows us to grasp the duration of involvement for the organizations in the field by looking at whether the latter were created before or after 1995. The presence of paid staff and the availability of office space are two indicators of the degree of internal structuring for the organizations. The former distinguishes between organizations that have more than one full-time or two part-time staff and those that have none. The latter differentiates organizations that either own or rent their office space from those that do not. Finally, the scope of action distinguishes organizations whose actions are limited to a neighborhood, city, or region from those that stretch beyond these areas.

Political opportunties and the political mobilization of civil society organizations

Table 4.1 shows important variations across the seven cities along each of the four dimensions of political opportunity structures. In particular,

Table 4.1 Summary scores for the political opportunity structures in the seven cities

	Cologne	Geneva	Karlstad	Kielce	Lisbon	Lyon	Turin
Unemployment regulations	−.125	.250	.500	−.750	−.500	.625	−.500
Labor market regulations	.125	.375	.375	.125	.000	.250	.000
Unemployment-specific POS	.600	.800	.200	−.200	−.200	.200	−.800
General POS	.200	.800	−.600	−.600	−.400	−.400	−.200

the analysis of unemployment regulations shows the large gulf that exists between contexts characterized by exclusion, such as Kielce, Lisbon, and Turin, and contexts where policies and institutional devices work in favor of inclusion for the unemployed, such as Lyon and Karlstad. Geneva and Cologne fill in the intermediate area between the two poles. Variations along the second dimension of labor market regulations are less drastic but still relevant. All of the cities are in the flexibility camp, except for Lisbon and Turin, which are just on the border between flexible and rigid. This could be seen, among other things, as a sign of the overall move toward more flexible labor markets that has taken place across Europe. Yet, some cities (Geneva, Karlstad) are characterized by more flexible labor markets than others (Cologne, Kielce, Lyon). That is, results show that the opposition between a flexible (newer and more virtuous) model, on the one hand, and a rigid (older and more vicious) model may well be overstated in the daily rhetoric of politics, as countries align along a gradual continuum, rather than in a bipolar fashion. Nevertheless, differences do exist (at least at the end of spectrum) between cities where the divide between the insiders and outsiders of the labor market has clearly weakened, and cities where workers' rights are still the basis of overall political consensus.

Regarding the specific unemployment-opportunity structure, the analysis shows crucial differences between open and closed political contexts. On the one hand, Geneva and Cologne stand out for their open political contexts, owing to the facilitated institutional access they grant to actors in the field of unemployment and precarity through a wide range of participatory mechanisms. On the other hand, Turin stands out for its closeness. The low power of this city, in terms of unemployment policy vis-à-vis the national and regional levels, poor spending for specific measures targeting the unemployed and the precarious, and marginal inclusion of civil society organizations (including those of the unemployed and the precarious themselves) in unemployment policies account for the most constraining political context across all cities of our investigation. Lastly, the consideration of general political opportunities once again highlights the extensive openness of the Swiss system, owing to the longstanding tradition of bottom–up inclusion through the workings of subsidiarity, federalism, and various institutional devices, such as referenda and citizens' assemblies. By contrast, Karlstad and Kielce are placed on the opposite polar end, as a consequence of the centralized, top–down models of their own national states. Cologne, Lisbon, and Lyon fill in the intermediate area between the two extremes of closeness and openness.

At the same time, it is worth taking a more detailed look at the politicization of civil society organizations across the seven cities. The analysis of political activities, shown in Figure 4.1, suggests that politicization is prevalent in Turin and Cologne, and decreases in Lisbon and Lyon, before reaching its lowest levels in Kielce, Geneva, and Karlstad. Protest,

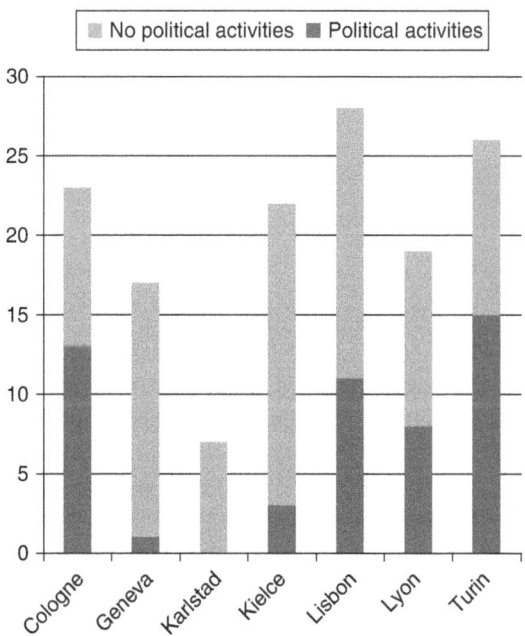

Figure 4.1 Political activities of civil society organizations in the seven cities (absolute numbers)

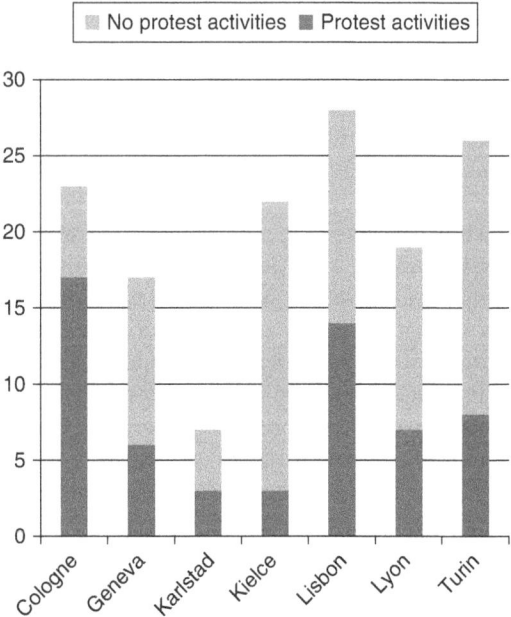

Figure 4.2   Protest activities of civil society organizations in the seven cities (absolute numbers)

however, follows a relatively different pattern, as we can see in Figure 4.2. In this case, the data suggest that, in some cities with high general politicization, such as Turin, protest may score relatively low – indeed, lower than in cities characterized by lower levels of general political activities, such as, for example, Lisbon.

In the two figures, it is noticeable that the variations are so extensive that our focus on seven cities is sufficient to identify distinct patterns whereby general political activities and protests are balanced at high (Cologne), intermediate (Lisbon and Lyon), or low levels (Kielce). Alternatively, political activities and protests can also combine in ways where one dimension of politicization prevails over the other. This is the case for Turin (where political activities prevail over protest) and Geneva (where protest prevails over political activities). Lastly, the case of Karlstad can be singled out as being characterized by very low levels of both general political activities and protest. Overall, the evidence shows the need for a more detailed analysis that can shed light upon the complex relationship between different dimensions of politicization and their distinct *explanans*. Hence, the next section discusses the results of a series of regression analyses that were conducted to assess the impact of the four dimensions of political opportunities on both dimensions of politicization.

The impact of political opportunities on the political mobilization of civil society organizations

As we have seen thus far, the seven cities under study vary extensively, in terms of the political opportunity structures they offer civil society organizations in the fields of unemployment and precarity for political activities and protest, whether in terms of unemployment regulations, labor market regulations, unemployment-specific opportunities, or general institutional opportunities. Similarly, civil society organizations vary in the forms and the extent to which they politicize. In this last explanatory part of our analysis, we want to ascertain (1) whether such political mobilization by organizations depends on the opportunities available to them and (2) whether distinct patterns of influence link each dimension of opportunities, on the one hand, with different dimensions of politicization, on the other. We do so by means of regression analysis. Since we deal with two dependent dummy variables (engagement in any political activity and the specific use of protest), we use logistic models with coefficients shown as odds ratios.

The results concerning the impact of the four dimensions of political opportunity structures on general political activities are shown in Table 4.2. Each of them is treated in a separate model. Each dimension was operationalized as a categorical variable measuring the two extreme situations (inclusive/exclusive, rigid/flexible, and open/closed), as well as an intermediate situation, in order to capture the potential curvilinear relationship between any given dimension of political opportunity structures and the involvement of organizations in political activities. In addition, we have included in each model four control variables pertaining to organizational characteristics: the age of the organization (year of foundation), their degree of professionalization (paid staff), their level of resources (owned or rented office space), and their scope of action (city level). In doing so, we keep the potential impact of main endogenous resources on organizational mobilization under control.

Overall, the findings point to a strong impact of political opportunity structures on the political activities of civil society organizations. We can thus provide a straightforward answer to our first question: political mobilization by organizations does depend on the opportunities available

Table 4.2   Effects of political opportunity structures on political activities by civil society organizations (odds ratios)

	Model 1	Model 2	Model 3	Model 4
Year of foundation (1 = after 1995)	1.11	.92	.95	1.19
Paid staff (1 = more than 1 full-time or 2 part-time)	.72	.67	.56	.65
Office space (1 = owned or rented)	.72	.83	.87	.95
Scope of action (1 = neighborhood, city, or region)	2.64*	1.48	2.16†	1.78
Unemployment regulations (ref.: exclusive)	***			
Inclusive	1.69			
Intermediate	12.07***			
Labor market regulations (ref.: rigid)				
Flexible		.99		
Intermediate		1.46		
Specific POS (ref.: closed)			**	
Open			4.18**	
Intermediate			1.73	
General POS (ref.: closed)				*
Open				5.45**
Intermediate				2.66
Constant	.40	.92	.51	.23
Nagelkerke R^2	.19	.03	.12	.12
−2 log-likelihood	161.497	179.362	169.951	170.309
N	135	135	135	135

† $p \leq .10$; * $p \leq .05$; ** $p \leq .01$; *** $p \leq .001$.
Standard errors between parentheses.

to them. In particular, unemployment regulations stand out as the most crucial dimension of opportunities, since it has the highest odds ratio and level of significance. However, this answer to our first general question needs to be substantiated in further detail by answering the second question about the existence of distinct patterns of influence that link opportunities with politicization.

Firstly, while inclusive unemployment regulations increase the chances that organizations politicize, as compared to exclusive ones, the effect is significant – and very strong – only for the intermediate category (Model 1). We thus observe a curvilinear relationship between this dimension of political opportunities and the use of political activities: relatively inclusive unemployment regulations favor the politicization of civil society organizations, whereas both strongly exclusive and strongly inclusive ones do not. Most likely, institutional arrangements and policy-making over unemployment may be challenged arduously when they are indisputably shaped according to opposite conceptions of welfare and unemployment regimes (Cinalli and Giugni 2011, 2013). By contrast, envisaging political change is easier when unemployment regulations are not based on uncompromising legal and normative assumptions of one shape or another. However, labor market regulations do not seem to have an impact on political activities (Model 2). Flexible labor market regulations do not push organizations toward becoming more political, rather than becoming involved in social, cultural, or other kinds of activities. Contrary to the possibility that the formulation of active measures and ongoing reforms over flexibility may be the most crucial issues at the core of overall unemployment policies, we instead find an overall predominance of consensual dynamics for this second dimension of opportunity, which does not account for variations of politicization in any of its values between rigid, intermediate, and flexible.

Open unemployment-specific opportunity structures greatly increase the likelihood that an organization makes use of political activities. The coefficient for the intermediate category is not significant, while the odds for the extreme category of openness are more than four times higher than for closed unemployment-specific opportunities. Hence, the more the institutional access available and participatory mechanisms are present in the field, the more the actors take advantage of them to become more politicized. This linear relationship is not surprising, given that the variations in the independent variable refer, in this case, to straightforward quantitative disparities between situations or poor and rich opportunities, respectively, rather than to opposition between two equally hegemonic political approaches (both leaving little room for challengers). Lastly, the pattern of influence linking general opportunities to politicization follows a similar linear relationship. An increase in general opportunities brings about an increase in general political activities. The coefficient for the intermediate category is not significant, while the odds for the extreme category of openness are about five and a half times higher than for closed opportunities. Again, our finding here is that a linear relationship may prevail over a curvilinear relationship for dimensions of political opportunities that refer to quantitative differences between situations of poor and rich opportunities, respectively.

The control variables do not display any statistically significant effect across the four models, with the exception of the scope of action for the model referring to unemployment regulations (at the 5% level) and for specific opportunities (at the 10% level). These findings only convey limited information about the endogenous resources and characteristics of organizations in the field. Yet, the main point here is that the consideration of these control variables (which are not significant) reinforces our appraisal of the crucial impact of political opportunities, rather than contributing to a full understanding of the role of organizational characteristics.

General political activities are only one indicator of organizational politicization in the field of unemployment and precarity. Another more specific side refers to the use of more contentious forms of political engagement by civil society organizations. Table 4.3 shows the results for involvement in protest activities. Again, we present four

Table 4.3   Effects of political opportunity structures on protest activities by civil society organizations (odds ratios)

	Model 1	Model 2	Model 3	Model 4
Year of foundation (1 = after 1995)	.51	.51	.49	.66
Paid staff (1 = more than 1 full-time or 2 part-time)	.14***	.14***	.13***	.12***
Office space (1 = owned or rented)	1.42	1.49	1.72	2.10
Scope of action (1 = neighborhood, city, or region)	2.41†	1.46	2.07†	1.76
Unemployment regulations (ref.: exclusive)	*			
Inclusive	.63			
Intermediate	3.36*			
Labor market regulations (ref.: rigid)				
Flexible		.35*		
Intermediate		.66		
Unemployment-specific POS (ref.: closed)				
Open			1.26	
Intermediate			1.09	
General POS (ref.: closed)				*
Open				6.20*
Intermediate				7.50**
Constant	1.64	3.28†	1.69	.31
Nagelkerke R^2	.22	.18	.15	.24
−2 log-likelihood	153.717	157.452	161.197	151.007
N	135	135	135	135

† $p \le .10$; * $p \le .05$; ** $p \le .01$; *** $p \le .001$.
Standard errors between parentheses.

separate models, each showing the effects of one of the four dimensions of political opportunities, as well as the control variables.

Starting back from our first question about whether politicization depends on opportunities, our findings once again display the overall crucial impact of political opportunities on organizations' involvement in protest activities (although not all of the coefficients are statistically significant). Once again, the two dimensions relating to unemployment regulations (Model 1) and general political opportunities (Model 4) have the strongest effects.

Regarding our second question about different patterns of influence linking opportunities and politicization, we find some interesting similarities between protest and political activities. Civil society organizations are more likely to engage in protest when unemployment regulations are more inclusive, with a significant and strong effect in the intermediary category (and once again, with a non-significant effect for the extreme category). The odds of engaging in protest activities for an organization, within a context of relatively inclusive unemployment regulations, are nearly three and a half times higher than when it acts in the context of exclusive unemployment regulations. The findings for protests are thus consistent with the results for political activities. A curvilinear relationship exists between unemployment regulations and the involvement of organizations in protest activities, due to the major space left open for challengers within political contexts that are not shaped on either of the two opposite poles of undisputable exclusiveness and undisputable inclusiveness. In addition, our results concerning general opportunity structures confirm the significant and strong impact of this aspect of the institutional context upon the political behavior of civil society organizations (Model 4). The latter are much more likely to engage in protest activities when the institutionalized system is open than when it is closed (which is the reference category). In this case, we also find some (minor) evidence of curvilinearity, indicating that successive increases in political opportunities will make it possible for organizations to opt for other forms of political activities beyond the simple use of protest.

Yet, some interesting differences of protest vis-à-vis political activities emerge when considering our second dimension of political opportunity structures – that is, labor market regulations (Model 2). In this case, we find that an increase in flexible labor market regulations is matched by a decrease in the protest activities of civil society organizations, as opposed to rigid labor market regulations (which is the reference category). Crucially, the choice of flexibility may follow the establishment of a free-market style of politics focused on macro-economic issues that may shrink the traditional space for workers' protests (Cinalli 2012; Cinalli and Statham 2005). The differences in protests vis-à-vis political activities are even stronger when focusing on the dimension of unemployment-specific opportunity structures (Model 3). With no significant effect, having open, specific opportunities make the use of protest activities by organizations neither more nor less likely, as opposed to closed opportunities (which is the reference category).

Only one control variable displays a statistically significant effect across the four models: paid staff. Professional organizations (e.g., those with paid staff) are less likely to engage in political mobilization than less professionalized organizations. Although the other control variables were not significant overall (except for the scope of action in the model referring to unemployment regulations and in the model referring to unemployment-specific opportunities, both at the 10% level), the main point to stress, once again, is that all these variables were included so as to gain a more robust evaluation of the impact of political opportunities and not to better understand the role of organizational characteristics.

Conclusion

This chapter has dealt with the potential impact of four main aspects of the political context – the degree of inclusiveness or exclusiveness of unemployment regulations, the degree of rigidity or flexibility of labor market regulations, the unemployment-specific political opportunity structure, and the general political opportunity structure – upon the politicization of civil society organizations that are active in the field of unemployment and precarity. Our conceptualization of politicization made us interested in two main dimensions: involvement in political activities, as measured through organizing targeted political events, and the use of more contentious activities, as measured through mobilizing members through protest, demonstrations, and direct actions. By comparing seven European cities, we assessed the extent to which the political opportunities that are specific to the field of unemployment and precarity, alongside more general opportunities stemming from certain features of the institutionalized system, influence the degree of politicization for civil society organizations. We also inquired into specific patterns of influence between different types of opportunities and different dimensions of politicization, by looking at the various directions of the effects and overall trajectories, whether linear or curvilinear.

Our results provide overall evidence of an important role of political opportunity structures for organizational positioning in the field of unemployment and precarity. Despite the non-significant effects of some of the variables, all four dimensions of opportunities influence the politicization of civil society organizations in some way. The findings also support the argument that there is sometimes a curvilinear, rather than a linear, relationship between political opportunity structures and political mobilization, which is in line with most recent analyses of the impact of political opportunities on protest actions in the field of unemployment politics (Cinalli and Giugni 2010). This is an important point of our argument, since similar non-linear patterns were also found, with regard to the impact of certain dimensions of political opportunity structures and the political participation of migrants and their descendants (Cinalli and Giugni 2011). From this viewpoint, the dimension pertaining to unemployment regulations can be singled out, since it shows a clear curvilinear effect on both of the dimensions of politicization considered here.

By focusing more closely on policy implications for unemployment, our findings show that inclusive unemployment regulations go quite far in favoring the bottom–up involvement of unemployed organizations themselves. In this case, no contradiction is found between general political activities and protest activities, since both dimensions of politicization coexist with similar patterns. Yet, curvilinearity also pinpoints the potential rigidity that inclusive policy approaches share with exclusive policy approaches. This is not surprising, when one considers that a clear-cut approach to unemployment regulations may be embedded within a powerful system of facts, norms, and ideas that shrink the space for any imaginable challenges. By contrast, politicization is expected to be stronger when policies stand out as the center of challenges coming from both sides of the exclusive/inclusive divide. Regarding the impact of labor market regulations, our analysis suggests that flexibility has no effect on involvement in political activities, while at the same time shrinks the use of protest. This is in line with the acquiescence of workers and the final establishment of a free-market style of unemployment politics. Lastly, unemployment-specific opportunities only have a significant effect on political activities, while general political opportunities are crucial to allow for increases in politicization altogether.

Finally, our analysis opens up space for further research to be conducted on the impact of complex political contexts made of different dimensions and their interactions. The way is now paved for more investigations that systematically combine different dimensions of opportunities, following on the footstep of previous research that has focused on the interplay of unemployment and labor market regulations (Giugni et al. 2009). Future research also needs to account for further interactions between specific and general opportunities at the intersection of the national and the sub-national levels, in order to evaluate the role of variable dynamic alignments in the multi-layered structures of political opportunities.

Notes

1. We also interviewed political parties; however, these actors were excluded from the present analysis, since we focus on civil society organizations (including trade unions). The final analysis is based on 142 cases. The regression analyses include 135 cases (seven organizations had to be excluded due to missing information on certain variables).
2. It should be emphasized that our indicators include not only hard legislation and public policies but also softer, informal aspects for each dimension. The main aim was to unveil the effect of hidden constraints or facilitations that may operate behind the façade of formal regulations. For example, the number of people that receive sanctions for abusing the benefit system is useful to indicate the true application of the formal provision: a strong force of sanction in the rhetoric of law may well be counterbalanced by its weak implementation.
3. The first three indicators come from the three components of the OECD's Employment Protection Legislation Index.
4. In addition to these four dimensions of opportunities, we also collected information on a fifth dimension dealing with related issue fields, such as education, child care, and antidiscrimination. However, these indicators are not included in the present analysis.
5. "How frequently has your organization engaged in the following activities in the last two years?" The interviewees went through more specific questions about cultural, social, intellectual, educational, and political events. We selected only the latter category, including lobbying, demonstrations, public meetings, and strikes.
6. "Could you please tell me which main actions among those listed below are used by your organization, in order to reach its aims?" We focused on mobilizing members through protest, demonstrations, and direct actions, dichotomizing along the yes/no distinction.

References

Bagguley, P. (1991) *From Protest to Acquiescence?* (London: Macmillan).
Bagguley P. (1992) "Protest, Acquiescence and the Unemployed: A Comparative Analysis of the 1930s and 1980s," *British Journal of Sociology*, 43 (3): 443–461.
Bassoli, M. and M. Cinalli (forthcoming) "Political Participation of Local Publics in the Unemployment Field: A Comparison of Lyon and Turin," *Social Movements Studies*.

Bay, A. H. and M. Blekesaune (2002) "Youth, Unemployment and Political Marginalisation," *International Journal of Social Welfare*, 11, 132–139.

Bonoli, G. (2003) "Social Policy through Labour Markets: Understanding National Differences in the Provision of Economic Security to Wage-Earners," *Comparative Political Studies*, 36, 1007–1030.

Cinalli, M. (2012) "Contention over Unemployment in Britain: Unemployment Politics versus the Politics of the Unemployed," in Chabanet, D. and J. Faniel (eds), *The Mobilization of the Unemployed in Europe: From Acquiescence to Protest?* (New York and Basingstoke: Palgrave Macmillan).

Cinalli M. (2010) "National Multi-Organisational Fields and Unemployment in Europe: A Comparison of Britain and France," in F. Royall and D. Chabanet (eds), *Mobilising Against Marginalisation in Europe* (Newcastle upon Tyne: Cambridge Scholars Publishing).

Cinalli, M. and M. Giugni (2010) "Welfare States, Political Opportunities, and the Claim-Making in the Field of Unemployment Politics," in M. Giugni (ed.), *The Contentious Politics of Unemployment in Europe* (Houdmills: Palgrave).

Cinalli, M. and M. Giugni (2011) "Institutional Opportunities, Discursive Opportunities, and the Political Participation of Migrants in European Cities," in Morales, L. and M. Giugni (eds), *Social Capital, Political Participation and Migration in Europe* (Houndmills: Palgrave).

Cinalli, M. and M. Giugni (2013) "New Challenges for the Welfare State: The Emergence of Youth Unemployment Regimes in Europe?" *International Journal of Social Welfare*, 22, 3, 290–299.

Cinalli, M. and P. Statham (2005) "Final Report for the United Kingdom," *Final Report for the 5th Framework Programme of the European Commission project UNEMPOL*, http://www.eurpolcom.eu/exhibits/ch3-UK.pdf, accessed 15 October 2009.

Demazière, D. and M.-T. Pignoni (1998) *Chômeurs: Du silence à la révolte* (Paris: Hachette).

Eisinger, P. K. (1973) "The Conditions of Protest Behavior in American Cities," *American Political Science Review*, 67, 11–28.

Esping-Andersen, G. (1990) *The Three Worlds of Welfare Capitalism* (Princeton, NJ: Princeton University Press).

Esping-Andersen, G. (1999) *Social Foundations of Postindustrial Economies* (Oxford: Oxford University Press).

Eurofund (2008) *More and Better Jobs: Patterns of Employment Expansion in Europe* (Luxembourg: Office for Official Publications of the European Communities).

European Commission (2009) *EU Youth Report 2009* (Brussels: European Communities).

Ferrera, M. (1996) "The 'Southern Model' of Welfare in Social Europe," *Journal of European Social Policy*, 6, 17–37.

Gallie, D. and S. Paugam (2000) *Welfare Regimes and the Experience of Unemployment in Europe* (Oxford: Oxford University Press).

Giugni, M. and F. Passy (eds) (2001) *Political Altruism? Solidarity Movements in International Perspective* (Lanham, MD: Rowman & Littlefield).

Giugni, M., M. Berclaz, and K. Füglister (2009) "Welfare States, Labour Markets, and the Political Opportunities for Collective Action in the Field of Unemployment: A Theoretical Framework," in Giugni, M. (ed.), *The Politics of Unemployment in Europe* (Aldershot: Ashgate).Green-Pedersen, C. and

M. Haverland (2002) "The New Politics and Scholarship of the Welfare State," *Journal of European Social Policy*, 12, 43–51.

Kitschelt, H. (1986) "Political Opportunity Structures and Political Protest: Anti-Nuclear Movements in Four Democracies," *British Journal of Political Science*, 16, 57–85.

Kriesi, H. (1996) "The Organizational Structure of News Social Movements in a Political Context," in McAdam, D., J. D. McCrthy, and M. N. Zald (eds), *Comparative Perspectives on Social Movements* (Cambridge: Cambridge University Press).

Kriesi, H. (2004) "Political Context and Opportunity," in Snow, D. A., S. Soule, and H. Kriesi (eds), *The Blackwell Companion to Social Movements* (Oxford: Blackwell).

Kriesi, H., R. Koopmans, J. W. Duyvendak, and M. G. Giugni (1995) *New Social Movements in Western Europe* (Minneapolis, MN: University of Minnesota Press).

McCarthy, J. D. and M. N. Zald (1977) "Resource Mobilization and Social Movements: A Partial Theory," *American Journal of Sociology*, 82, 1212–1241.

Meyer, D. S. (2004) "Protest and Political Opportunities," *Annual Review of Sociology*, 30, 125–145.

Oberschall, A. (1973) *Social Conflict and Social Movements* (Englewood Cliffs, NJ: Prentice-Hall).

Paugam, S. and D. Gallie (2004) "L'expérience du chômage: éléments pour une comparaison européenne," *Swiss Journal of Sociology*, 30, 3, 441–460.

Piven, F. Fox and R. A. Cloward (1979) *Poor People's Movements* (New York: Vintage Books).

Richards, A. (2002) "Mobilizing the Powerless: Collective Action of the Unemployed in the Interwar Period," Working Paper, Juan March Institute (January).

Tarrow, S. (2010) *Power in Movement* (3rd ed.) (Cambridge: Cambridge University Press).

Taylor-Gooby, P. (1991) "Welfare State Regimes and Citizenship," *European Journal of Social Policy*, 1, 93–105.

Tilly, C. (1978) *From Mobilization to Revolution* (New York: Random House).

van Deth, J. W., J. R. Montero, and A. Westholm (eds) (2007) *Citizenship and Involvement in European Democracies* (London: Routledge).

van Kersbergen, K. (2002) "Comparative Politics and the Welfare State," in H. Keman (ed.), *Comparative Democratic Politics* (London: Sage).

Warner Weil, S., D. Wildemeersch, and T. Jansen (2005) *Unemployed Youth and Social Exclusion in Europe* (Aldershot: Ashgate).

Zald, M. N. and J. D. McCarthy (eds) (1987) *Social Movements in an Organizational Society* (New Brunswick, NJ: Transaction Books).

Part II
Networks

5
Networks within the Multi-Organizational Field of Unemployment and Precarity: A Tale of Seven Cities in Europe

Matteo Bassoli and Manlio Cinalli

Introduction

The different contributions of this volume show that unemployment and precarity are crucial matters of concern in Europe, with a large number of actors mobilizing over issues pertaining to the labor market, social protection, and services. The unemployed and the precarious themselves have mobilized so as to advance their demands and defend their own interests. Institutions, decision-makers, and political elites have put the issues of unemployment and precarity at the core of their political strategies. And a number of additional actors – including political parties, trade unions, churches, and a range of charities and independent organizations – have engaged with unemployment and precarity. One should also focus on the organizations that speak and act on behalf of unemployed people and the precarious. While their members are not necessarily unemployed or precarious, these pro-beneficiary organizations take the fight against unemployment and precarity as their own main *raison d'être*. Their role is important, since the unemployed and the precarious themselves may be too "weak" to make their voice heard (Cinalli 2007; Giugni and Passy 2001).

This chapter deals with the large plurality of actors that enter multi-organizational field of unemployment and precarity, by focusing on their inter-organizational exchanges. We deal in particular with (a type of) networks of cooperation. Yet, the broader argument is that inter-organizational exchanges, whether they are contentious or based on consensus, translate into meaningful relational patterns that can be matched against cross-national variations of policy-making and political processes. The study of these relational patterns is essential for appraising the intermediating processes at the intersection between the multi-organizational field of unemployment and precarity on the one hand and the role of single organizations on the other. There are two main implications that follow from our relational approach. First, we show that networks interact with other major variables that are treated in the other contributions of this volume. For example, looking at "political opportunities," networks may allow for capitalizing on political access to agents who play a critical role in decision-making. As regards "resources," networks allows for appraising the resources that actors can control through mutual connections, beyond the depletory assets which each actor possesses. The second implication follows from the first one, since we show the crucial impact that networks have upon actors' decisions within the multi-organizational field of unemployment and precarity (see also Bassoli et al. in this volume).

Having tackled the theoretical bases of our work in the first part, we engage with a systematic cross-national assessment of multi-organizational fields and their relational structures. Throughout this assessment, we also address a number of methodological issues that rise in the analysis of incomplete and asymmetrical networks. Afterwards, our attention is focused on the relationship between networks and the political access of organizations within contexts of "inclusion" or, alternatively, "exclusion." A brief section of conclusions sums up the main output of this chapter.

The multi-organizational fields of unemployment in Europe

Our analysis focuses on the invisible aspects of the politics of unemployment and precarity. On the one hand, we shed light on hidden ties that link actors to each other within whole multi-organizational fields (Curtis and Zurcher 1973; Galaskiewicz 1985). The study of these networks is considered to be especially important to appraise the construction of relational patterns across the public and the policy domain. While the policy domain includes institutions and policy elites, the public domain refers, in the context of our argument, to the "city publics" that are the target of policy-making (Bassoli and Cinalli forthcoming; Cinalli 2004). On the other hand, we focus on the (mis)matching between relational structures and the broader political process. By referring to the crucial distinction between countries that facilitate and countries that constraint the inclusion of the unemployed (Cinalli and Giugni 2010, 2013), we assess the extent to which the facilitating policies of France, Sweden, and Switzerland translate into similar relational patterns. The same inquiry is conducted in Germany, Italy, Poland, and Portugal, since these countries endorse constraining policies of exclusion and low social protection vis-à-vis the unemployed and the precarious. Our comparison may also reveal some evidences of cross-national synergies (in terms of relational structures) across countries that are different for their approaches to welfare and the labor market.

Network analysis (Knoke and Kuklinsky 1982; Scott 2000; Wasserman and Faust 1994) provides us with the key conceptual and methodological tools for examining the multi-organizational field of unemployment and precarity. Following on the footsteps of previous research on unemployment politics and relational structures (Bassoli and Cinalli forthcoming; Cinalli 2004; Cinalli and Füglister 2008), the multi-organizational field is operationalized in terms of networks of ties among units, that is, a set of nodes which are entrusted to actors who, through their reciprocal interactions, contribute to shape the overall relational structure. In particular, we define our networks as sets of ties of cooperation to common projects. Each organization is thus seen as a focus from which lines radiate to other nodes of the multi-organizational field, that is, the other organizations with which ties of common projects are shared. This relational approach to the politics of unemployment and precarity also responds to the pressing need to use networks as an effective instrument of empirical analysis, rather than as a simple heuristic device (Christopoluos 2008).

We can thus proceed to evaluate cross-national variations of networks, so as to see whether they fit our distinction between countries that facilitate the political access of the unemployed and the precarious on the one hand and countries restricting political access on the other. The expected differences between a model that promotes some inclusion (France, Sweden, and Switzerland) and a model that more strongly promotes exclusion (Germany, Italy, Portugal, and Poland) are tested through the analysis of a number of relational measures, including (1) "scope" of the multi-organizational field, (2) "heterogeneity" of actors, (3) "reciprocity" of exchanges, as well as (4) "coreness," (5) "centralization," (6) "dispersion," and (7) "positioning."

The two measures of "scope" and "heterogeneity" enable us to assess the extent to which the multi-organizational field includes a large variety of organizations. Drawing upon teachings of governance (Faerman et al. 2001; Storper and Christopherson 1987), we know that field borders, as well as the need for "specializing," are stronger when policy-making focuses on a specific issue. In this case, the access of specialized stakeholders is facilitated so as to avoid the creation of wider and looser multi-organizational fields (where coordination may be too costly).

As a consequence, we expect that contexts that fit an inclusive model of unemployment politics have tighter borders and low organizational heterogeneity. By contrast, in countries where policy-making does not address unemployment and precarity, there cannot be a clear allocation of actors' position and responsibilities. This leads to the entrance of a larger volume of heterogeneous actors in the multi-organizational field (Bassoli and Cinalli forthcoming). In particular, the analysis of "heterogeneity" is useful to identify the presence of diverse actors, with no prevalence of a given type that fits the specific requirements of the field. The various aspects of heterogeneity may include cultural perspectives, political goals, and the different levels at which actors are active. Thus, heterogeneity is expected to increase when a large variety of actors from different fields and levels engage with unemployment and precarity.

Beside a relatively small number of homogeneous actors, a well-defined multi-organizational field requires that actors know each other, trust each other, and acknowledge explicitly their mutual interdependence (Ostrom 1990: 197–206; Rhodes 1996: 652). Hence, "reciprocity" stands out as a further relational measure at the core of our analysis. The main argument is that the mutual acknowledgement among actors, as well as their shared cooperation over common issues, is essential to strengthen bottom-up processes within the multi-organizational field, thus weakening the traditional forms of top-down intervention (Chisholm 1992). Direct government steering and the cogent intervention of policy elites become increasingly redundant when reciprocity is growing amongst actors.

The three measures of "coreness," "centralization," and "dispersion" can be valuable to appraise whether organizations are in full control of their own field – with actors interacting with each other in dense, dispersed, and highly decentralized patterns – or if alternatively the main control passes through one or few highly centralized brokers (Provan and Kenis 2007). Starting with our treatment of "coreness," it should be emphasized that a dedicated institutional approach to unemployment and precarity may go together with the establishment of an efficient coordinating core. As a consequence, a central group of actors that are densely tied with each other can easily communicate with the periphery, whose members have more ties to core members than to each other (Borgatti and Everett 2000). By contrast, the opposite situation of segmentation may translate into stronger top-down control and less inclusive dynamics across the public and the policy domain (see also the notion of "sectorization" in Peters and Wright 2001). As regards our assessment of "centralization," the main argument is that bottom-up inclusion requires that a large number of actors interact in a highly decentralized pattern of inter-organizational cooperation that prevents the hegemony of a (strongly interconnected) node on all the others. Lastly, weaker top-down control and self-management among stakeholders in the public domain are facilitated in contexts of high "dispersion," where actors can survive in isolation.

As a final step, our analysis focuses on "positioning" according to the legal status of organizations. In this case, we think that inclusive models of unemployment politics – based on the effective functioning of the multi-organizational field – place greater and more complex demands upon actors. These latter have to deal with a policy process that is articulated in a multiplicity of different stages, and hence, highly demanding in terms of actions that must be performed. So the expectation is that the most established actors are more likely to conquer the central positions of the multi-organizational field, while actors that are less established will occupy the peripheral positions.

Put simply, our analysis aims to match the seven cities against the two opposite ideal-typical poles that may be identified on the base of the variables just described (Table 5.1). This is useful to reduce complexity. It also provides the benchmark for appraising the relationship between cross-national variations of networks, on the one hand, and differences across the inclusive/exclusive spectrum of the political context on the other. We can thus assess the extent to which Cologne, Kielce, Lisbon and Turin also follow the ideal-typical pole of exclusion in terms of their networks, while at the same time matching Geneva, Karlstad and Lyon against the inclusive pole.

As said, our analysis of networks is focused on a specific type of tie, namely, cooperation of unemployed actors to common projects.[1] Our decision to focus on cooperation to common projects follows two main empirical findings of our research. First, cooperation to common projects is a strong tie as compared to other types of co-operative

Table 5.1 Expected relationship between unemployment regime and organizational fields

	Scope	Heterogeneity	Reciprocity	Core	Centralization	Dispersion	Positioning
Inclusive system	Few actors	Low	High	High	Low	High	Correlated
Closed system	Large number	High	Low	Low	High	Low	Uncorrelated

ties. Second, the measure of network centralization suggests taking the cooperation to common projects as a better proxy of what is going on in the city (Baglioni and Bassoli 2009). The recall of existing projects with specific partners helps to clarify the landscape of actual coopera-tion in the different cities. By contrast, overlapping memberships and the exchanges of information are more strongly dependent upon the perceived importance of the named actors.

Accordingly, we can give a full relational twist to most relevant questions of unemployment politics. What are the field borders being forged in each national case, and what is the organizational composi-tion within them? Do unemployment and precariousness stand out as contentious issues that divide certain types of actors from the others? Is reciprocity prevalent among organizations, reducing the traditional distance between actors of different type? And do actors themselves have a good control of their own field? Through the study of relational characteristics, we can evaluate whether unemployment politics relies on an effective multi-organizational field. Crucially, our evaluation of scope, heterogeneity, reciprocity, coreness, centralization, dispersion, and positioning can also tell us much more about contexts where traditional top-down forms of coordination are more likely to stay. Loose interaction in the multi-organizational field can give more force to traditional top-down politics, as government will have more room to point out and decide what has to be done (Majone 1996).

Data and operationalization

In what follows, we have engaged in a two-step methodology (see Baglioni and Giugni in this volume for a full account of methodologi-cal issues). First, we have established an exhaustive inventory of all actors within the multi-organizational field of unemployment and precarity. Second, we have interviewed those actors who were avail-able to be interviewed. The use of snowballing techniques, as well as the inclusion of both formal and informal organizations, have allowed for the identification of the largest number of active organizations in each national case. It has already been shown in this volume that, cross-nationally, the organizational universes differ not only in terms of numbers but also in terms of degree of heterogeneity. We have thus distinguished civil society organizations (CSOs), social movement organizations (SMOs), religious organizations (ROs), trade unions (TUs), and political parties (PPs). Our approach is thus different from other network approaches to social movements that have taken SMOs only as those informal groups that are part of a social movement (Diani and Bison 2004).[2]

At the same time, we have tackled a main methodological problem of network analysis, namely, the drawing of field boundaries (Wasserman and Faust 1994: 30–35). Our recourse to snowballing (Goodman 1961) refers to networks that are *de-facto* two-modes $(X*X+\varepsilon)$.[3] The difference between two-mode and one-mode networks is crucial in our analysis. Network analysis often focuses on one-mode networks with one set of nodes that are similar to each other. While it can be argued that ontologically our networks are one-mode $(X+\varepsilon*X+\varepsilon)$, they are of a particular kind, with two different sets of nodes, namely, the interviewed organizations (X) and the mentioned ones $(X*X+\varepsilon)$ which may be interviewed or not.[4] This common problem is often tackled by reducing the two-mode networks into one-mode networks by considering only the X interviewed organizations (Pilati 2012). Yet, in this chapter we have preferred the use of adjacent data $(X+\varepsilon*X+\varepsilon)$, accepting the more limited scope for their analysis (but see Everett and Borgatti 2005). A main advantage consists in the possibility to contrast core organizations with peripheral actors, providing a comprehensive picture of the unemployment multi-organizational field in each national case.

As regards the use of the specific tools of network analysis, we can start with the discussion of "scope" and "heterogeneity." "Scope" refers to the dimension of the field. We provide this measure through two main variables. First, we consider the number of interviewed and mentioned organizations. Whenever a city scores higher than the average, it receives a value of "1"; otherwise it receives a "0." Second, we control for the number of interviewed actors so as to take account of the impact of pendants (that is, nodes that have only been mentioned once – or that have mentioned only one alter).[5] As regards "heterogeneity," we focus on the legal status, in line with other chapters of this volume. The diverse composition in terms of legal status is strongly embedded within national welfare structures. Yet we use a relative measure so as to counterbalance the shape of national provisions (that may not favor the presence of certain types) as well as the sampling procedures and the maximum number of types of legal status that have been considered. Since our understanding of heterogeneity refers to both the number of types of actors and their relative balance, our measure consists in the number of the types which have at least three actors (n) divided by the cumulative percentage of the first three types (cum). This measure ranks between 0.001 and 0.270 (given the maximum number of actors 9 and the minimum cumulative percentage of 33.3%). Therefore the final measure of heterogeneity (H) is:

$$H = (n/cum)/0.27^6$$

The notion of "reciprocity" is operationalized through a simple measure of "dyad base reciprocity." According to this latter, "a tie is reciprocated if whenever a tie is connected from actor A to actor B then there is a tie from actor B to actor A. We can [...] count the number of dyads connected by a tie (which may or may not be reciprocated) and calculate the proportion of dyads that have reciprocated ties" (Borgatti et al. 2002). Given that the reciprocity (ρ) is the percentage of reciprocated dyads (r) divided by the number of adjacent dyads (t − r):

$$\rho = r/(t - r)$$

Our approach to "coreness" is based on the UCINET routing of core-periphery with correlation algorithm (Borgatti et al. 2002).[7] The routing allocates actors in a way to have a core-periphery structure, thereby creating two blocks of actors. In the first block, that is, the core, nodes are highly interconnected. In the second block, nodes are unconnected. However, coreness should also be hierarchical: the number of connections between peripheral and central nodes should be higher than those among peripheral nodes alone.

As regards "centralization," we consider how much central the most central node is in relation to how central all the other nodes are (Freeman 1978).[8] UCINET computes the network degree centralization of a binary network as:

$$\Sigma(c_{max} - c(n_i))/c_{max}$$

where c_{max} is the maximum value possible and $c(n_i)$ is the degree centrality of node n_i.[9] We then assess "dispersion" through the so-called level of fragmentation. This measure can be computed on the base of the proportion of nodes that cannot reach each other (Borgatti et al. 2002). In order to have a more fine-grained measure, we have opted for the distance-weighted fragmentation. This measure is equal to one minus "compactness," that is, a distance-based cohesion measure calculated as the harmonic mean of the normalized sum of the reciprocal of all the distances. Thus, it has a value of zero when the network is a clique (everyone is connected with everybody else) and one when the network is entirely made up of isolates.

Lastly, our notion of "positioning" refers to the concept of centrality based on the legal status. Since centrality may be measured using different variables, we have opted for controlling the four major directed variables: outdegree, indegree, out-Bonacich, and in-Bonacich. The first two variables are simple measures of the number of outgoing and incoming ties. The measures proposed by Bonacich consider that the outgoing/incoming centrality of a vertex is determined by the outgoing incoming/centrality of actors to which the same vertex is connected. Therefore it makes a crucial difference whether an actor is tied to more central or less central actors. A correlation test between all the four variables and the legal status has been conducted using the ANOVA routine in UCINET. The routine undertakes a standard analysis of variance using a permutation test to generate the significance level so that standard assumptions on independence and random sampling are not required. Thus we have found a significant distribution of legal status, given that some types of organizations are more central than the expected values given by the network composition.

Unemployed-related organizations and their project network

Given the cost of forging and maintaining connections as well as the cost of tight cooperation, we expected that the project network would be generally small, made of a highly interconnected network (almost a clique) or of a group of actors with many simmelian ties (triples of interconnected nodes)[10] and many reciprocated ties (Krackhardt 1998). Yet, project networks (Table 5.2 and following figures) are not

Table 5.2 Networks of project collaboration in cities of inclusion (white) and exclusion (grey)

	Interviewed organization	Number of nodes (universe)	Sample's representativeness (interviewed/ universe)	Density	Number of ties	Network centralization	
						Outdegree	Indegree
Geneva	21	50	42.0%	0.06	135	42.3%	9.0%
Karlstad	13	21	61.9%	0.07	31	29.0%	8.0%
Lyon	21	34	61.8%	0.04	49	20.5%	11.1%
Cologne	29	51	56.9%	0.06	149	20.6%	16.5%
Kielce	26	30	86.7%	0.07	56	14.7%	14.7%
Lisbon	30	74	40.5%	0.02	122	22.7%	21.3%
Turin	36	70	51.4%	0.05	225	24.7%	14.4%

built in this way. In Table 5.2 we present the key variables to compare networks: number of interviewed organization (X), size of the network (X+ε), sample's level of representation (X/X+ε), density and network centralization. While the level of representativeness gives only a simple measure of the number of interviewed organizations, the other measures are based on networks. Density is the most synthetic measure of a network (Wasserman and Faust 1994: 181): it gives the percentage of existing relationships out of all possible ties.[11] The number of nodes is relevant (bigger networks have lower density), yet some comparisons are striking. Lyon with a network dimension similar to the one of Kielce is much more sparse, whereas Turin scores higher with a double size. For this reason, given the low level of representativeness of our samples (Table 5.2), it is important to focus on the network centralization.[12] This latter provides an expression of how tightly the network is organized around its most central point (thus taking into account the network dimension). Since we are dealing with direct data (actor A may acknowledge a project with actor B, but this latter may not recognize it as a major collaboration), we opted for two measures: outdegree (measuring the number of outgoing ties) and indegree (measuring the number of incoming ties).

The importance of distinguishing between outdegree and indegree can be grasped by contrasting Kielce with Geneva. These two cities have similar interviewed samples (21 and 26), similar densities (6% and 7%) but different universe (50 and 30). The number of existing (outgoing) ties in Geneva is much higher than in Kielce. The reason is that the Geneva network is built around 21 well-connected actors, while Kielce have 26 not-so-well connected actors (out of 28 receiving actors and two isolates). Generally the variance of these measures is much higher in comparison with the measure of density. Moreover, there are key differences between indegree and outdregree. While the latter tends to be quite high (thus, there are only a handful of actors mentioning others), the same does not hold for the indegree. In addition, cities tend to be centralized around a few actors in terms of outdegree. Among the most centralized samples we find Geneva, Karlstad, and Turin. By contrast, incoming ties are especially centralized in Lisbon, followed by Cologne, Kielce, and Turin.

This overview of networks across the seven national cases provides our first picture to display divergences and similarities across different multi-organizational fields of unemployment and precarity. We can now move on to study more closely the city specific characteristics across the two models of inclusion and exclusion (that is, the white/grey distinction of Table 5.2).

Geneva

In Geneva the universe is large (50 actors) and the population is quite heterogeneous (value of 0.24). Figure 5.1 illustrates the structure of interactions between all actors. It emphasizes the high density and the level of interconnection. The location where each node is placed is given by the "scaling and composition" routine of UCINET (Borgatti et al. 2002). This routine finds a set of points in a bidimensional space such that the Euclidean distances among these points correspond as closely as possible to the distance given by the connections (MDS).[13]

Figure 5.1 shows that the network is grouped around five major organizations, namely, a12, a13, ch2, ch3, and c01. These five organizations receive either seven or six ties from their counterparts, suggesting the importance of their role in the whole field. By contrast, the association a07 and the political party pp2 send out more ties. The low correlation between indegree and outdegree (0.256) suggests that the outdegree is also measuring the ties with associations that are less relevant (for example, the pendants). The two nodes a07 and pp2 refer to a political party (pp2) and to an organization providing jobs and

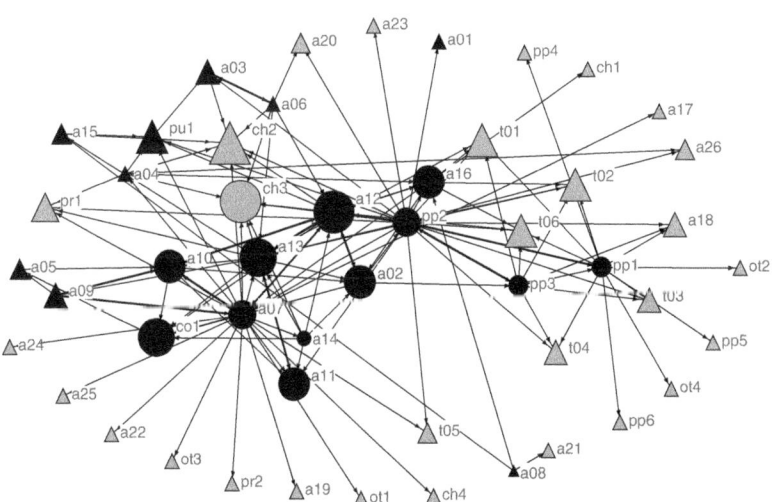

Figure 5.1 Network of organizations having common projects in Geneva (darker nodes are those interviewed, circles in the core, triangles in the periphery, size by indegree, darker lines are symmetric)

Source: Network graphed with Netdraw (Borgatti, 2002) according to MDS calculated by UCINET (Borgatti et al. 2002), with small adjustment.

in-kind help to people who suffer from various forms of precarity and exclusion (a07). These two nodes have both 23 outgoing ties. We then find the node pp1 with 12 ties and the two nodes a12 and a13 with 11 ties each. These latter two associations are also the most crucial in terms of the indegree measure.

The picture clearly displays a core-periphery structure as well as the relative importance of central actors (size according to the indegree). These aspects are also confirmed by more robust statistical tests. The core-periphery routine has a goodness of fit of 0.464. Moreover the density of the core is quite high (34.1%), thus showing some strong hierarchy (peripheral nodes are linked more to the center than among themselves). All these aspects conform to the ideal type of inclusive unemployment regime described before (Table 5.1).

The analysis of symmetric ties and simmelian ties add up some valuable information. Figure 5.1 makes use of darker lines to depict the presence of reciprocal ties. There are only 12 instances. This suggests that the conduction of common project is not a widespread experience. There are only two simmelian triples (a12, a07, a10) and (a09, a07, a10). As regards the "positioning," political parties and cooperatives play a brokerage role in the Swiss field. Yet associations and religious organizations are the most active segment of the civil society in line with rich civic participatory traditions of Swiss polity across the traditional cleavages of religion and nationality. As a legal type, the "association" stands out not only as the most frequent but also as the most active and most central. The main reason for this specific aspect seems to relate to the prevailing role of "service provision" developed by local CSO in Geneva.

Karlstad

As for Geneva, the case of Karlstad includes non-interviewed organizations, many of which are pendants, that is, organizations with connections to only one other node. Many "public" and "for-profit" organizations have also been included in order to draw the network. However, the number of mentioned alters allows for drawing only a small network of 21 nodes (that is, the smallest value for scope among all our networks). The main finding is that relational patterns in Karlstad do fit the ideal type of an inclusive unemployment regime. Figure 5.2 displays different (weak) components, that is, unconnected subnetworks. In particular, there is a big component in the upper part (circular nodes) and three smaller components in the lower part (triangles and squares). This relational structure has the highest scores for "coreness," with a goodness of fit of 0.476 and a core-density of 45.2%

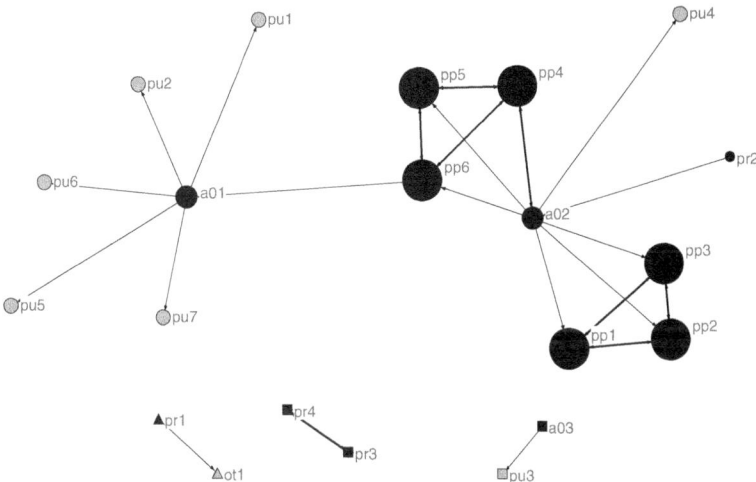

Figure 5.2 Network of organizations having common projects in the Karlstad (darker nodes are those interviewed, shape according to the different components, size by indegree Bonacich power, darker lines are symmetric)
Source: Network graphed with Netdraw (Borgatti, 2002) according to MDS calculated by UCINET (Borgatti et al. 2002), with small adjustment.

(confirming the fit with an inclusive regime). Yet the core-periphery structure in Karlstad is different in comparison with the other inclusive case of Geneva. In this latter city, peripheral nodes are interconnected rather than connected to the core (no clear hierarchy). As regards the level of heterogeneity and positioning, components tend to confirm the legal status differences among actors. Thus, in the main components, there are only parties (two cliques and one pendant), two bridging associations (a01 and a02), and the public/private pendants of these organizations (confirming the crucial role of political parties in Karlstad).

Another crucial feature is the structural aspect of the main component (the one with political parties), which is made of two parties' cliques connected through brokerage (see Bassoli et al. in this volume). The two cliques are ideologically based. Three right-wing parties and three left-wing parties, respectively, are connected via association a02, which at first sight takes the role of a broker. This association has only one reciprocal tie shared with one of the left-wing parties. At the same time, the two cliques increase the number of reciprocated ties in a way to make the network in Karlstad as the one with the highest level of reciprocity (35%). This structure also explains why the network has the lowest value of (indegree) centralization, given that the central nodes have all similar indegree, and hence similar size (Figure 5.2).

It is also important to emphasize that the inclusive system in Geneva strongly relies on service providers (not-for profit) which are the actors forging the borders of the unemployment field. By contrast, in Karlstad the higher importance of the for-profit sector and direct public provision of services may account for a crowding-out effect in the unemployment field. This latter is not composed by third-sector organizations but by the public sector, for-profit organizations (e.g., job coaches) and political parties that mainly play a rhetoric role.

Lyon

The analysis of relational patterns in Lyon provides us with findings that do not fit the French inclusive political context. Figure 5.3 displays a rather small network with low scope (34). We find no core-periphery structure, nor do we find a high level of centralization (11%). Comparatively, there are strong similarities with Karlstad. Overall the network is the second most fragmented (82% of unconnected nodes)

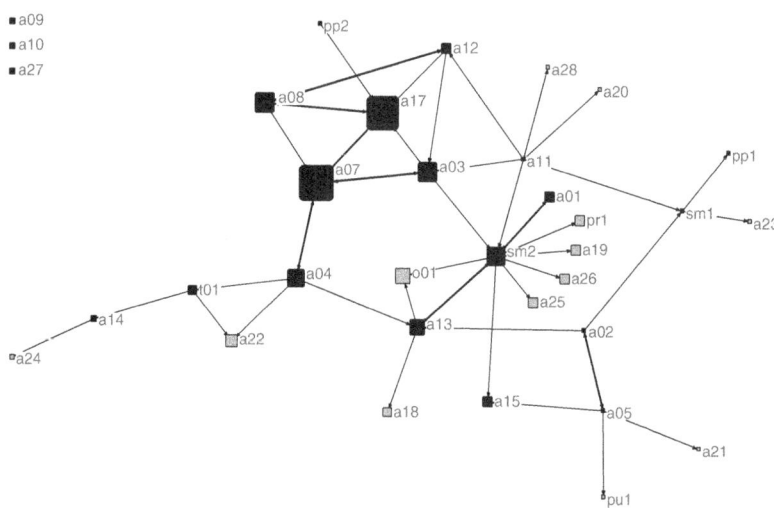

Figure 5.3 Network of organizations having common projects in the Lyon (darker nodes are those interviewed, size by indegree Bonacich power, darker lines are symmetric)

Source: Network graphed with Netdraw (Borgatti, 2002) according to MDS calculated by UCINET (Borgatti et al. 2002), with small adjustment.

yet with a good proportion of reciprocated ties (20%). No simmelian ties can be found.

As regards heterogeneity and positioning, the network in Lyon is quite peculiar compared to every other city. Out of seven different types of actors, only one (civil society organization) reaches the threshold of three. The number of associations is remarkably high (26) so that the cumulative percentage of the first three legal types amounts to 88%. Therefore the centrality has not a clear correlation with the legal status, given the fact that associations are both central (a17, a07, a03) and pendants (a24, a28, a21). Another crucial factor to consider is the presence of different key actors that play the role of brokers. The nodes a04, sm2, and a11 split the network into two distinctive parts, while a04 is also gate-keeping the right-hand side of the network.

Cologne

The network in Cologne is quite different from what we have found in Geneva and Lyon. Although scope is similarly high (51), the level of heterogeneity is much higher as expected by a system of exclusion (0.26). Overall there are seven types of actors, five of which count at least three units. This partially explains the high score of heterogeneity. However, the crucial reason is the rather small size of the first three types. There are six social movement organizations (sm), twenty-five civil society organizations (a), six political parties (pp), seven trade unions (t), one cooperative (co), five church-related institutions (ch), and one private enterprise (pr).

Figure 5.4 clearly displays the different (quasi-cohesive) subgroups in the network, which are characterized by high level of connection and relative low distance. This structure shows a tendency toward a core-periphery, albeit this is not a purely core-periphery (goodness of fitness equal to 0.421). There is a relative high level of indegree centralization (16.48%) with a low level of dispersion (0.117). On the left side of the network we notice a cluster that is completely made up of social counseling centers (pr1, a05, a07, a13, a14). On the right side, there is a second subgroup of actors that is mainly composed of labor unions (t01, t02, t03, t06), one social movement organization (sm2)[14] and a leftist political party (pp4). These latter two actors are also those that are connected with the first (service provider) subnetwork.

Some other actors are also important and have similar features that connect the different subgroups (pp5, a08, a04, sm1). This network illustrates that, in general, there is a tendency to interact with similar others, such as members of their own type of organization.[15] Nonetheless

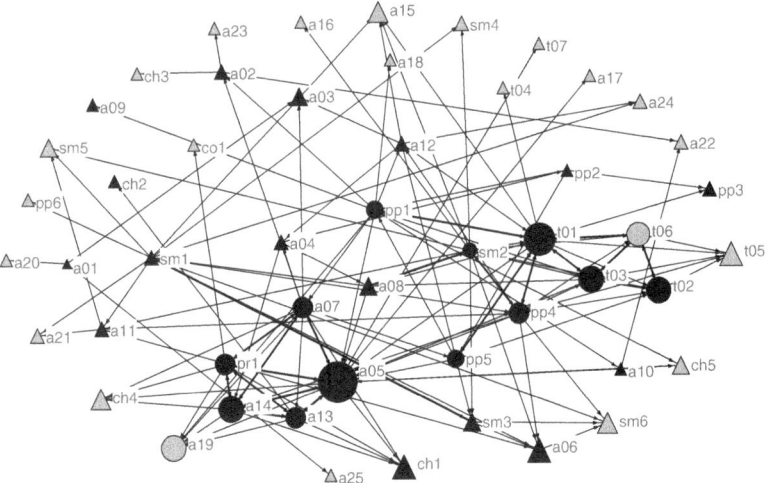

Figure 5.4 Network of organizations having common projects in Cologne (darker nodes are those interviewed, circles in the core, triangles in the periphery, by indegree Bonacich power, darker lines are symmetric)

Source: Network graphed with Netdraw (Borgatti, 2002) according to MDS calculated by UCINET (Borgatti et al. 2002), with small adjustment.

there are two crucial features: (1) the most central actors are not of any particular kind (positioning) and (2) the linkages are rarely matched (see darker arches in Figure 5.1). These findings thus confirm our expectation about closed unemployment regimes, which should be matched by large numbers, high heterogeneity, low reciprocity, and the absence of a clear core. This latter exists, at least to some extent. Yet the network is centralized and central actors are not of any specific kind (although trade unions play a major role on the right-hand side of the figure and associations play a major role on the left-hand side).

Kielce

The situation of Kielce (Figure 5.5) refers to a weakly interconnected single-component graph. While Kielce is characterized by an unemployment regime of exclusion, its network structure is not fully consistent with this ideal type. On the one hand, the situation is similar to Cologne in terms of the general structure, while, on the other, the network is rather small in terms of scope (30) and homogenous (0.12), with only three types including more than three actors. There is a low level of general reciprocity (6%) and low cohesion among the organizations (see darker arches in Figure 5.5), with only three reciprocated ties and no simmelian triples. Apart from the very low level of cohesion of this network, there are only few horizontal links based on trust and partnership. During the interviews it was clear that to mention "alters" was a way to projecting the organizational strength. Having a strong partner was considered as a way to gain visibility for more marginal organizations, whereas visible actors tended to underplay the existence of ties with more marginal actors. In the words of a representative of a main organization: "we know that they maintain to cooperate with us, but we deny; they are very weak."

Emphasis should also be put on the relative importance of some actors (with high levels of centralization) and the absence of a core-periphery structure. As regards positioning, religious organizations are clearly identifiable as central nodes. Some of them have a high level of indegree (ch1, ch3, ch5, and a03) showing their perceived importance within the field. This subnetwork is centralized around Caritas (ch1) (see also Bassoli and Theiss in this volume). The cluster of Caritas consists of its services provision centers (ch2, ch3, and ch4) and other

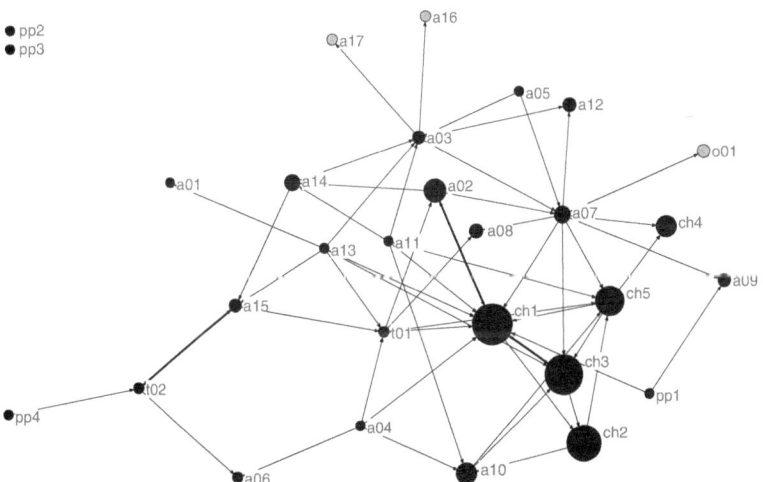

Figure 5.5 Network of organizations having common projects in the Kielce (darker nodes are those interviewed, size by indegree Bonacich power, darker lines are symmetric)
Source: Network graphed with Netdraw (Borgatti, 2002) according with lightening procedure, with small adjustment.

organizations that are relatively right-wing oriented (a14, ch5, a03). In this cluster we also find the presence of the labor union Solidarność (t01). Generally speaking, all the organizations in this "central" area are linked to the Solidarność tradition. When describing the network, interviewed organizations of this cluster often pointed out to the similar background or tradition (saying, for example, phrases such as "we have similar roots" or "we stem from the same post-Solidarność group"). Hence, this historical heritage has had a crucial impact on networks, which are shaped according to an unexpected pattern. Instead of favoring a decentralized network with no clear role-positions, the political context of exclusion in Kielce is matched by the presence of a core that is made of church-related institutions. This core is not linked to the efficient service provision of an inclusive unemployment regime, but it stems from the historical development of the Polish civil society.

Lisbon

The Portuguese network (Figure 5.6) is the largest one, with a scope of 74 nodes. It is also very fragmented (98% of nodes cannot reach each

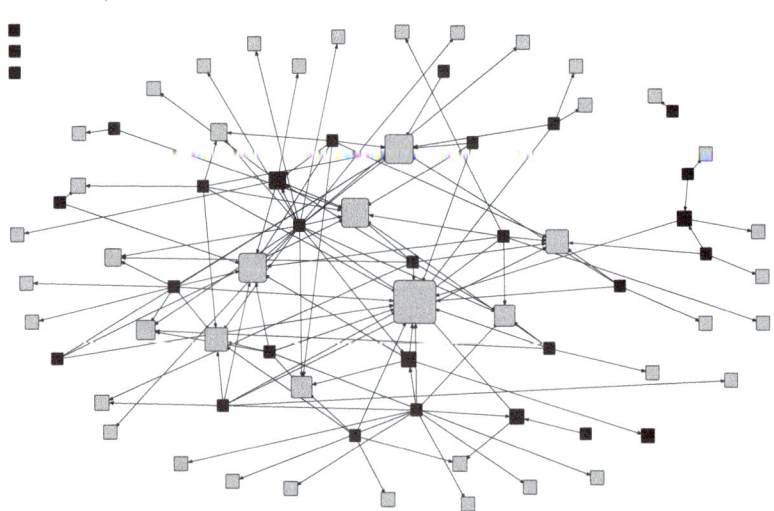

Figure 5.6 Network of organizations having common projects in the Lisbon (darker nodes are those interviewed, size by indegree Bonacich power, darker lines are symmetric)

Source: Network graphed with Netdraw (Borgatti, 2002) according to MDS calculated by UCINET (Borgatti et al. 2002), with small adjustment.

other) compared to the previous ones. However, Lisbon is a case that we must treat on the base of incomplete information. The legal status was not retrieved for many organizations, while a number of major actors could not be interviewed. Thus, scores are sometimes missing (as in the case of heterogeneity and positioning) and in general must be treated cautiously.

The network has a very centralized structure (21%), with no reciprocal ties, and it does not have a clear core/periphery. There is a large volume of pendants (32) and isolates (3). Yet it should be emphasized that the (indegree) centralization is around an actor that could not be interviewed. This limits the scope of our results and their potential interpretation. As it is clear by the different shades of grey in Figure 5.6, the interviewed organizations are not as central as they are in the previous networks. So, for example, in Geneva we find a similar sample's robustness (42% against 41%), but interviewed organizations are central (though non-interviewed organizations are also important). By contrast, the network in Lisbon suggests a lack of clear centrality among the interviewed organizations that may be not as representative as in the other samples.

Turin

The Italian network is much wider, fragmented and sparse as compared to all the other networks. It is much more similar in scope to the Lisbon one (70 nodes), but it shows some quite distinctive characteristics. As in the case of Kielce, the field of unemployment and precarity in Turin does not fit the ideal type of an unemployment regime of exclusion. Due to the strong ideological associational background, the network mixes opposite characteristics. On the one hand, it is large, heterogeneous, and dispersed, while on the other, it has a centralized structure with a clear core and a high level of reciprocity. The overall relational structure is quite similar to Cologne, given the presence of a cohesive network with a single component and no evident broker. Turin has an analogous level of indegree centralization (14%), as well as no clear sign of fragmentation (26% of unconnected nodes) and a weak tendency towards core-periphery. The network scores quite well in the core-periphery routine. It has a fitness of 0.384, with a tendency towards centralization (14%). Given its size, the core density is low (22%) and, as in the case of Cologne, there is a strong tendency for clustering among similar actors. However, actors are not grouped according to legal status as expected but according to political orientation and ideological legacies (see also Bassoli and Theiss in this volume). The right-wing organizations are relatively isolated (t02, t12, pp2, pp3, pp7), whereas there is a clear "core-periphery" structure created by the leftist and Catholic institution (circles vs nodes in Figure 5.7). Many nodes are embedded in simmelian ties (as opposed to the German and Swiss structures). Moreover, the level of reciprocity is comparable to the French and Swedish cases, since 21% of connections are reciprocated.

The network in Turin is composed of two tightly connected subnetworks, that is, a core central network on the one hand and a relatively small network on the other. In Figure 5.7 the triangles are part of the so-called periphery (density 7%), while circles are part of the core (density 22%). As expected, the right-wing organizations are part of the periphery together with many social movements. These latter organizations need to be described with further details. Indeed, there is a large volume of these organizations both in the Italian sample and in the Italian universe. Yet they do not seem to be so relevant in the structure. Often, they are not interviewed (sm8, 9, 10, 11, 12, 13) because they are not

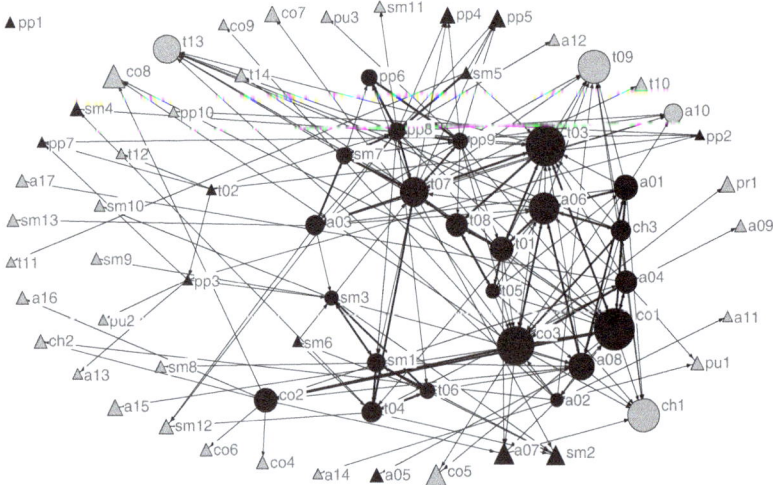

Figure 5.7 Network of organizations having common projects in the Turin (darker nodes are those interviewed, circles in the core, triangles in the periphery, size by indegree Bonacich power, darker lines are symmetric)

Source: Network graphed with Netdraw (Borgatti, 2002) according to MDS calculated by UCINET (Borgatti et al. 2002), with small adjustment.

mentioned. Alternatively, they are part of the periphery (sm2, 4, 5, 6). Only in three cases (sm1, sm5, sm7) they do play a role. Clearly, they are part of the outer layer of the core. Figure 5.7 also shows that the size of the social movement nodes is smaller compared to other "central nodes." A number of final features can be highlighted. Turin scores the highest level of heterogeneity with 0.41. We find the presence of seven legal types with more than three actors as well as a very low cumulative percentage (63%). Cooperatives and trade unions are very central (Bonacich indegree) while political parties are not.

Relational dynamics: context of inclusion vs contexts of exclusion

Having appraised the main relational characteristics of the multi-organizational field of unemployment, we can give a closer look at the fit of networks with major institutional approaches in Europe. As said, a key difference exists between, on the one hand, countries where the unemployed and the precarious have been put at the core of a relatively generous system of benefits and inclusive policy-making and, on the other, countries where the unemployed and the precarious face more constraining arrangements. In particular, countries diverge when looking at various indicators of state intervention in terms of unemployment regulations – for example, the prerequisites for obtaining social provisions, the level and extension of benefit coverage, the role of employment agencies, and the scope of sanctions (Cinalli and Giugni 2010; Giugni et al. 2009). Accordingly, processes of (mis)matching between relational and political factors need to be investigated with a particular reference to the distinction between more inclusive and less inclusive models of "unemployment regimes" (Berclaz et al. 2004; Cinalli and Giugni 2013; Gallie and Paugam 2000). Focusing on the national cases of our research, it is thus crucial to consider more explicitly whether an inclusive policy approach in Geneva, Karlstad, and Lyon translates into similar cross-national relational characteristics. The same type of inquiry needs to be conducted for Cologne, Kielce, Lisbon, and Turin so as to look for hidden relational patterns of similar models of exclusion and low social protection.

Table 5.3 completes and sums up systematically the information about the network characteristics that have been discussed in previous sections. Each column gives a value on each relational characteristic for each city,[16] but it also dichotomizes the same values in a way to assign national cases to a same, or alternatively, to an opposite camp.

Table 5.3   Cross-national comparison of relational characteristics in the field of unemployment and precarity

	Heterogeneity	Reciprocity	Coreness	Centralization	Dispersion	Positioning
Inclusive	0	1	1	0	1	1
Geneva	.24 (1)	.10 (0)	.32 (1)	.09 (0)	.83 (0)	yes (1)
Karlstad	.18 (0)	.35 (1)	.45 (1)	.08 (0)	.88 (1)	yes (1)
Lyon	.04 (0)	.20 (1)	.07 (0)	.11 (0)	.90 (1)	no (0)
Exclusive	1	0	0	1	0	0
Cologne	.26 (1)	.16 (0)	.34 (1)	.16 (1)	.83 (0)	no (0)
Kielce	.12 (0)	.06 (0)	.10 (0)	.15 (1)	.81 (0)	yes (1)
Lisbon	N/A	.00 (0)	.10 (0)	.21 (1)	.98 (1)	no (0)
Turin	.41(1)	.20 (1)	.22 (0)	.14 (1)	.84 (0)	yes (1)

Findings point to some interesting relationship between political and relational factors. Thus, heterogeneity brings together, as expected, Lyon and Karlstad (but not Geneva) on the side of inclusion, as well as Cologne and Turin (but not Kielce) on the side of exclusion. Reciprocity brings together, as expected, Lyon and Karlstad (but not Geneva) on the inclusive side, as well as Cologne, Kielce, and Lisbon (but not Turin) on the side of exclusion. Coreness brings together, as expected, Geneva and Karlstad (but not Lyon) on the inclusive side, as well as Kielce, Lisbon, and Turin (but not Cologne) on the side of exclusion. As regards centralization, this measure shows a common relational pattern across all the three national cases on the inclusive side, but also across all the four national cases on the side of exclusion. Dispersion brings together, as expected, Lyon and Karlstad (but not Geneva) on the inclusive side, as well as Cologne, Kielce, and Turin (but not Lisbon) on the side of exclusion. Lastly, the analysis of positioning brings about the weakest results, yet it still brings together, as expected, Geneva and Karlstad on the inclusive side, as well as Cologne and Lisbon on the side of exclusion.

Overall, a good fit is found within the camp of exclusion. Yet Turin and Kielce have more than a single variable that do not conform to the model of exclusion. It should be emphasized that in these two cities the network is strongly influenced by the ideological legacy which triggers the correlation between legal status and centrality (see Bassoli and Theiss in this volume). As regards the inclusive camp, one also finds some crucial differences: for example, Geneva has a heterogeneous sample, small reciprocity, and low dispersion. Yet a general picture of good fit is still prevailing. Karlstad stands out for its full consistency with the ideal-typical network configuration of inclusion, while Lyon presents only some minor discrepancies (mainly due, possibly, to the large volume of interviewed associations).

Hence, a strong relationship emerges between the relational characteristics of our multi-organizational fields of unemployment and precarity on the one hand and the exogenous characteristics of the political context on the other. Findings about the (mis)matching amongst relational characteristics and city contexts are most often consistent with our expectations. Heterogeneity is more constrained within political contexts of (relative) inclusion – and vice-versa, it is facilitated within political contexts of stronger exclusion. This also indicates the likely incidence of an organizational type that may prevail in a scenario where unemployment is at the core of an established multi-organizational field. The analysis of reciprocity indicates that policies of exclusion vis-à-vis the unemployed and the precarious do very little to foster trust and mutual acknowledgement in the field. In fact, they contribute to restrict the space for bottom-up inclusion, preventing the weakening of traditional forms of top-down intervention. As regards "coreness," "centralization," and "dispersion," these relational characteristics show that self-management and full control – with the prevalence of a dense, yet dispersed and highly decentralized, pattern of interaction – is more likely with an inclusive approach to unemployment.

Of course, one also finds some evidences that go in the opposite direction of our expectations. However, a more detailed analysis often reveals that some specific reasons may hide behind the inconsistent mismatching between the relational characteristics of the multi-organizational field on the one hand and, on the other, the two opposite contexts of relative inclusion and stronger exclusion. Take for example the inconsistent results for Turin and Kielce in our analysis of positioning. In these two cities the more established groups define the field. Yet this happens not just because these groups have an official status, but because they provide specific services and share a specific ideological background (see Bassoli and Theiss in this volume).

Conclusions

This chapter has shown that network analysis is valuable for examining the multi-organizational field of unemployment and precarity in Europe. Our main point was that even the most articulated sets of policies targeting the unemployed and the precarious need to be appraised by considering the relational characteristics of the multi-organizational field of unemployment and precarity. Following our nexus between the two opposite political contexts of inclusion and exclusion on the one hand, and the relational characteristics of the multi-organizational field on the other, we have thus opened up space for more empirical research (and further theorization) on the relationship between policy processes and fields of contentious politics.

In particular, we have argued that a number of crucial questions have to be answered about the complex interactive dynamics that enable various actors and stakeholders to engage across the public and the policy domain so as to strengthen their position within multi-organizational fields. In so doing, we have proved that the analysis of networks is especially important to evaluate the role of relational structures in different fields, where different policy approaches may prevail. Different unemployment policies – summed up in the two opposite models of relative inclusion and stronger exclusion – have been matched against the relational shape of the unemployment field.

We have appraised cross-national variations of networks through an extensive number of measures. Some of them, such as centralization, have displayed the same relational pattern across all national cases within both camps of inclusion and exclusion. Other measures have shown much weaker results (in particular, positioning). Taken together, however, these measures have suggested some extensive matching between networks and the political context, with a good overall fitting of each city to its relational ideal type. At the same time, the study of these network measures has told us a lot about the unaffected dominance, or alternatively the ongoing weakening, of traditional forms of top-down politics in Europe. An inclusive unemployment approach is more likely matched by a homogeneous multi-organizational field where a given organizational type prevails, with high levels of trust, mutual acknowledgement, self-management, and full control by actors themselves.

Ultimately, this chapter has shown that the relational characteristics of multi-organizational fields of unemployment and precarity in Europe do fit the distinction between countries that facilitate the political access of the unemployed and the precarious on the one hand and countries restricting the same type of political access on the other. In line with our expectations, crucial relational differences hide behind the distinction between an unemployment policy model that promotes a relative inclusion on the one hand and an opposite policy model that more strongly perpetuates the exclusion of the the unemployed and the precarious on the other.

Notes

1. The question was asked directly through direct listing of all organizations that had been mapped but at the same time providing the interviewee with the possibility to add up further names of other project partners that were not in the list.
2. Furthermore, fieldwork has not detected any clear social movement related to unemployment under the same terms.
3. The X-interviewed organizations of each city have mentioned some other ε organizations, creating a X time X+ε matrix.
4. The mapped universe is a X+ε times X+ε matrix. However, there are information only connecting X organization with the corresponding X+ε organization. Thus for ε organizations we have only incoming ties, because they have not been interviewed.
5. Once the variable scope has been created, its ranking has been controlled for the ranking of the variable counting the number of interviewed organizations only. As ranking was consistent, no additional correction has been put in place.
6. This measure is now more disperse and range from 0.04 to 1.
7. The fit function is the correlation between the permuted data matrix and an ideal matrix consisting of ones in the core block interactions and zeros in the peripheral block interactions. This value is maximized (Borgatti et al. 2002).
8. Our measure is based on "indegree" centrality, as opposed to "outdegree" centrality, because indegree centrality provides a good measure of the popularity and the reliability of a node. By contrast, the outdegree also considers ties that are less relevant (in particular, the ties with the so called "pendants," that is, actors who have no other connections).
9. Given that the "star" is the most centralized network (all the actors but one have degree of 1, and the "star" has degree of the total number −1), the centralization can also be taken as a measure of the degree of variance as a percentage of that of a "star" of same size (Hanneman and Riddle 2005: 65).
10. Simmelian ties are strong reciprocated ties shared by three actors, thus indicating the presence of three actors reciprocally interconnected.
11. Given the problem of boundaries we faced, the recorded densities are very low since the non-interviewed organizations increase the number of theoretical ties but not the one of the recorded one.
12. "For a given binary network with vertices v1 ... vn and maximum degree centrality cmax, the network degree centralization measure is $\Sigma(c_{max} - c(vi))$ divided by the maximum possible value, where c(vi) is the degree centrality of vertex vi" (Borgatti et al. 2002).
13. Metric multidimensional scaling of a proximity matrix.
14. It is a social movement fighting for basic income. It is quite new and is not part of the traditional leftist milieu of Köln.
15. Although it is not reasonable to measure homophily with such a numerous partition, the E-I index is smaller than expected (0.178 vs 0.443), yet not statistically smaller than by chance alone.
16. Cf. Appendix I for further details about the computation of each measure.

References

Baglioni, S. and M. Bassoli (eds) (2009) *Addressing Work Instability. Organizational Activation on Youth Unemployment and Precariousness in European Cities*, www.younex.unige.ch/Products/Reports/WP2_INTEGRATEDREPORT_D7.pdf, accessed 18 February 2012.

Bassoli, M. and M. Cinalli (forthcoming) "Political Participation of Local Publics in the Unemployment Field: A Comparison of Lyon and Turin," *Social Movement Studies*.

Berclaz, M., K. Füglister, and M. Giugni (2004) "Etats-providence, opportunités politiques et mobilization des chômeurs: une approche néo-institutionnaliste," *Swiss Journal of Sociology*, 30, 421–440.

Borgatti, S. P. (2002) *NetDraw Software for Network Visualization* (Lexington, KY: Analytic Technologies).

Borgatti, S. P. and M. G. Everett (2000) "Models of Core/Periphery Structures," *Social Networks*, 21, 4, 375–395.

Borgatti, S. P., M. G. Everett, and L. C. Freeman (2002) *Ucinet for Windows: Software for Social Network Analysis* (Harvard, MA: Analytic Technologies).

Chisholm, D. (1992) *Coordination without Hierarchy: Informal structures in Multiorganizational Systems* (Berkley: University of California Press).

Christopoulos, D.C. (2008) "The Governance of Networks: Heuristic or Formal Analysis? A Reply to Rachel Parker," *Political Studies*, 56, 475–481.

Cinalli, M. (2007) "Between Horizontal Bridging and Vertical Governance: Pro-Beneficiary Movements in New Labour Britain," in Purdue, D. (ed.), *Civil Societies and Social Movements: Potentials and Problems* (London: Routledge).

Cinalli, M. (2004) "Horizontal Networks vs Vertical Networks within Multi-Organisational Alliances: A Comparative Study of the Unemployment and Asylum Issue-Fields in Britain," *Centre for European Political Communication Working paper 8/04*, http://www.curpolcom.cu/exhibits/paper_8.pdf, accessed 2 July 2013.

Cinalli, M. and K. Füglister (2008) "Networks and Political Contention over Unemployment: A Comparison of Britain, Germany and Switzerland," *Mobilization*, 13, 259–276.

Cinalli M. and M. Giugni (2013) "New Challenges for the Welfare State: The Emergence of Youth Unemployment Regimes in Europe?" *International Journal of Social Welfare*, 22, 290–299.

Cinalli M. and M. Giugni (2010) "Mapping the Contentious Politics of Unemployment in Europe," in Giugni, M. (ed.), *The Contentious Politics of Unemployment in Europe: Welfare States and Political Opportunities* (Houndmills: Palgrave).

Curtis, R. L. and L. A. Zurcher (1973) "Stable Resources of Protest Movements: The Multi-Organizational Field," *Social Forces*, 52, 53–61.

Diani, M. and I. Bison (2004) "Organizations, Coalitions, and Movements," *Theory and Society*, 33, 281–309.

Everett, M. and S. P. Borgatti (2005) "Extending Centrality," in Carrington, P. J., J. Scott and S. Wasserman (eds), *Models and Methods in Social Network Analysis* (Cambridge: Cambridge University Press).

Faerman, S. R., D. P. McCaffrey, and D. M. V. Slyke (2001) "Understanding Interorganizational Cooperation," *Organization Science*, 12, 372–388.

Freeman, L. C. (1978) "Centrality in Social Networks Conceptual Clarification," *Social Networks*, 1, 215–239.

Gallie, D. and S. Paugam (2000) *Welfare Regimes and the Experience of Unemployment in Europe* (Oxford/New York: Oxford University Press).

Giugni, M., M. Berclaz, and K. Füglister (2009) "Welfare States, Labour Markets, and the Political Opportunities for Collective Action in the Field of Unemployment: A Theoretical Framework," in Giugni, M. (ed.), *The Politics of Unemployment in Europe: State and Civil Society Responses* (Aldershot: Ashgate).

Giugni, M. and F. Passy (eds) (2001) *Political Altruism? Solidarity Movements in International Perspective* (Lanham, MD: Rowman and Littlefield).

Goodman, L. A. (1961) "Snowball Sampling," *The Annals of Mathematical Statistics*, 32, 148–170.

Hanneman, R. and M. Riddle (2005) *Introduction to Social Network Methods: Table of Contents* (Riverside, CA: University of California Riverside) http://faculty.ucr.edu/~hanneman/nettext/, accessed 6 June 2012.

Knoke, D. and J. H. Kuklinski (1982) *Network analysis* (Beverly Hills: Sage Publications).

Krackhardt, D. (1998) "Simmelian Ties: Super Strong and Sticky," in Roderick Moreland, R. K and Neale, M. A. (eds), *Power and Influence in Organizations* (Thousand Oaks, CA: Sage).

Majone, G. (1996) *Regulating Europe* (London/New York: Routledge).

Ostrom, E. (1995) *Governing the Commons: The Evolution of Institutions for Collective Action* (Cambridge: Cambridge University Press).

Peters, G. and V. Wright (2001) "The National Co-ordination of European Policy-Making: Negotiating the Quagmire," in Richardson, J. (ed.), *European Union: Power and Policy-Making* (Thousand Oaks, CA: Routledge).

Pilati, K. (2012) "Network Resources and the Political Engagement of Migrant Organisations in Milan," *Journal of Ethnic and Migration Studies*, 38, 671–688.

Provan, K.G. and P. Kenis (2007) "Modes of Network Governance: Structure, Management, and Effectiveness," *Journal of Public Administration Research and Theory*, 18, 2, 229–252.

Rhodes, R. A. W. (1996) "The New Governance: Governing without Government," *Political Studies*, 44, 652–667.

Scott, J. (2000) *Social Network Analysis: A Handbook* (Los Angeles/London: Sage).

Storper, M. and S. Christopherson (1987) "Flexible Specialization and Regional Industrial Agglomerations: The Case of the U.S. Motion Picture Industry," *Annals of the Association of American Geographers*, 77, 1, 104–117.

Wasserman, S. and K. Faust (1994) *Social Network Analysis: Methods and Applications* (Cambridge: Cambridge University Press).

6

Cliques, Cleavages and Conflicts: Local Civil Societies in Cologne and Turin

Christian Lahusen and Bettina Grimmer

Introduction

Unemployment is a social problem that implies multiple hardships, because joblessness leads to a loss not only of income but also of work-related recognition and self-esteem, professional identities, and social relations (e.g., Jahoda et al. 1971), which may result in a process of marginalization and exclusion (Kieselbach et al. 2001). However, marginalization is not limited to the unemployed. It may also be evoked by precarious employment, because like joblessness, insecure employment situations are often connected with the experience of financial troubles, the inability to earn a livelihood, and the impossibility of making plans for the future. Among these problems, research has also centered on the observation that long-term unemployment is closely linked to a loss of "social capital" and a state of "social poverty" that implies a reduced number of contacts to friends, family members, and acquaintances; limited participation in public life (e.g., through organizations and initiatives in the realm of culture, leisure, politics, or social matters); and a reduced level of trust in public institutions and fellow citizens (Jahoda et al. 1971; van Oorschot et al. 2006; Cainzos and Voces 2010).

This strand of research converges with public debates in the conviction that civil society can help to prevent or ameliorate social marginalization and exclusion (Putnam et al. 2003; Gerometta et al. 2005). Most of these organizations provide services to the unemployed and precariously employed and thus help them to relieve deprivations and/or overcome joblessness or job insecurity. Moreover, they provide opportunities to participate in public life, thus combating isolation, apathy, and mistrust. Finally, they often advocate on behalf of the unemployed and precarious, or help to mobilize and organize them. According to this line of reasoning, therefore, the ability to combat or overcome social marginalization depends on the availability, organizational strength, and structural composition of local civil societies, among other factors.

In spite of the importance attributed to civil societies, we do not know a great deal about the field of civil society in the realm of unemployment and precarity, and even less about their potential role or impact. So far, research has tried to reconstruct the organizational field of civil society at large, by conducting empirical surveys in all areas of activity, such as culture and education, sports and leisure, social and health services, and professional and political interest representation (see Anheier and Toepler 2010; Edwards 2011). With regard to unemployment issues, a number of studies have been conducted on the role of civil society organizations in protest actions and the related mobilization and organization of the jobless (Reiss and Perry 2011; Giugni 2010; Chabanet and Faniel 2012). However, they center on only one part of a more pluralized and fragmented field of local civil societies.

This chapter aims at generating empirical evidence on the structure of local civil societies in the area of unemployment and precarious employment. It strives to reconstruct the field of local civil societies by describing the types of organizations involved and analyzing the structure of organizational relations in two specific cities: Cologne, Germany, and Turin, Italy. These empirical insights do not allow us to answer the question of if and how local civil societies are used by the jobless and precarious, and whether they succeed in ameliorating deprivations and overcoming marginalization. However, this method allows a reconstruction of the "supply-side" and thus the organizational opportunities provided to and the constraints imposed on the unemployed and precarious population. For this purpose, we will try to answer the following three research questions.

- Which types of organizations are part of local civil societies in the field of labor market issues?
- How do contacts and collaborations structure the organizational field? Is it marked by widespread cooperation, or divided by cleavages and cliques?
- Finally, how can we explain these patterns? Which factors govern the structure of organizational relations and collaborations?

To answer these questions, we will analyze the two organizational fields with regard to network structures. Secondly, we will explain homophilic relationships between organizations by testing the impact of the organizations' action repertoires, their governance structures, and their relations to the organizational environment (i.e., to public authorities and the political arena) on project collaboration. Finally, we will discuss our findings and draw conclusions.

Research assumptions: organizational networks and homophily

This chapter will use concepts and tools of network analysis in order to study the organizational structure of local civil societies. In that manner, we can describe and explain this structure along the patterns of organizational ties (e.g., contacts, collaborations, and so on) within the field of unemployment and employment issues. Studies of organizational networks share the conviction that we live in an organizational society, within which social reality is strongly shaped by organizations and their mutual relations. This applies to the field of unemployment as well, because unemployment is a social problem that is defined, administered, or tackled by a number of interrelated organizations (public authorities, welfare associations, political parties, social movement organizations, etc.). Scholars of policy networks, for instance, have argued that democratic politics relies on the basic notion of participation by the people. However, they raise our awareness of the fact that individual participation is mediated (e.g., enabled, motivated, controlled, or suppressed) by many different organizations (political parties, interest groups, think tanks, mass media, and so on). Politics is thus determined by the structure of policy networks and the dynamics of organizational relations of power, exchange, or deliberation (Knoke 1990; Knoke et al. 1996; Perrucci and Potter 1989). This applies in particular to the problem of individual participation and collective action in the political sphere, as indicated by social movement research. Proponents of resource mobilization theory, for instance, have insisted on the fact that political protest is a rational and purposeful collective action that requires resources and organization (Zald and McCarthy 1987). Social movements are a particularly powerful instrument of political participation and collective action because they consist of "industries" (Zald and McCarthy 1987) or "networks" (della Porta and Diani 1999: 124–127) of cooperating and/or competing organizations, whose mission is to mobilize, organize, and represent constituencies.

The structure and dynamic of social movements are thus strongly determined by the intensity of cooperation and/or competition between organizations, although social movements always exhibit a combination of factionalism and consensus, antagonism and division of labor, albeit with a different grading.

Organizational fields are also important in the realm of welfare services. Each unemployed person has stipulated rights and is usually entitled to receive social benefits. However, the access to these rights and entitlements is strongly mediated by the availability of welfare associations and advocacy groups that provide information and advice, organize and implement public programs, and represent the interests of the jobless and precariously employed (Chabanet and Faniel 2012). In addition, this field of action is patterned by interorganizational relations. Indeed, welfare service delivery requires networking and cooperation between various service organizations, as argued by resource dependence theory (Aldrich 1976), because organizations depend on securing resources for their organizational work (e.g., information, funds, qualified personnel, support). Moreover, human service and community organizations are often interrelated due to overlapping memberships and leaderships with similar social and ethnic backgrounds (Laumann et al. 1978; Galaskiewicz and Shatin 1981). These interorganizational relations are beneficial for individuals as well, because they improve access to available services and increase the chances of community organization and political empowerment (Hendryx et al. 2002; Andrews and Edwards 2004).

In sum, local civil societies comprise a dense web of organizations dealing with different dimensions of the problems of unemployment and precarity: the political, administrative, legal, social, or cultural aspects of the everyday lives of persons in precarious situations. But what can we say about these local civil societies, their organizational structures, and the forces driving them? Before we turn to network analysis in order to answer these questions in empirical terms, we need to lay the theoretical groundwork for this analysis by presenting our guiding assumptions. For this purpose, we want to refer to various factors identified in previous research. In first instance, the authors highlight external factors. Neo-institutionalist studies of the organizational field have pointed to the fact that organizational structures are strongly molded by the state or dominant professions, and these actors have a homogenizing or streamlining impact on them (Meyer and Rowan 1977; Powell and DiMaggio 1991). We assume that "isomorphism" implies an increase in organizational contacts among these actors. Others have highlighted the impact of the immediate community by stressing the importance of a similar social background, such as race, residence, or social class, among members or leaders of various organizations. These societal structures facilitate and channel interorganizational relations (Galaskiewicz and Shatin 1981; McPherson and Smith-Lovin 1987; Ruef et al. 2003).

With regard to factors internal to organizational networks, earlier research has identified three different forces. First, organizational relations are governed by a utilitarian logic, whereas organizations maintain contacts in order to exchange resources, optimize their organizational functioning, and maximize their chances of reaching their organizational goals (Albrich 1976; Laumann and Knoke 1989; Knoke 1990). In this sense, the structure of organizational fields is determined by the specific issues at stake, the various organizational interests and resources, and the related rational choices involved. Second, organizational relations are also governed by relations of solidarity and ideological affinity, as implied in the concepts of "policy-communities" (Richardson and Jordan 1979: 73–74) or "advocacy coalitions" (Sabatier 1988). According to these concepts, the structure of organizational fields is not governed only by volatile and changing issues and interests but by a more enduring "set of normative and causal beliefs" (Sabatier 1988). Third, organizational relations are structured by mutual affiliations and overlapping memberships, also at the level of activists and leaders (della Porta and Diani 1999: 119–124), as mentioned before. At this level, however, the focus is rather on the argument that the structure of organizational fields is strongly shaped by interpersonal networks and their specific traits of familiarity, trust, and solidarity.

These explanatory factors tend to converge in one research assumption that has been explicitly developed within network analysis: the thesis of homophily (e.g., McPherson et al. 2001). This hypothesis argues that network ties are more common between similar actors than between dissimilar ones, leading to the conclusion that networking exposes a strong tendency toward homogeneity. This assumption has been recurrently verified in the context of interpersonal networks, such as in classrooms, workplaces, or local communities (Lazarsfeld and Merton 1954; McPherson and Smith-Lovin 1987; Ibarra 1992; Currarini et al. 2009; Wimmer and Lewis 2010; Burgess et al. 2011). In many areas of everyday life, people tend to associate with fellow citizens with similar demographic characteristics (e.g., race and ethnicity, education and social class, age, and gender) and with similar values, attitudes, and beliefs. But the same assumption also seems to apply to organizational networks, as alluded to by the explanatory factors discussed above. Organizations tend to maintain more contacts to other organizations with similar issues and interests (Knoke et al. 1996); with similar values, ideas, and knowledge bases (Sabatier 1988; Powell and DiMaggio 1991); and with similar constituencies and leadership groups (Galaskiewicz and Shatin 1981; Lincoln and McBride 1985; Ruef et al. 2003). Moreover, homophily seems to be based also on organizational features like the degree of formalization and professionalization and the size and power of the organizations (Spires 2011). For instance, it has been demonstrated that large, formal, and highly professionalized movement organizations tend to interact more among themselves than with informally structured grass-roots groups (Rucht 1989).

In this chapter, we want to test the assumption that local civil societies in the realm of unemployment and precarity issues are structured along organizational similarities. According to this assumption, we expect that this organizational field will be governed by alliances and cliques of entities with similar organizational features and missions. More specifically, we will argue that local civil societies are structured along two "cliques"' – social movement and social welfare organizations. This structure increases the subjacent antagonism between competing organizational communities: a confrontational strategy of contentiousness on the one side and a conciliatory strategy of professional service delivery on the other. This assumption needs to be validated empirically and critically. For this purpose, two tasks have to be accomplished, one descriptive and one explanatory. On the one hand, we will need to examine the structure of the organizational field of civil society; on the other hand, we will identify those organizational characteristics that are responsible for homophily.

These explanatory attempts will rely on a number of research hypotheses. As a starting point, we will argue that civil society organizations (CSOs) normally fulfill two functions: service delivery and political advocacy. These functions have implications for the organizational field, because it is argued that different types of organizations will prioritize these two functions differently. For this reason, it makes sense to distinguish social movement organizations from social welfare associations, because they follow different missions and goals, organizational forms, and repertoires of action. Hence, even if both areas of work (service and advocacy) are complementary, we argue that organizations often make choices as to their priorities, and that these choices are responsible for homophily within the network.

This general assumption, however, needs to be specified, because the distinction introduced above is quite broad and refers implicitly to a series of organizational characteristics. Three different hypotheses will thus be tested in order to explain homophily, following the theoretical arguments introduced above. The first hypothesis argues that organizations with similar activities or action repertoires will maintain more ties because it is easier for them to identify common projects and events with which to collaborate. In this regard we will compare the network ties of organizations involved in mobilization and political protest activities against those active in the area of service provision and advice. Our second hypothesis assumes that the network divides into groups with different governance structures, depending on the degree of formalization and professionalization. It is quite probable that formal organizations with full-time staff and professional management structures interact more easily and more often among themselves and thus dissociate from informal grass-roots organizations. The third hypothesis assumes that ties are determined by the relations of CSOs to their environment, in this case to public authorities, and their access to the political arena. We will argue that organizations that maintain close contact with public authorities (in terms of funding, consultation, information, and participation in local decision-making bodies) will tend to form a separate group, while entities detached from the local administration will associate among themselves more often.

Methods and data

To test these hypotheses, we used data collected in an organizational survey that aimed at uncovering network structures within the field of local civil societies (for details, see Baglioni and Giugni in this volume). Organizational representatives were asked about four types of network ties: exchange of information, collaboration in projects or events, personal links through common members, and major disagreements. For the following analysis, we will center on the question of shared projects or events, because this presupposes the most demanding form of networking and allows underlying group patterns to be unveiled more clearly.

This chapter will focus on the civil society networks of Cologne and Turin. Both cities are comparable in terms of size and density of the organizational landscape. We chose them because unlike other cities, in which service-oriented organizations clearly dominate the field, both Cologne and Turin contain a pluralized field of CSOs, including welfare associations, political parties, trade unions, self-help groups, and social movement organizations. Hence, these two cities are well suited for testing the homophily hypothesis, because their organizational fields involve both similar and dissimilar organizations, thus providing enough variance to verify or falsify our propositions. In the city of Cologne, our mapping identified 50 organizations within the wider field of unemployment issues and precarious employment. Interviews were conducted with the 31 organizations that actually committed to work with jobless and/or precariously employed people in a structured way and had been named most recurrently as visible players in the field. In Turin, the mapping yielded 49 CSOs active in the field, of which 35 took part in the survey, following the same sampling decisions.

The analysis will make use of descriptive and explanatory tools of network analysis. First, we will use network graphs to visualize and describe the organizations and the distribution of network ties across our sample. In a second step, we will identify homophilic subgroups or cliques on the basis of the E-I index (Krackhardt and Stern 1988; McGrath and Krackhardt 2003). The coefficient measures the degree to which network ties tend to divide into different groups sharing predefined features, by comparing the numbers of ties within and between groups. This index measures homophily at the level of the whole network, each group, and the individual organization involved. The values range from −1 to +1: the former indicates perfect homophily (i.e., all ties are restricted to members within the group), while the latter indicates that contacts are held exclusively between members of different groups. This method enables us to investigate whether there are distinct groupings within the network and whose members maintain more internal contacts than external ones.

For the explanatory purposes of our paper, we identified several organizational traits that might be responsible for homophily in this organizational network, following the research assumptions and hypotheses introduced above. In a first step, we will compare network ties between service- and policy-oriented organizations. This variable assimilates various information (e.g., the official mission and the main activities) in order to identify a basic difference of organizational orientation that might have an effect on group formation. In a second step, we will calculate the effect of different and more specific organizational characteristics on clique formation. We selected those organizational traits that allowed operationalizing the three hypotheses mentioned above:

(a) the organization's action repertoire is measured by some of the CSO's main actions used to further the organization's aims (mobilization of members through protest, demonstrations, and direct action; services for members; advisory/counseling activities; and services for clients) and by political and protest-oriented events (i.e., organizing political events in the last two years and conducting rallies for the unemployed and the precarious);

(b) the degree of formalization and professionalization is operationalized by the existence of a board, a treasurer, and full-time staff; a less professionalized structure is grasped by the presence of unemployed members in the most important decision-making body;

(c) the relations to the organizational environment (here, public authorities) is classified according to the CSO's activities (does the organization manage or implement public programs?), the presence of government funds within the organizational budget, the existence of contacts (e.g., information and consultation) to local public authorities, and by formal participation in the political arena as a temporary or permanent member of a city or district council or committee working on a specific local issue.

Empirical findings: cleavages and cliques

Figure 6.1 shows the network graph of the city of Cologne. It demonstrates an organizational field with a series of collaborations among various types of actors. However, a closer look reveals that the field is separated into three different groups. First, the right side is made up of social movement organizations (sm1–3) and unemployed associations

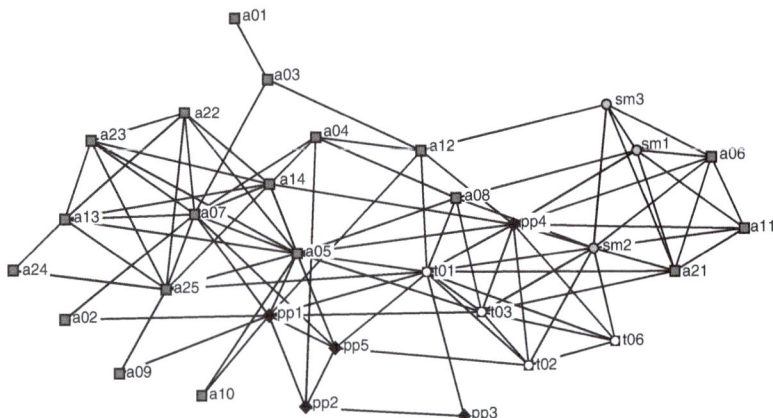

Figure 6.1   Cologne: network structure of project collaboration

with a clear affinity to political mobilization and protest (a06, a11, and a21). Second, on the left, there are welfare associations or unemployment centers that focus more on providing services (training, placement, legal advice, etc.), like a07, a13, a14, a22–25, and a05, which plays a particularly important role in this subgroup. Finally, there is an intermediate group consisting of local trade union branches, their youth associations (t01–03, t06), and the socialist party (pp4) that provide an interface between both groups. These organizations collaborate with social movement organizations and affiliated associations on the right hand but cooperate also with a number of service-oriented organizations, among them the most important welfare association (a05). Moreover, they also collaborate with left-wing parties (pp1 and pp5), a socialist self-help group (a12), and an initiative rallying for a basic income (a08).

A similar pattern holds for the organizational network of Turin. The network shows a high number of collaborations as well, but it is divided into four different sub-networks. On the left side, there is a web of service-oriented welfare associations active in the realm of social integration, training, and placement (a01, a02, a04–08) on the one hand, and trade unions (t01, t03, t05, t08) on the other, in which the cooperatives co1 and co3 take the central position. The second network clique is located in the upper middle part of the graph. It comprises the left-wing political parties (pp4–pp6, pp8, pp9) and two social movement organizations of precarious workers (sm5, sm7), and it is connected to the service-oriented group through the trade unions t03 and t07. A third group is composed of social movement organizations and can be found in the lower middle part. This group consists of more anarchic movement organizations and militant trade unions that contest conventional leftist party politics and traditional unionism (sm1–3, sm6, t04, t06). Their connection to the left-wing group described above is mediated again through the union t07, which is a traditional branch union, but also by one of the communist parties (pp8) and an international activist network (a03). Their contacts to the service-oriented group are also made through an organization working with young migrants (a08). On the right hand side, finally, there is a loosely connected clique of political right-wing parties (pp2, pp3, pp7) and a conservative union (t02).

Both network graphs illustrate that the local field of CSOs seems to be patterned along specific features: organizational missions, activities, and ideological orientations. To verify this initial observation, we will test our hypotheses by making use of the E-I index. Table 6.1 shows that in both cities the field of civil society organizations is rather weakly

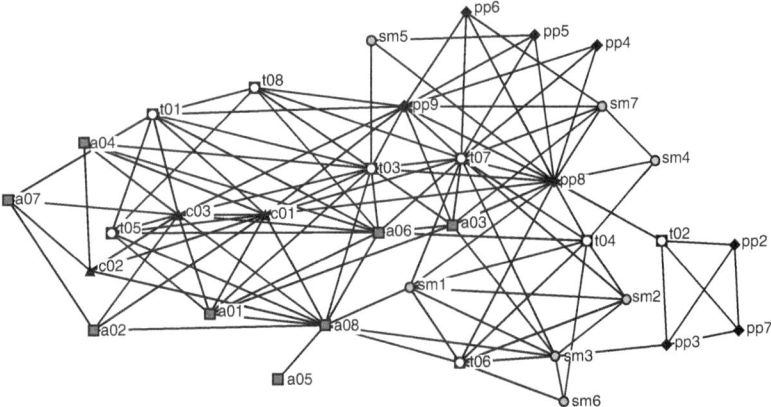

Figure 6.2   Turin: network structure of project collaboration

Table 6.1   Network structure along the organizations' main orientation

Organizational mission	Cologne			Turin		
	Density	Centrality (out-/indegree)	E-I Index	Density	Centrality (out-/indegree)	E-I Index
Whole network group level[a]:	.160	21.0%/27.9%	−.237*	.195	29.4%/23.4%	−.287
policy-oriented	.186		−.444	.138		−.503
service-oriented	.136		.213	.200		.262
	[a]n=29 (2 organizations could not be categorized)			[a]n=33 (2 organizations could not be categorized)		

*E-I Index is significant ($p < 0.05$).

interrelated and feebly centered on specific organizations. This finding conforms to the expectations because we are dealing with organizational fields comprising quite different CSOs. Moreover, our analysis focuses on a rather demanding form of cooperation, namely collaboration in regard to common projects or events. This raises the question of whether network ties conform to the assumption of homophily. The calculations highlight that in Cologne some homophily is given on a statistically significant level. However, we are speaking of a moderate degree of clique-formation among peers. Moreover, networking among organizations with similar missions seems to be stronger with respect to policy-oriented organizations, while service-oriented associations maintain a greater number of contacts to the other group as well. Homophily is particularly pronounced on the right hand of the network chart, among social movement organizations and sympathizing associations, and the trade unions (see Figure 6.1). In the city of Turin, in contrast, the E-I index is not statistically significant. However, a look at the figures shows that the organizational field seems to follow a similar pattern here. Homophily is rather given among policy-oriented organizations, while the service-oriented organizations maintain more ties outside their own group.

Table 6.2 summarizes the main findings in regard to the various organizational traits that we assume to have an impact on homophily.

Table 6.2 Organizational traits and homophily

Variable	Cologne E-I Index		Turin E-I Index	
	Whole network	Group level	Whole network	Group level
Activities and action repertoires				
Mobilization of members (no/yes)	−.485*	−.020/−.650	−.322*	−.037/−.477
Rallies (no/yes)	−.278*	−.067/−.412	−.409	−.595/.097
Political events (no/yes)	−.732*	.529/−.853	−.026	−.138/.120
Services for members (no/yes)	−.175	.429/−.420	−.322*	.418/−.554
Advisory/counseling activities (no/yes)	−.196	.279/−.414	.009	−.017/.036
Services for clients (no/yes)	−.216	−.073/−.321	−.148	.273/−.359
Formalization/professionalization				
Board (no/yes)	−.258	.500/−.507	−.391	.707/−.630
Treasurer (no/yes)	.031	.042/.020	−.130	.667/−.412
Full-time staff (no/yes)	−.155	−.274/.012	−.061	.038/−.143
Unemployed represented in decision-making body (no/yes)	−.381	−.605/.429	−.148	−.434/.719
Relations to environment				
Management/ implementation of public programs (no/yes)	−.155	−.188/−.118	−.078	.050/−.178
Budget: dependence of government grants (no/yes)	−.299*	−.485/−.097	−.374*	−.514/−.122
Contacts to local authorities (none/regular)	−.402*	−.247/−.504	−.461*	−.361/−.534
Participation in political arena (no/yes)	.031	−.123/.250	−.235	−.380/.000

*E-I Index is significant ($p<0.05$).

According to our data, the patterns are very similar in both cities. First, we can generally dismiss the assumption that the governance structure has a decisive impact on network ties. Neither the existence of a board or treasurer, nor the inclusion of full-time staff has a significant impact on homophily in both cities. The role of constituencies and members is negligible as well, because the involvement of unemployed people in the CSO's main decision-making body does not make a significant difference when collaborations are at stake.

Second, activities do play a role in explaining homophily, although not all of the variables tested are significant. Only specific activities seem to make a difference. In Cologne, homophily is significant particularly among those organizations involved in political activities such as mobilizing members and organizing political events and rallies. In Turin, mobilization of members makes a difference as well, while specific political activities like events and protests are not significant. Instead, here we find homophily among those organizations that provide services to members.

Third, the relation to the organizational environment is also useful to explain homophily. Indeed, the implementation of public programs does not allow identifying homophilic groups, because this activity seems to be part of everyday business for many different organizations. However, there is a strong effect of the financial (in)dependence of the organization on networking in both cities, particularly because organizations with no public funding in their budget seem to collaborate more strongly, while this is much less apparent among those organizations relying on public funding. The strongest impact derives from the organizational relations to local public authorities. On the one hand, organizations that report that they do not seek contacts and are ignored or sometimes treated with hostility by public authorities collaborate more often among themselves. More homophily, however, is apparent among those organizations that say they are treated in a friendly manner and frequently asked for advice. In contrast, formal participation in the political arena does not have an impact in either of the two cities.

Discussion of empirical findings

The findings point to a tendency within the local civil societies of Cologne and Turin to collaborate preferably among similar organizations. As we have seen, the degree of formalization or professionalization does not have an impact on project collaborations. Homophily can rather be explained through activities and relations to public authorities.

Concerning the latter, it is interesting that formal access to the political arena does not influence project cooperation among organizations. Very different CSOs are temporary or permanent members of city or district councils, or of committees or working groups, the exception being social movement organizations in Cologne, of which none has ever formally participated in a public decision-making process. Hence, it is not the formal access to the political arena but the quality of the informal contacts to public authorities at the local level that makes a significant difference. Organizations with regular and irregular or no contacts tend to form separate cliques. However, homophily is stronger among those who have regular and/or good contacts with the authorities, while those organizations whose relationship is either bad or non-existent expose a somewhat weaker tendency to collaborate with their peers. Thus, there is a division between "insiders" and "outsiders" in both cities. A look at the data shows that the group of insiders is composed of the more conciliatory organizations such as service-oriented associations and prominent trade unions, while the outsider group comprises some smaller and more radical organizations such as social movement and self-help groups and – in Turin – some trade unions. This cleavage tends to determine interorganizational relations and points to the fact that organizational missions and ideologies seem to have an important impact on clique formation. We will come back to this issue below.

Government grants had some significant effects on project collaboration. However, homophily is restricted to those organizations not receiving government funds. That is, CSOs relying on government grants do not collaborate only among themselves but also with those organizations working without public support, while the latter tend to restrict their project cooperation to organizations in similar financial situation circumstances. This clique does exhibit some similarities to the group of "outsiders" named before, but it is more heterogeneous because it is composed of social movement organizations, all trade unions and all political parties. This finding is less plausible because CSOs with public funding could tend to cooperate more often among themselves as well, possibly only for the simple reasons that they are engaged in common projects funded by public authorities. We propose two interpretations. First, public funding seems to support the divide between insiders and outsiders mentioned before, albeit only in part. The group of "outsiders" not maintaining regular working contacts with public authorities are also those who operate without state funding, whether this situation is imposed or voluntary. Homophily is then a necessary consequence of the smaller range of collaborations among organizations in a similar situation of (voluntary or imposed) marginalization. "Insiders" receiving public funds are less exposed to this group-forming process; more than that, public funding seems to interrelate with a wider range of project collaborations. Second, we expect that the clique-formation between "outsiders" is due to organizational activities as well, thus leading us back to the first explanatory factor. CSOs centered on political advocacy and protest might not be able or willing to receive funding from local authorities. In this case, homophily is due to the fact that these advocatory CSOs cooperate more often in regard to political events and activities, for which they do not get or seek any public funding. Service-oriented welfare associations and CSOs with a broader range of activities, projects, and events will have a different and/or a more heterogeneous budget structure with at least some public funding. In this sense, organizational activities seem to be strongly interrelated with funding patterns.

In regard to this explanatory factor of organizational activities, mobilization of members has proven to be the most important type of action explaining homophily in both cities. Project collaboration occurs very often among organizations that are active in member mobilization, (i.e., political parties, trade unions, and social movement organizations). Those who do not mobilize, in contrast, do not cooperate significantly more among themselves than with others. This finding thus corroborates the result shown in Table 6.1: there is rather strong homophily among the policy-oriented organizations, while their counterparts, the service-oriented, maintain ties both inside and outside their groups. Regarding service-related activities, the provision of services for members was significant only in Turin, which refers to the group on the left side of the network chart, consisting of welfare associations, cooperatives, and trade unions (see Figure 6.2). Service activities do not seem to be important because most of the organizations do provide some kind of services either to members or to clients or both. The types of services offered vary strongly along the organizations' goals and missions and may range from in-kind support, employment, training, and placement to legal advice or self-help. Hence, service provision is too broad a category to unveil different cliques. In regard to activities, we can thus conclude that homophily is rather restricted to more politicized, advocatory, and militant CSOs. In this respect, the role of social movement organizations seems to be crucial to understand the implicit cleavages within the organizational fields of both cities and their respective specificities.

In sum, our data exhibits an organizational network structured along two groups of organizations within a system of complementary cleavages. In Cologne, the organizational field is marked by a conflict that has its roots in the intense mobilizations against the labor market reforms since the late 1990s and early 2000s, when unemployment policies were substantially changed toward a more "activating" approach curtailing especially the entitlements of long-term unemployed. These policies have divided local civil society. On the one hand, some organizations did not fully agree with the intention and outcome of the reforms but took a pragmatic approach and collaborated with the public authorities in implementing the new policies. Here, we can name the first generation of unemployed groups, which emerged during the 1980s and in the meantime professionalized and developed to service centers, as well as many other service-oriented associations. On the other hand, a new movement of advocatory protest groups (social movement organizations and associations) evolved in an attempt to combat these policies. The protest groups criticize welfare associations to be part of the alienating and exploitative establishment and thus part of the problem, while the latter disapprove of the advocatory groups by arguing that they unnecessarily radicalize the conflict and divide forces. This cleavage has led to a situation in which political dialogue between CSOs and public authorities is restricted to the service-oriented agencies and welfare associations, while many of the advocatory groups report exclusion from policy deliberations, in spite of the fact that they claim to be one important political voice of the jobless. As a consequence, they tend to form a group of dissenting outsiders.

In Turin, the politically contested issue is precarity rather than unemployment. Although Italy traditionally had a rather rigid system of labor market regulation with pronounced employment rights, these rights were curtailed successively during the past two decades in order to make the labor market more flexible (Baglioni 2013; Jessoula et al. 2010). For the opponents, this development leads to increasingly precarious employment and living conditions, thus furthering a social problem of which unemployment is only a single aspect. The issue of precarity has deepened political cleavages within the local civil society of Turin in a similar way as in Cologne. On the one hand, there is a group of service-oriented welfare associations and cooperatives that focus more strongly on unemployment than on precarity and are much less politicized. In Figure 6.2 they were placed at the left side of the network chart. On the other hand, there is a group of CSOs mobilizing against the mushrooming problem of precarity. However, and in contrast to the situation in Cologne, there is a further division that separates this advocatory type of CSOs into two cliques along ideological lines.

There is a group of social movement organizations and leftist political parties with a more "reformist" approach, and on the other side, there are the more radical social movement groups (some of them *centri sociali*) and militant trade unions aiming at a more outspoken and combative way of organizing workers' interests, the precariously employed and the jobless included.

This dynamic explains why setting up political events and organizing rallies with unemployed and/or precarious people has a significant impact on clique formation in Cologne, but not in Turin. In Cologne, the organizations are ideologically quite homogenous, thus increasing homophily, and the main conflict is between welfare associations and social movement organizations. In Turin, there is more heterogeneity within the organizational field, and an ideological divide separates social movement organizations and trade unions into two different cliques. It is interesting that ideological disagreements in this city impede collaborations between CSOs sharing an advocatory mission and protest-oriented action repertoires, while CSOs not organizing political events and rallies (i.e., welfare associations and cooperatives and more moderate interest groups) tend to collaborate quite often.

Overall, we can identify two explanatory factors that tend to determine the formation of the two cliques in a rather marked way. On the one side, activities (i.e., mainly political and protest-oriented actions and events) are responsible for the development of an advocatory group of CSOs – among them primarily social movement organizations as well as some trade unions and political parties – that maintains its distance from the service-oriented welfare associations. Additionally, this advocatory group of CSOs does not only share a similar action repertoire but also a financial independence from public funding, which might be due either to an explicit choice or to an imposed constraint. On the other side, we have seen that close working relations with public authorities help distinguish a second group of service-oriented CSOs with strong internal collaborations with other "insiders" and little contact with "outsiders." This two-sided structure of the organizational network of local civil societies is true for both cities, although the empirical constellation of actors varies somewhat between Cologne and Turin.

Conclusions

This chapter focused on reconstructing the network structures within local civil societies in the field of unemployment and employment issues. It has demonstrated through a case analysis of the cities of Cologne and Turin that a proper field of civil society organizations has been established, which comprises actors with very different missions, action repertoires, and identities. These organizations cooperate with each other, but organizational collaborations tend to be restricted to CSOs with similar organizational traits. In particular, we identified two factors impinging on homophily. The organizational environment has an impact on network structures: the relations a CSO maintains with local public authorities make a significant difference in the readiness to collaborate with CSOs with regard to projects and events in both cities. That is, organizations with regular and close contacts to public authorities collaborate very often among themselves, and organizations with no contact do the same, although less intensively. At the same time, there is more collaboration between CSOs with a more pronounced policy and protest orientation. Hence, homophily is also stronger among the more politicized yet also more marginalized groups of the local civil society because these organizations are said to be heard less by local and regional authorities.

These findings support the theoretical argument of neo-institutionalism (Meyer and Rowan 1977; Powell and DiMaggio 1991) because the organizational structure of local civil societies seems to be strongly patterned by the societal environment in general, and by the organizational relations between CSOs and public authorities in particular. However, this theory assumes that homogenization affects organizational fields at large, thus neglecting the differential impact of the (local) state on organized civil societies. Our own observations highlight the need to consider existing power structures within the local field of labor market policies in order to decipher the network dynamics mirrored by our findings. In fact, the power structures of the local policy domain have a differentiating impact on network ties. On the one hand, power structures seem to force CSOs to choose a side: that is, they need to opt for a conciliatory approach of cooperation with local authorities or for a confrontational strategy and a fundamental criticism of the status quo. On the other hand, the policy domain pushes advocatory CSOs into a minoritarian group of radicalizing peers, while expanding the range of action – and the array of potential collaborations – for the more moderate and service-oriented organizations. Within this cleavage structure, the trade unions play a particularly central role in the organizational field of both cities. Indeed, they act as mediating interfaces between the service-oriented welfare associations and the politicized advocacy and protest groups.

These findings raise questions about the implications of these network structures for the local constituency of the unemployed and precariously employed. On the one side, the availability of CSOs is a promising fact, because the jobless and precarious can make their voices heard with important instruments of empowerment and participation in public life. In fact, our analysis has demonstrated that they can rely on many different organizations with various missions, activities, and identities, providing them with numerous organizational opportunities for social and political participation. The segregated and confrontational structure of the organizational field in the cites of Cologne and Turin is not necessarily a problem because it offers various access points to individual jobless people and entails a highly differentiated division of labor with regard to service provision, social advocacy and, political protest. On the other side, our data suggests that a process of political marginalization of specific organizations is underway. This tends to limit the possibilities of networking by restricting advocatory CSOs to collaboration among peers. The opportunities for social and political participation by the unemployed and precarious within the organizational field of local civil societies are thus greatly biased toward individualized service delivery, to the detriment of more politically outspoken forms of collective action.

Note

We wish to thank Eva-Maria Kolb for preparing the network charts and running the calculations that were the basis of Tables 1 and 2.

References

Aldrich, H. (1976) "Resource Dependence and Interorganizational Relations: Relations between Local Employment Service Offices and Social Services Sector Organizations," *Administration and Society*, 7, 419–454.

Andrews, K. T. and B. Edwards (2004) "Advocacy Organizations in the US Political Process," *Annual Review of Sociology*, 30, 479–506.

Anheier, H. and S. Toepler (eds) (2010) *The International Encyclopedia of Civil Society* (Hamburg: Springer).

Baglioni, S. (2013) "Alike but Not Alike: Welfare State and Unemployment Policy in Southern Europe: Italy and Portugal Compared," *International Journal of Social Welfare*, 22: 319–327.

Burgess, S., E. Sanderson, and M. Umaña-Aponte (2011) School Ties. An Analysis of Homophily in an Adolescent Friendship Network. Centre for Market and Public Organisation (CMPO Working Paper Series, No. 11/267).

Cainzos, M. and C. Voces (2010) "Class Inequalities in Political Participation and the 'Death of Class' Debate," *International Sociology*, 25, 383–418.

Chabanet, D. and J. Faniel (eds) (2012) *The Mobilization of the Unemployed in Europe: From Acquiescence to Protest?* (Houndmills: Palgrave).

Currarini, S., M. O. Jackson, and P. Pin (2009) "An Economic Model of Friendship: Homophily, Minorities, and Segregation," *Econometrica*, 77, 1003–1045.

della Porta, D. and M. Diani (1999) *Social Movements. An Introduction* (Oxford: Blackwell).

Edwards, M. (2011) *The Oxford Handbook of Civil Society* (Oxford: Oxford University Press).

Galaskiewicz, J. and D. Shatin (1981) "Leadership and Networking among Neighborhood Human Service Organizations," *Administrative Science Quarterly*, 26, 434–448.

Gerometta, J., H. Haussermann, and G. Longo (2005) "Social Innovation and Civil Society in Urban Governance: Strategies for an Inclusive City," *Urban Studies*, 42, 2007–2021.

Giugni, M. (ed.) (2010) *The Contentious Politics of Unemployment in Europe: Welfare States and Political Opportunities* (Houndmills: Palgrave).

Hendryx, M. S., M. M. Ahern, N. P. Lovrich, and A. H. McCurdy (2002) "Access to Health Care and Community Social Capital," *Health Services Research*, 37, 87–103.

Ibarra, H. (1992) "Homophily and Differential Returns. Sex Differences in Network Structure and Access in an Advertising Firm," *Administrative Science Quarterly*, 37, 422–447.

Jahoda, M., P. F. Lazarsfeld, and H. Zeisel (1971) *Marienthal: The Sociography of an Unemployed Community* (Chicago, IL: Aldine).

Jessoula, M., P. R. Graziano, and I. Madama (2010) "'Selective Flexicurity' in Segmented Labour Markets: The Case of Italian 'Mid-Siders'," *Journal of Social Policy*, 39, 561–583.

Kieselbach, T., K. von Heeringen, M. La Rosa, L. Lemkow, K. Sokou, and B. Starrin (eds) (2001) *Living On the Edge: An Empirical Analysis on Long-Term Youth Unemployment and Social Exclusion in Europe* (Opladen: Leske + Budrich).

Knoke, D. (1990) *Political Networks: The Structural Perspective* (New York: Cambridge University Press).

Knoke, D., F. U. Pappi, J. Broadbent, and Y. Tsujinaka (1996) *Comparing Policy Networks: Labor Politics in the U.S., Germany, and Japan* (New York: Cambridge University Press).

Krackhardt, D. and R. Stern (1988) "Informal Networks and Organizational Crises: An Experimental Simulation," *Social Psychology Quarterly*, 51, 123–140.

Laumann, E. and D. Knoke (1989) "'Policy Networks of the Organizational State: Collective Action in the National Energy and Health Domains'," in Perrucci, R. and H. Potter (eds), *Networks of Power. Organizational Actors at the National, Corporate, and Community Levels* (New York: de Gruyter).

Laumann, E., J. Galaskiewicz, and P. Marsden (1978) "Community Structures as Interorganizational Linkages," *Annual Review of Sociology*, 4, 455–484.

Lazarsfeld, P. F. and R. K. Merton (1954) "Friendship as a Social Process: A Substantive and Methodological Analysis," in Berger, M. (ed.) *Freedom and Control in Modern Society* (New York: Van Nostrand).

Lincoln, J. R. and K. McBride (1985) "Resources, Homophily, and Dependence. Organizational Attributes and Asymmetric Ties in Human Service Networks," *Social Science Research*, 14, 1–30.

McGrath, C. and D. Krackhardt (2003) "Network Conditions for Organizational Change," *Journal of Applied Behavioral Science*, 39, 324–336.

McPherson, J. M. and L. Smith-Lovin (1987) "Homophily in Voluntary Organizations: Status Distance and the Composition of Face-to-face Groups," *American Sociological Review*, 52, 370–379.

McPherson, M., L. Smith-Lovin, and J. M. Cook (2001) "Birds of a Feather: Homophily in Social Networks," *Annual Review of Sociology*, 27, 415–444.

Meyer, J. W. and B. Rowan (1977) "Institutionalized Organizations: Formal Structure as Myth and Ceremony," *American Journal of Sociology*, 83, 340–363.

Perrucci, R. and H. Potter (eds) (1989) *Networks of Power: Organizational Actors at the National, Corporate and Community Levels* (New York: de Gruyter).

Powell, W. W. and P. J. DiMaggio (eds) (1991) *The New Institutionalism in Organizational Analysis* (Chicago, IL: The University of Chicago Press).

Putnam, R., L. M. Feldstein, and D. Cohen (2003) *Better Together: Restoring the American Community* (New York: Simon & Schuster).

Reiss, M. and M. Perry (eds) (2011) *Unemployment and Protest: New Perspectives on Two Centuries of Contention* (Oxford: Oxford University Press).

Richardson, J. J. and G. Jordan (1979) *Governing under Pressure: The Policy Process in a Post-Parliamentary Process* (Oxford: Martin Robertson).

Rucht, D. (1989) "Environmental Movement Organizations in West Germany and France: Structure and Interorganizational Relations," In Klandermans, B. (ed.), *International Social Movement Research*, Vol. II: *Organizing Change* (Greenwich, CT: JAI Press).

Ruef, M., H. E. Aldrich, and N. M. Carter (2003) "The Structure of Founding Teams. Homophily, Strong Ties, and Isolation among U.S. Entrepreneurs," *American Sociological Review*, 68, 195–222.

Sabatier, P. A. (1988) "An Advocacy Coalition Framework of Policy Change and the Role of Policy-Oriented Learning Therein," *Policy Sciences*, 21, 129–168.

Spires, A. J. (2011) "Organizational Homophily in International Grantmaking: US-Based Foundations and their Grantees in China," *Journal of Civil Society*, 7, 305–331.

van Oorschot, W., W. Arts, and J. Gelissen (2006) "Social Capital in Europe: Measurement and Social and Regional Distribution of a Multifaceted Phenomenon," *Acta Sociologica*, 49, 149–167.

Wimmer, A. and K. Lewis (2010) "Beyond and Below Racial Homophily: ERG Models of a Friendship Network Documented on Facebook," *American Journal of Sociology*, 116, 583–642.

Zald, M. N. and J. McCarthy (1987) *Social Movements in an Organizational Society* (New Brunswick, NJ: Transaction Books).

7
Who Are the Powerful Actors?
An Analysis of Brokerage in the
Networks of Organizations Dealing
with Unemployment and Precarity

Matteo Bassoli, Manlio Cinalli, and Marco Giugni

Introduction

Other contributions to this book have examined the impact of political
context on political behavior in the field of unemployment and precarity
and have focused on the multi-organizational nature of the unemployment and precarity field and its network dynamics. This chapter consists
of a research design that analyzes the impact of the actors' networks on
the various types of political engagement of organizations in the field
of unemployment and precarity politics while taking into consideration
the key role of welfare regimes. We performed a comparative analysis of
Cologne, Kielce, and Turin. While they differ in their degree of flexibility
in labor market regulations, these three national cases are comparable in
terms of their restrictive approach vis-à-vis the unemployed and precarious workers. Relationally, we have singled out the role of brokerage as a
main network attribute of the actors. The primary point that we would
like to emphasize is that brokerage stands out as a valuable measure that
captures actors' capacity to foster exchanges within the field in terms of
both bonding in the public domain and creating linkages between the
public and the policy domains (Cinalli 2004, 2007). We have focused on
three main variables of political engagement: mobilizing members, lobbying, and general involvement in political activities.

The main results of this chapter follow from the combination of
inter-organizational networks and political opportunities. We contend
that inter-organizational network patterns may lead to variations in
political engagement in spite of similar conditions in the political
arena. Networks may allow for capitalizing on political access to policy
elites and to crucial sites of decision-making while at the same time

reinforcing communication, belonging, and exchange among civil society organizations in the public domain. Ultimately, we have proved that networks can be valuable in filling the gap between the institutional sites of policy-making and the political engagement of actors in the public domain.

Drawing on the scholarly literature, we begin with a discussion on the role of brokerage in the multi-organizational field of unemployment and precarity. We then present our data and provide further details on our specific operationalization of brokerage. In the next two sections, we present our empirical findings. First, we illustrate cross-national variations on three types of network brokerage: coordination, gatekeeping, and representation. Second, we look at the impact of each of these types of brokerage on the three variables of political engagement that we have selected: mobilizing members, lobbying, and involvement in political activities. The final section wraps up our analysis and discusses some of its broader implications for future scholarly research.

Brokerage in the multi-organizational field of unemployment and precarity

As discussed in other network contributions to this book, the study of the unemployment and precarity multi-organizational field may profit from the application of a relational approach. In this chapter, we continue to engage with teachings on network analysis (Knoke and Kuklinski 1982; Scott 2000; Wasserman and Faust 1994) that are in line with previous network research on unemployment and precarity politics (Cinalli and Füglister 2008). Our definition of networks is consistent with the other contributions to this book. Our networks depict sets of ties that organizations forge through participation in common projects. We thus consider each actor as being connected with and sharing common projects with other actors in the multi-organizational field of unemployment. Our aim is to single out the various impacts of networks on the actors, focusing in particular on measures of brokerage (Burt 2005). Actors with strong brokerage capabilities are expected to be crucial nodes even when their capabilities that are related to other, more common network measures are not as strong, for example, in the areas of local and global centrality. This is particularly true when looking at political engagement in multi-organizational fields that are divided because the role of brokers becomes essential to the circulation of information, resources, trust, ideas, and so forth (Christopoulos and Quaglia 2009). Our major concern here is with brokerage that takes place across the division between the public space and the policy domain.

Brokerage can be linked to the idea of social capital, which consists of the resources that actors can access through their own networks (Bourdieu 1986; Coleman 1988, 1990; Putnam 1993, 2000). In particular, actors control communication and exchanges between different parts of the network based on the two different directions that their brokerage may take: brokers can reinforce identity and internal belonging and they can foster the reaching out to different groups (Burt 2005). Because "the *tertius* is literally an entrepreneur who adds values by brokering connection between others" (Burt 2005: 18), we consider brokerage to be the action of bonding civil society in the public domain, as well as the linking of the public domain of civil society with the policy domain of political elites and policy-makers (Cinalli 2007). This means that the analysis of brokerage is especially important when discussing networks that are shaped along crucial divisions.

Hence, we need to say more about the types of brokerage at the core of our analysis and the reasons for focusing attention on the divide between the public and policy domain. Policy-makers and political elites sequester institutional and political resources that are not available to civil society organizations. Brokerage is thus crucial when a civil society organization makes connections between the public space and the domain of policy. In this case, a kind of vertical brokerage develops along two directions. Bottom–up, civil society organizations may foster exchanges between civil society "senders" in the public domain and institutional "receivers" in the domain of policy. Top–down, civil society brokers may strengthen the flow of communication that proceeds from the domain of policy to the public domain. Brokerage, however, also occurs when a civil society actor reinforces bonding horizontally, thus reinforcing the flow of communication and co-operation among civil society organizations in the public domain that would otherwise remain disconnected.

Our choice of specific types of brokerage follows from the previous argument. Network analysis provides us with a number of measures that are valuable in examining horizontal and vertical brokerage. Horizontal brokerage can be assessed in terms of coordination. This measure is crucial in appraising the function of bonding that a civil society organization plays when brokering with other civil society organizations. Vertically, network analysis provides us with two specific measures. First, gatekeeping is the top–down brokerage that a civil society organization engages in between the greatest number of institutions and policy-makers and any civil society actor. Second, representativeness appraises the extent to which a civil society organization permits bottom–up brokerage between the greatest number of civil society actors and any policy actor. Taken together, coordination, gatekeeping, and representativeness enable civil society organizations to access more resources and opportunities and thus increase their influence on policy-makers and institutions, establish their position in the public domain, and reinforce their broader societal support. This is expected to have a key impact on political engagement.

As a consequence, the last research step has been to examine the extent to which variations in our three types of brokerage can account for variations in our selected forms of political engagement. The relationship between resources embedded in social networks and the purposeful action of actors has already been studied by scholars who specialize in social capital, social movements, and contentious politics (Diani and McAdam 2003; Gould 1995; Lin 2001).[1] Accordingly, we take networks as an *explanans* that may account for variations in political engagement in different nations. We have tested variations in brokerage against variations in mobilization, lobbying, and involvement in the political activities of the actors while controlling for important organizational attributes such as the presence of paid staff, the scope of activities, and so forth. In addition to looking at simple variations in terms of the degree of each form of political engagement, we have also appraised whether the prevalence of any specific type of brokerage can be linked to the prevalence of a specific form of political engagement in the field.

Our main expectation has been that vertical brokerage has the strongest impact on political engagement. Within the restrictive political context of the exclusive unemployment regulations in Cologne, Kielce, and Turin, key channels for political access become available through extensive networks that cut across the divide between the public domain and the policy domain. In this case, the capacity to mediate between the largest number of policy actors and civil society reveals the crucial standing of an organization in the field in spite of the overall lack of opportunities at the level of institutional systems and the specific policy field (Cinalli and Giugni 2010; Giugni et al. 2009). In particular, top–down brokerage allows for communication across the public and the policy domains even when political access to the policy domain depends on a limited number of highly specialized gatekeepers. In this latter case, many civil society organizations in the field remain disconnected from the policy domain, so the situation does not necessarily translate into pacified forms of co-optation that pre-empt unemployment and precarity politics (Cinalli 2004, 2007). In fact, we expect that the coupling of high gatekeeping and high coordination will foster a broader recourse to direct forms of mobilization that extend beyond the general growth of political activities. Political mobilization relies on extensive bonding within the public domain but also on vertical linking across the divide between the public domain and the domain of policy. Ultimately, this chapter follows in the footsteps of the previous chapter in order to advance a relational approach to the study of the multi-organizational field of unemployment and precarity. Beyond what we have learned, what can the study of networks, the investigation of political context, and the use of the standard variables of contentious politics tell us? Do national cases with similar, restrictive policies vis-à-vis the unemployed and precarious workers look different when attention is focused on more hidden connections? And does brokerage matter? Does it influence political engagement? The primary conclusion that we have drawn from our research is that a relational approach allows us to assess the extent to which similar institutional contexts translate into different sets of political opportunities for civil society actors. And hence, the study of brokerage is useful in identifying restrictive contexts where exclusionary practices are more likely to be lasting ones as well as being useful in identifying contexts in which political exclusion will most likely conflict, at some stage, with the relational agency of civil society.

Data and operationalization

As in previous chapters, we have followed a two-step methodology involving the use of snowballing techniques. This chapter, however, distinguishes between only a few statuses of actors and focuses on brokerage between different actors of the civil society in the public domain, as well as between civil society actors and public authorities, political parties, and publicly owned entities. In particular, we have opted for a specific conceptualization of brokerage that emphasizes the importance of triadic relationships over larger sub-networks (Gould and Fernandez 1989). Given a network with some partition of nodes (in our case, actors in the policy and in the public domain, respectively), we have built the triad of nodes A, B, and C in a transitive fashion, that is, A has a tie to B and B has a tie to C, but A has no tie to C:

$$A \rightarrow B \rightarrow C$$

Because A needs B in order to reach C, B acts as a broker. Thus, according to our conceptualization of brokerage in the public and policy domains, we can distinguish three main types of brokerage that are particularly relevant. According to Borgatti et al.'s terminology regarding "social roles" (2002):[2]

- Gatekeepers are those brokers, defined as B, in the public domain who belong to the same group as the civil society actors, defined as C, but who have a source node belonging to a different group of policy actors. In simpler words, they provide a flow of communication from the policy domain towards the public domain,

$$a \rightarrow B \rightarrow C$$

- Representatives are those brokers, defined as B, in the public domain who belong to the same group as the civil society actors, A, but who have a destination node belonging to a different group of policy actors. In simpler words, they allow for the flow of communication in the opposite direction, from the public domain toward the policy domain.

$$A \rightarrow B \rightarrow c$$

- Lastly, coordinators are those brokers, B, in the public domain belonging to the same group of civil society actors A and C. In simpler words, they are brokers for their own constituency of civil society within the public domain.

$$A \rightarrow B \rightarrow C$$

Through UCINET we have computed not only the number of times that a civil society organization B acts as a broker but also the alternative routes that the nodes A and C may use to avoid the intermediation of B. Accordingly, B receives only partial credit as a broker when it is not the only intermediate node between A and C. For example, we have given half a point for brokerage to B if the intermediation between A and C is also possible through another actor (Borgatti et al. 2002). In particular, we have examined the brokerage of B beyond the consideration of its own network. Given the cross-national dimension of our comparison, it is important to compare the brokerage role of any actor B to its expected value in a way that considers the number of sub-groups (two in our study) as well as their size, which varies for Cologne, Kielce, and Turin. Final scores consist of brokerage values divided by expected values, thus controlling for network specificities across different national cases.

Regarding the group dimension, it is important to point out the different sizes of the two groups in the three cities. While the number of relevant political actors is very high in Turin, the same is not true for either Kielce or Cologne. Since this strongly influences the possibility of civil society actors serving as gatekeepers of any kind, it is important to take into account the different levels of heterogeneity. The best tool for assessing the level of heterogeneity is the Gini index, normalized. Given that the variable is dichotomous, that is, it has two degrees of freedom, the minimum amount of heterogeneity is reached if all actors are of the same kind, meaning that the index equals 0 while the maximum level of heterogeneity is reached if the number of political actors and civil society are the same, meaning that the index equals 1. From Table 7.1, the third row, it is clear that the level of heterogeneity is quite low in absolute terms, and yet there is a big difference between Turin and the other two cases.

As indicated, the dependent variable focuses on three forms of political engagement. The first form involves the mobilization of membership, allowing for testing the link between different types of brokerage and the recourse to a contentious form of intervention over unemployment and precarity politics. The second form is lobbying; we thus consider the relationship between different types of brokerage and more hidden forms of political engagement in the unemployment and precarity multi-organizational field. The third form is a more general category of political engagement. In this case, interviewed organizations were asked whether they engaged in any political event over the course of the previous two years.

Our analysis of political engagement relies on regression analyses that include four main control variables (all dummy variables) in addition to the specific measures referring to our three types of brokerage. The four control variables include some main endogenous characteristics of civil society organizations, namely, the presence of paid staff, the availability of office space, the scope of action, and the year of foundation. This last variable refers to the length of activation of organizations in the field

Table 7.1 Political partition and heterogeneity level (absolute values and percentages)

	Cologne	Kielce	Turin
Political actors	6	4	13
Civil society actors	45	25	57
Normalized heterogeneity Gini index	.42	.48	.60
N	51	29	70

and considers whether their year of foundation is before or after 1995. Paid staff and office space are useful in accounting for the degree of internal structuring of the organizations. We thus distinguish structured organizations – those having at least one full-time or two part-time staff members, and that own or rent their office – from other, less structured organizations that rely exclusively on volunteers to function and have to borrow office space. Finally, the scope of action distinguishes between organizations whose action stretches up to the national level and actors that engage only at the sub-national level, including the neighborhood, the city, and the region.

Brokerage in Cologne, Kielce, and Turin

We will now discuss the main findings through the use of graphs. Each figure (Figure 7.1, Figure 7.2, and Figure 7.3) represents the specific situation for each national case and consists of three distinct graphs that refer to each type of brokerage, respectively. Civil society actors are round-shaped while institutions and political elites in the policy domain are square-shaped. The size of nodes is based on their in-degree (the number of times a node is mentioned), while connecting lines between actors are darker when they are symmetric (i.e.,, reciprocated by both connected nodes). All actors have different shades of grey according to their brokerage role. For each figure, the first graph uses darker nodes to portray the gatekeepers; the second graph uses darker nodes to portray the representatives; and the third graph uses darker nodes to portray coordinators.

The crucial finding of Figures 7.1, 7.2, and 7.3 consists of the high cross-national variation of degrees and types of brokerage. Our analysis of Cologne reveals that there are ten gatekeepers that also acted as representatives on three occasions. Furthermore, the size of the nodes indicates that these ten gatekeepers are all centrally located in the network, which allows for extensive communication in the field. The German network is populated by different types of actors that tend to interact, especially with similar actors of their own type. Moreover, only two additional actors act as representatives. So, overall, there are five actors engaging in the representative type of brokerage. Thus, it is clear that gatekeeping is highly prevalent when looking at vertical brokerage. That is, it is much more common for civil society actors to be receivers of ties from policy actors than to be senders to the public domain. As regards coordination, its extensive presence is noticeable. Almost all civil society gatekeepers (with only two exceptions) and representatives

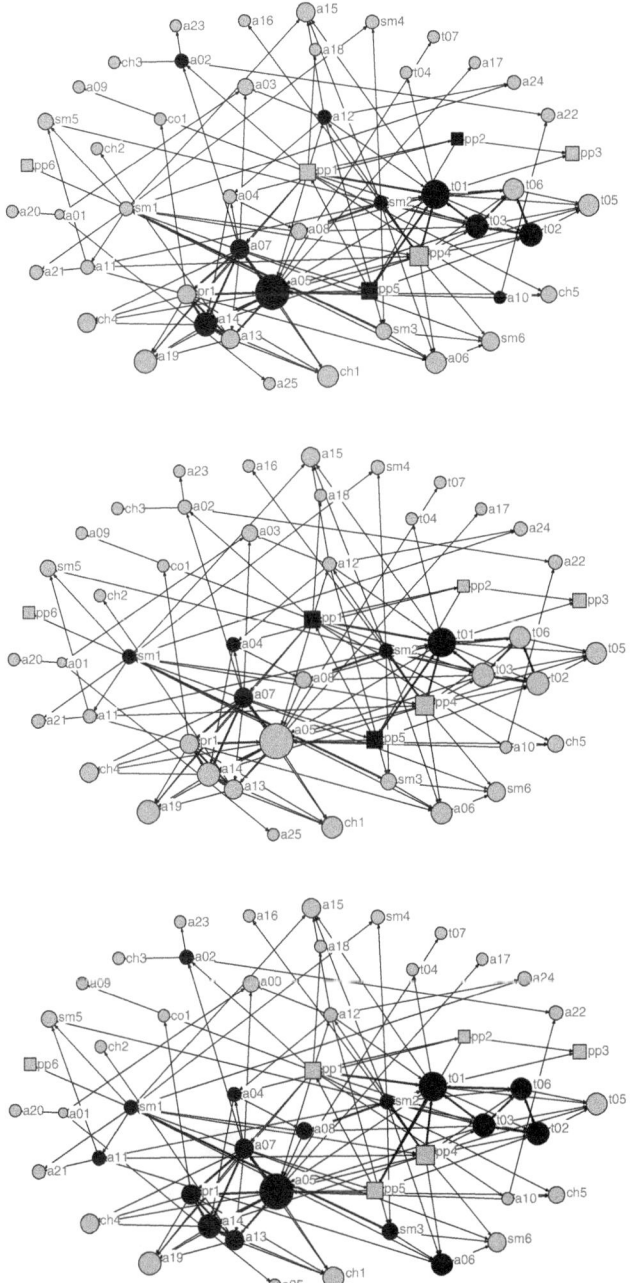

Figure 7.1 Network of organizations having common projects in Cologne
Source: Network graphed with Netdraw (Borgatti 2002) placed according to MDS calculated using UCINET (Borgatti et al. 2002), with small adjustment.

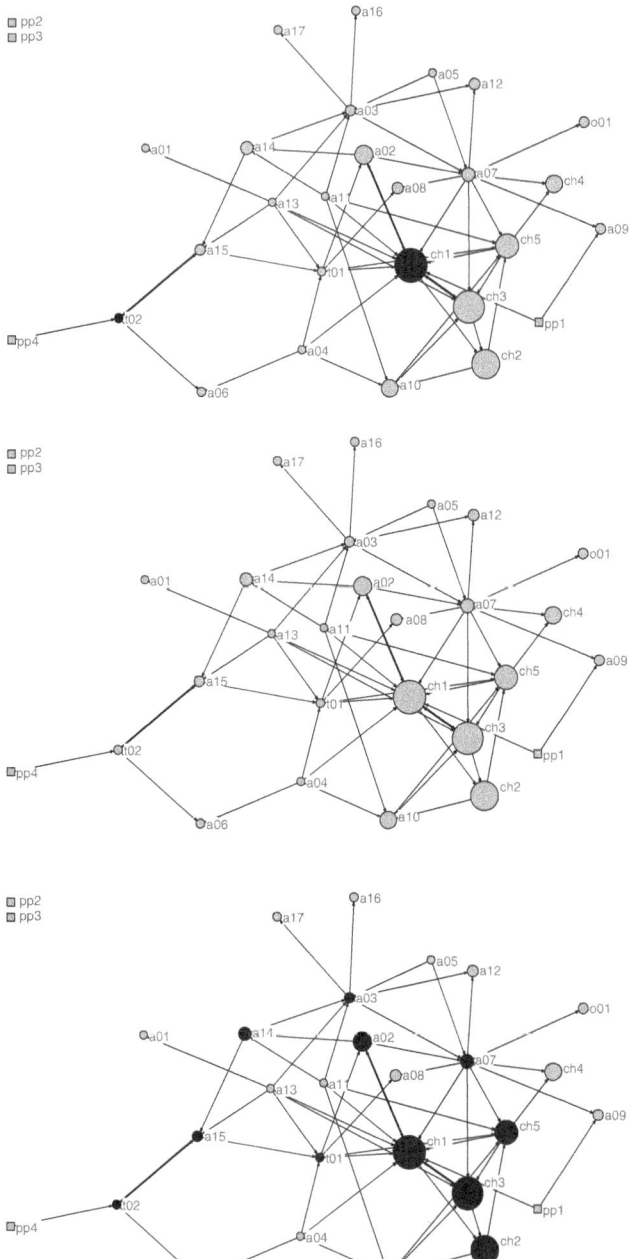

Figure 7.2 Network of organizations having common projects in Kielce
Source: Network graphed with Netdraw (Borgatti 2002) placed according to MDS calculated using UCINET (Borgatti et al. 2002), with small adjustment.

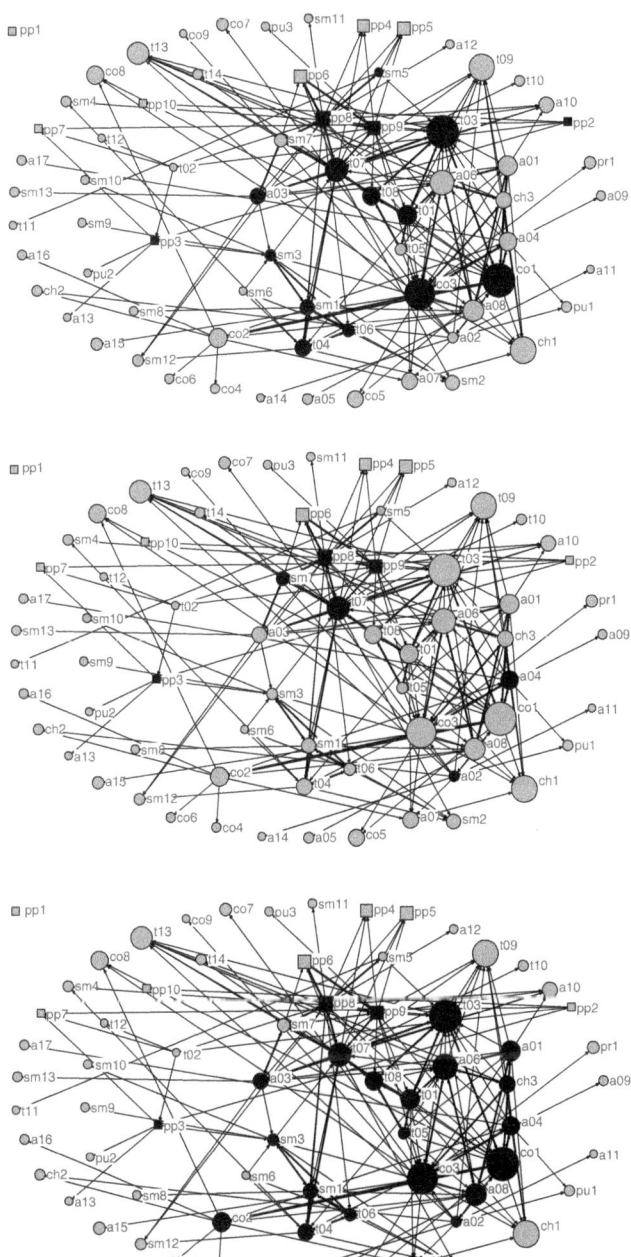

Figure 7.3 Network of organizations having common projects in Turin

Source: Network graphed with Netdraw (Borgatti 2002) placed according to MDS calculated using UCINET (Borgatti et al. 2002), with small adjustment.

act as coordinators at the same time. These overlapping roles point to the importance of the civil society network, suggesting that brokers are embedded in dense social exchange. Therefore, only rarely are civil society actors either only receiving ties from (pure gatekeeper) or only sending ties to (pure representative) other actors in the policy domain.

Vertical brokerage is poor in the case of Kielce especially when one compares it with the German case. Yet, we do find a similar prevalence of top–down on bottom–up vertical brokerage. There is not even a single representative, but there are two gatekeepers. The strong horizontal structure of the Polish network is evident when looking at coordination. All gatekeepers also act as coordinators, with a larger additional number of civil society senders playing this role. The strong presence of horizontal brokers is also in line with the fact that the Polish network is smaller and less homogenous than the German network. The prevalence of horizontal brokerage in Kielce may also be linked to the minor mobilization of political parties in terms of project development and implementation. Two civil society actors have become central in the public domain by playing a gatekeeping role, namely, ch1 and t02. The first actor is Kielce Caritas, which is at the center of a large sub-group of service providers. The second is the trade union, Solidarność.

In the third case, that of Turin, it is interesting to see that along the vertical dimension of analysis, top–down brokerage still prevails over bottom–up brokerage. In fact, this trend is even more pronounced than in the other two national cases owing to the larger volume of political parties in the policy domain. In the first graph of Figure 7.3, 12 nodes act as gatekeepers, while in the second graph only four nodes stand as representatives. In addition, the small nodal size of representatives demonstrates that they are not central in the multi-organizational field. By contrast, gatekeepers stand out for their high centrality, displaying their crucial role in fostering communication within networks that are characterized by strong clustering among similar actors. However, the coordination of horizontal brokerage is very diffuse in the Italian multi-organizational field, overlapping to a great extent with other types of brokerage. Put simply, the combination of horizontal and vertical brokerage is more balanced in Turin than in Kielce given the poor amount of vertical brokerage in the Polish network. It is also important to notice that several civil society organizations that are quite central in Turin–they are either in the core or they have a high degree centrality–do not act as brokers but rely instead on other actors in order to have access to the policy domain. This is the case for a01, a04, a06, a08, ch3, c02, and sm7. It is quite interesting that most of these organizations, such as ACLI, Casa della Carità, GIOC, KAIROS, and the Diocese, are Catholic.

Explaining the political engagement of organizations: the impact of brokerage

Having examined different patterns of brokerage in the multi-organizational field of unemployment and precarity in our three cities, we now turn to the analysis of the political engagement of civil society organizations. Does the degree of political engagement vary in the three cities, and if yes, to what extent? Do the three forms of brokerage that we distinguished earlier affect such political involvement, and if yes, how? We will attempt to answer these questions in this section.

Table 7.2 illustrates the degree of political engagement of civil society in the unemployment and precarity field. As we mentioned earlier, we have looked at three forms of political engagement: a first variable relating to publicly visible mobilizing activities, a second one referring to more hidden forms of lobbying activities, and a third comprehensive variable related to political action. We observed important variations in the three forms of political engagement both across the three cities and across the three forms of political engagement in each city. Clearly, civil society organizations are less politically involved in Kielce than in the two other cities. This holds true in particular for mobilizing activities and for the more general indicators of political activities. Meanwhile, lobbying is relatively similar in Kielce and Turin, and both are well below the level displayed in Cologne. Cologne is indeed the city where organizations are most active overall, although the difference in mobilizing activities is about the same as in Turin.

At the same time, the relative weight of each of the three forms of political engagement is not the same in all of the cities. In Cologne, a large majority of the organizations make use of lobbying activities, and most are involved in more broadly defined political activities while mobilizing activities are a bit less widespread. Lobbying is also the form

Table 7.2 Political engagement of organizations across countries (percentages)

	Cologne	Kielce	Turin
Mobilizing members	56.5	13.6	57.7
Lobbying	87.0	45.5	42.3
Political activities	73.9	13.6	30.8
N	23	22	26

of political engagement that is used most often in Kielce, but overall involvement in political activities is as low as mobilization. Finally, in Turin, we observe a distinct pattern again because mobilization is a strategy that is preferred over lobbying while overall engagement in political activities is even lower. Thus, in sum, organizations involved in the field of unemployment and precarity politics seem generally politically very active in Cologne, especially in the form of lobbying activities, and quite inactive in Kielce (although not when it comes to lobbying), with those in Turin standing somewhere in between and characterized by a focus on mobilizing activities.

These crucial, cross-national differences can hardly be explained by the ways in which these three cities cope with unemployment and precarity because they each have a rather exclusive approach vis-à-vis the unemployed and precarious workers. While the differences might be explained by the broader political opportunity structures, which students of social movements have repeatedly demonstrated as being a major aspect of channeling political mobilization (see Kriesi 2004 and Meyer 2004 for overviews), we would like to stress the that the differences in the political engagement of organizations can be linked to the structure of the multi-organizational field of unemployment and precarity and, more specifically, to the position of broker within such a network. To test this hypothesis, we analyzed the effect of the three forms of brokerage as distinguished by the degree of political engagement of organizations. Table 7.3 lays out the results of three regression analysis models for this effect, one for each variable of political engagement. Obviously, we do not observe so many statistically significant effects as the number of cases is quite limited. Therefore, in this case, we have considered a 10% level of significance to be acceptable.[3]

The analysis yields three important findings in this context. First, of the three models, the model referring to mobilizing activities has the most explanatory power. This can be seen in the measures of the quality of the models: Nagelkerke R squared and -2 log-likelihood, or, in other words, the set of selected predictors, including the measures of network brokerage, accounts more readily for the fact that organizations engage in activities aimed at mobilizing rather than in lobbying or political activities in general. This, however, is probably due primarily to the effect of the control variables rather than to that of the three measures of brokerage.

Second, the effects of the control variables vary across the three models. In particular, there is a significant effect of paid staff in the model concerning mobilizing activities, while this variable has no effect in the models referring to the other two forms of political engagement.

Table 7.3 Effects of brokerage on three forms of political engagement by organizations (odds ratios)

	Mobilizing members	Lobbying	Political activities
Year of foundation (1 = after 1995)	.505	1.380	.907
Paid staff (1 = more than 1 full-time or 2 part-time)	.063**	1.669	.424
Office space (1 = owned or rented)	.561	.653	.544
Scope of action (1 = neighborhood, city, or region)	2.679	.515	.765
Coordinator	.980	.957	.970
Representative	1.217	.974	1.017
Gatekeeper	1.380*	1.337†	1.231†
Constant	5.464	1.474	2.078
Nagelkerke R^2	.442	.160	.161
−2 log-likelihood	66.092	84.182	82.734
N	71	71	71

†$p \le .10$; *$p \le .05$; **$p \le .01$; ***$p \le .00$.
Standard errors between parentheses.

Thus, organizations that have no or very few paid staff members are much more likely to engage in activities aimed at mobilization. In other words, the more formalized an organization is, the less likely it is to mobilize its members. None of the other control variables had any significant effect on any of the three indicators of political engagement.

Third and most importantly, we observe a consistent positive effect of one of the three measures of brokerage across the three models, namely gatekeeping. Organizations that have a gatekeeping role are more likely to be politically active, and this applies to all three variables of political engagement. In contrast, neither representativeness nor coordination matters. What does this tell us about the relationships between network brokerage and the political engagement of organizations in the field of unemployment and precarity politics? It tells us that certain network properties, and more specifically, the position of an actor in the multi-organizational field of unemployment and precarity politics, have a clear impact on the degree of political engagement of civil society organizations. However, only a particular type of brokerage plays a role. What matters in order for organizations to become politically active is that they act as gatekeepers, that is, they link policy actors and other civil society actors by allowing for the flow of exchanges from the former to the latter. The more they perform this role the more they become politically engaged. Crucially, the consistent, positive effect of gatekeeping may also link with the potential effect of other types of brokerage. Thus, the presence of strong or weak gatekeepers may come to reinforce or, otherwise, deactivate horizontal brokerage in the public domain. After all, the strong bonding in the public domain that one finds in Turin and Kielce seems to lead to contrasting scenarios. The extensive presence of gatekeepers couples with that of coordinators, meaning that strong bonding in the public domain goes hand in hand with access points to the policy domain. This probably leads to the extensive use of mobilizing activities at the level of the whole field. At the same time, the scarce presence of gatekeepers couples with extensive coordination and reduces the potential of bonding to translate into widespread mobilization through the seizing of crucial opportunities in the policy domain.

Conclusion

This chapter has discussed how network analysis at the actor level, and in particular the computation of brokerage, is valuable in examining the multi-organizational field of unemployment and precarity in Europe. Our main contention is two-fold. First, *prima facie*, similar sets of policies targeting the unemployed and precarious workers can translate into different sets of opportunities for civil society actors depending on their own brokerage in the field. We have thus argued that a crucial question needs to be answered about the unique position that each actor has at the intersection of the public and the policy domains so as to control communication and the flow of exchanges across both the horizontal and the vertical dimension. In particular, we have found that gatekeeping has a consistent, positive effect at the actor level. That is, the more civil society organizations play a role in top–down linking in the field the more politically engaged they are in terms of mobilization, lobbying, and general activities. In addition, similar sets of policies targeting the unemployed and precarious workers have different impacts at the level of the whole field based on the particular shape that actors give to the field via their different relational properties. In particular, the presence of a number of mighty gatekeepers has emerged as a crucial priority at the whole field level that is beyond the relationship between brokerage and political engagement at the actor level.

Findings are more difficult to interpret under the second fold given the counter-intuitive direction that they may take. For example, we have found that the presence of strong coordinators, which leads to strong bonding in the public domain, is not linked in itself to mobilizing activities. Instead, for mobilization to occur, horizontal brokerage among civil society actors also requires that crucial political opportunities be circulated through vertical linking with the policy domain. This view is consistent when comparing Turin with Kielce. In the Italian city, gatekeeping and coordination reinforce each other, leading to the necessary mix of bonding and linking that is behind the operation of mobilizing activities. In the Polish case, by contrast, loose gatekeeping constrains the flow of political opportunities across the divide between the policy domain and the public domain, leaving room for forms of political engagement such as lobbying that are in fact run behind the curtains and in solitude. In Cologne, the concurrent presence of gatekeepers and coordinators accounts for the high degree of political engagement in general. Overall, then, the picture is quite consistent at the actor and fields levels, with civil society being quite active in Cologne, quite inactive in Kielce, and standing somewhere in between – with its focus on mobilization – in Turin.

Following our nexus between political engagement and brokerage, we have thus opened up space for more scholarly research to be conducted on the impact of networks in contentious fields of unemployment and precarity politics. Different institutional and policy dynamics, summed up in an inclusive vs. an exclusive model, can be matched against specific findings that shed light on major relational characteristics in the multiorganizational field. Therefore, the study of networks can tell us a lot about the unaffected impact of a given policy approach upon variations of political engagement, or, alternatively, its on-going weakening.

Notes

1. But see scholarship that takes networks as a dependent variable (Diani 1995; Diani and Bison 2004).
2. The partition is between capital letters, non-capital letters, letters in italics and letters in non-italics.
3. Because we are discussing dependent variables that are measured as dummies, the coefficients shown in the table are odds ratios (exponentials of the unstandardized regression coefficient). A value greater than 1 indicates a positive effect, a value lower than 1 a negative effect, and a value equal to 1 no effect on the independent variable.

References

Borgatti, S. P. (2002) *NetDraw Software for Network Visualization* (Harvard, MA: Analytic Technologies).

Borgatti, S. P., M. G. Everett, and L. C. Freeman (2002) *Ucinet for Windows: Software for Social Network Analysis* (Harvard, MA: Analytic Technologies).

Bourdieu, P. (1986) "The Forms of Capital," in J. G. Richardson (ed.), *Handbook of Theory and Research for the Sociology of Education* (New York: Greenwood).

Burt, R. S. (2005) *Brokerage and Closure: An Introduction to Social Capital* (Oxford/ New York: Oxford University Press).

Christopoulos, D. and L. Quaglia (2009) "Network Constraints in EU Banking Regulation: The Capital Requirements Directive," *Journal of Public Policy*, 29, 179–200.

Cinalli, M. (2004) "Horizontal Networks vs. Vertical Networks within Multi-Organisational Alliances: A Comparative Study of the Unemployment and Asylum Issue-Fields in Britain," *Centre for European Political Communication Working paper 8/04*, http://www.eurpolcom.eu/exhibits/paper_8.pdf, accessed 2 July 2013.

Cinalli, M. (2007) "Between Horizontal Bridging and Vertical Governance: Pro-Beneficiary Movements in New Labour Britain," in Purdue, D. (ed.), *Civil Societies and Social Movements: Potentials and Problems* (London: Routledge).

Cinalli, M. and K. Füglister (2008) "Networks and Political Contention over Unemployment: A Comparison of Britain, Germany and Switzerland," *Mobilization*, 13, 259–276.

Cinalli, M. and M. Giugni (2010) "Welfare States, Political Opportunities, and the Claim-Making in the Field of Unemployment Politics," in Giugni, M. (ed.), *The Contentious Politics of Unemployment in Europe* (Houdmills: Palgrave).

Coleman, J. S. (1990) *Foundations of Social Theory* (Cambridge, MA: Harvard University Press).

Coleman, J. S. (1988) "Social Capital in the Creation of Human Capital," *American Journal of Sociology*, 94, 95–120.

Diani, M. (1995) *Green Networks: A Structural Analysis of the Italian Environmental Movement* (Edinburgh: Edinburgh University Press).

Diani, M. and I. Bison (2004) "Organizations, Coalitions, and Movements," *Theory and Society*, 33, 281–309.

Diani, M. and D. McAdam (2003) *Social Movements and Networks: Relational Approaches to Collective Action* (Oxford: Oxford University Press).

Giugni, M., M. Berclaz, and K. Füglister (2009) "Welfare States, Labour Markets, and the Political Opportunities for Collective Action in the Field of Unemployment: A Theoretical Framework," in Giugni, M. (ed.), *The Politics of Unemployment in Europe* (Aldershot: Ashgate).

Gould, R. V. (1995) *Insurgent Identities: Class, Community, and Protest in Paris from 1848 to the Commune* (Chicago, IL: Chicago University Press).

Gould, R. and R. Fernandez (1989) "Structures of Mediation: A Formal Approach to Brokerage in Transaction Networks," *Sociological Methodology*, 19, 89–126.

Knoke, D. and J. H. Kuklinski (1982) *Network Analysis* (Beverly Hills, CA: Sage).

Kriesi, H. (2004) "Political Context and Opportunity," in Snow, D. A., S. Soule, and H. Kriesi (eds), *The Blackwell Companion to Social Movements* (Oxford: Blackwell).

Lin, N. (2001) *Social capital a theory of social structure and action* (Cambridge, NY: Cambridge University Press).

Meyer, D. S. (2004) "Protest and Political Opportunities," *Annual Review of Sociology*, 30, 125–145.

Putnam, R. D. (1993) *Making Democracy Work: Civic Traditions in Modern Italy* (Princeton, NJ: Princeton University Press).

Putnam, R. D. (2000) *Bowling Alone: The Collapse and Revival of American Community* (New York: Simon & Schuster).

Scott, J. (2000) *Social network analysis a handbook* (Los Angeles: SAGE).

Wasserman, S. and K. Faust (1994) *Social Network Analysis: Methods and Applications* (Cambridge: Cambridge University Press).

8

Inheriting Divisions? The Role of Catholic and Leftist Affiliation in Local Cooperation Networks: The Case of Italy and Poland

Matteo Bassoli and Maria Theiss

Introduction

Catholic and (post)Communist organizations play a crucial role in the political traditions and functioning of civil society both in Italy and in Poland. The Catholic and (post)Communist affiliation of an organization still plays a crucial role from both a social and a political point of view, with a consequent rise of tension between these two ideological and institutional traditions. During the post-WWII period, most civil society organizations in Italy were connected either to the Communist Party or to the Christian Democrats (Biorcio 2007) as a result of a deliberate political effort to influence civil society more broadly. Similarly in Poland, the majority of older civil society organizations were either quangos, officially acknowledged by the Communist regime, or organizations that stemmed from the Catholic Solidarność movement (Rose-Ackerman 2008: 54, Leś 2000: 193).

The aim of this chapter is to investigate if (and to what extent) values shared by civil society organizations influence the creation of cooperative networks. We intend to operationalize values as the ideological and institutional affiliation of an organization and to limit the scope of our analysis to Catholic and (post)Communist affiliations of organizations in two local settings. Treating the official principles and the tradition of an organization as a three values variable (Catholic, leftist, and non-affiliated) allows us to evaluate to what extent the ideological affiliation may result in structural divisions and power asymmetry within the civil organizations network. The focus on these two ideological affiliations stems from our attempt to assess whether the political cleavage, developed as early as the first decades after

WWII, still matters in the local cooperative networks of civil society organizations.

In the first part of the chapter we present different theoretical notions of values in their relation to network structure. We identify contradictory concepts assuming that actors' norms are marginal to predict network structure as well as approaches based on the idea that values are a fundamental source of organizational network dynamics. The second part of the text describes two (post)Communist and Catholic coalitions (intended as groups of organizations) in Turin and Kielce, as well as their origins and the broader political context of their development. The third part presents the quantitative data, the fourth treats empirical investigation aimed at assessing to what extent organizations in two researched local settings exchange information with those sharing similar norms. The fifth section presents the impact that the ideological cleavage has on the social predominance of actors and coalitions. Finally, the last paragraph delineates the general conclusions on the relative role of ideological affiliation in modern times.

The role of values in cooperation networks

The theoretical discussion on the role of values in the cooperation networks of organizations reveals a paradox. The difficulty in presenting the state of art of the empirical data related to this problem may be attributed to the fact that on the one hand, in classical network theory, actor's values are perceived as non-relevant and, on the other hand, the assumption of the crucial role of values is a cornerstone of some perspectives within Social Movement Theory (Snow 2004, Oliver and Johnston 2000) or Advocacy Coalition Framework.

In network theory,[1] individuals' values are explicitly (Knoke and Yang 2008: 6, Borgatti and Halgin 2011: 1, Thatcher 1998: 409) or implicitly (Adam and Kriesi 2007) considered as individually attributed. They are considered unproblematic features because their methodological order differs from that of network aspects. By way of example, Thatcher (1998: 409) stresses that "in network explanations shared beliefs are not a precondition to coordinated action and indeed (...), they arise from coordinated action." Thus, one of the presumptions of the network approach is to regard the social structure apart (and not the values system) as an independent variable producing certain outcomes. Actors' values are considered in the same way as any attribute; thus they may be treated as a precedent (pre-independent) variable or a broader context leading to certain shape of the network. However, the use of individual attributes is well developed in the network field. One of the classic issues within network theory is that of homophily – the grouping of cooperating actors along given features: either "neutral" and stable (social status, age, and gender) or more subtle and value loaded (left-right orientation). The underlying idea is that the principle of homophily is socially pervasive; it structures network ties of different type, including marriage, friendship, work, advice, support, information transfer, exchange, and many other types of relationships. "The result is that people's personal networks are homogeneous with regard to many socio-demographic, behavioral, and intrapersonal characteristics" (McPherson et al. 2001). When it comes to organizations, the concept is applied in a similar way. Organizations can forge ties either because they share a common background (as we are going to assess) or because they work in a similar way or any other reasonable source of action strategy (see Lahusen and Grimmer in this volume). A proverb such as "birds of a feather flock together" thus may serve as a hypothesis that similar values enable interconnections and cooperation among actors.

Whereas network theory seems to treat values as either peripheral or "static" variables, the frameworks of organizational networks regard values as an important aspect of the networking process. This is apparent in the Advocacy Coalition Framework (ACF) (Sabatier and Weible 2007; Zafonte and Sabatier 1998). The ACF regards values as crucial variables structuring policy subsystems and leading to coordinated action. It assumes that policy actors aim to translate components of their normative system into policy. As deep core beliefs (general normative assumptions regarding human nature, the state, the market, etc.) span most policy subsystems, according to ACF it is the "policy core beliefs" (actors' notion on whose welfare counts, on authority of government, on proper roles of citizens, elected officials, seriousness of policy problems, etc.) that enable the distinguishing of at least two advocacy coalitions within a policy subsystem. Thus, the divergent preferences ("policy core policy preferences") might be, as Sabatier and Weible stress, "the stickiest glue that binds coalition together" (Sabatier and Weible 2007: 195).

Finally in the Social Movement approach (extensively on the role of values in Social Movement Literature, see della Porta and Diani 2006), the role of values in a network is further-reaching than in ACF. Not only are shared values a basis for shared identities to arise, but they also lead to political conflict. As Sabatier and Zafonte used the metaphor of "glue" when describing the role of shared beliefs, in Diani and Bison's they could be compared to an "engine." As they stress, "a social movement process is occurring to the extent that long-term bonds and shared identities translate into sustained networks (...) movement action has to do much with the constant redefinition of identity" (Diani and Bison 2004: 304). Thus, they explicitly differentiate coalitions (note however that advocacy coalitions are closer to a social movement than non-advocacy coalitions) from social movements.

Research methodology

Taking inspiration from the contradictory concepts on the role of values in network structures, this study intends to examine two research questions:

1. If values are important in shaping networks, do Catholic and (post) Communist organizations tend to form exclusive groups?
2. To what extent do organizations' shared values influence their power within the network? Does a certain ideological affiliation prevail in the two contexts?

As mentioned, we chose to operationalize the values shared by an organization as its ideological affiliation and historical tradition. We coded an organization as Catholic if its charter explicitly mentions Catholic values. In many cases, these are organizations that are institutionally linked to the Catholic Church and in Poland they often have their origins in anti-communist opposition. As a (post)Communist or Leftist organization, we labelled those organizations that were "official" during the Communist time in Poland and those which are their immediate inheritors, whereas in Italy Communist organizations are those which were considered a social expression of the PCI (Italian Communist Party) during the period 1921–1991 or those more recent groups which are acknowledged as being of Leftist background.

In our study, we investigate organizations in two cities that are included in the YOUNEX project – Turin in Italy and Kielce in Poland. The comparative form is based on the assumption that Turin and Kielce share some common features in relation to the role played both by Catholic and (post)Communist tradition in the social sphere but are at the same time substantially different in terms, for instance, of the strength and length of civic tradition as well as the impact of communist heritage. Thus, similar outcomes confirm the actual and universal importance of values in shaping civil society organizations in European Catholic countries, whereas different outcomes do not fully falsify the hypothesis because findings may be attributed to the different levels of "civicness" and the impact of the communist legacy in Poland.

Our analysis is confined to civic organizations (including trade unions) that deal with labor market issues and combat youth social exclusion. The parties are not included in the study, as our focus was to "extract" the influence of the ideological affiliation of organizations from the context of party influence. As regards the network selection, we opted to analyze information networks because it allows for a more robust test of our hypotheses. This is the widest network and the one that should be less influenced by the ideological cleavage. Indeed, in both the project network and personal-contact network a greater impact of values could be expected. On the one side, projects are often developed with partner organizations (trust and values may be an asset for the selection of partners), while on the other personal contacts are often informed by common background at the individual level. For these reasons, the information network is therefore best suited to assess the impact of ideological cleavage (as opposed to Bassoli and Cinalli's chapter, which assesses the most stable structure).

We deliberately chose to use the term "coalitions" with a broad and figurative meaning, claiming that such a notion is justified here as the contemporary history of civil society organizations in both countries, and the researched cities suggest the existence of both collective origins and goals of both groups.

Inspired by the "homophily hypothesis" of our first research question, we want to test whether the ideological affiliation of organizations plays a certain role in shaping the network structure. Generally, when measuring homophily at a systemic level, two phenomena are possible: a polarized or a not-polarized system. In the first case, third organizations would take either a pro-Catholic or pro-Leftist political stand, which means they would cooperate exclusively either with Catholic or with Leftist organizations. In the latter, the average third organization would cooperate with both coalitions; thus third organizations would make cross-cleavage ties in the network. In order to control for the impact of this third group (the non-affiliated), we use two different measures of homophily (the homophily index and the external-internal index) based on different partitions: Catholic vs. non-Catholic, Leftist vs. non-Leftist, Catholic vs. Leftist vs. others. The two measures are different as regards their statistical nature. While the homophily index measures only the tendency toward homophily,[2] the E-I (external-internal) index[3] (Krackhardt and Stern 1988) assesses the statistical difference between the actual homophily and the null hypothesis (the observed value is due to chance alone and not a systematic cause).

The "ideological division" among civil society actors in Turin and Kielce cannot be reduced to the issue of a complete polarization of local civil society, which is measured by the homophily indexes. The tendency of grouping together can be also traced to the presence of strong ties among organizations within groups (Krackhardt 1998). One of the possible ways of understanding strong ties is controlling for the presence of simmelian ties – thus interconnected triads – as in Bassoli and Cinalli (this volume). The reason to choose this indicator is the fact that homophily only suggests the presence of a division between Leftist organizations and Catholic ones, whereas it does not infer any strong relationship within the group. On the contrary, the presence of simmelian ties among actors of the same affiliation implies that the impact of the ideological tradition is still very strong not only in clustering actors but in forging strong relationships within the respective "ideological world."

Our second research question focuses on the impact of homophily on the distribution of power among organizations. We understand power as the ability to influence others' behaviors; in network terms, this is translated into the concept of centrality (Bassoli and Cinalli forthcoming; Everett and Borgatti 2005; Christopoulos 2006). Which coalition scores higher in group centrality? Which one has, on average, the most central actors? Centrality can be measured using different variables (Freeman 1978), all based on the intuition that the more connection a node has, the better it is. The more a node is connected, the higher its ability to reach other nodes and have higher access to information and resources. Centrality can be measured in incoming ties or in outgoing ties. In the first case, the connection represents the prestige of the actor; in the second it represents the outreaching capacity of the actors (or the desire of being acknowledged). Therefore both incoming and outgoing ties are different aspects of power. While incoming ties represent the power perceived by alters, outgoing ties may suggest a power based on influencing capacity perceived by the actors themselves.

However, it is important to highlight that homophily is a network property (shared by all actors or by a group of actors), while centrality is an individual characteristic, which may extend to the group only under certain conditions (Everett and Borgatti 2005). In order to measure the centrality of groups, different approaches may be employed. We opted for the two most widely used: the group average centrality and the group centrality. The former is the simple average of actors' centralities belonging to the group. Average centrality is strongly influenced by the number of internal ties, because if a group has a lot of internal ties the group average centrality rises accordingly. The latter measure, called group centrality, is the number of alters that are connected to the group. Therefore it tries to assess the impact of the coalition on the wider network. The combination of mentioned measures results with four indicators we deployed to assess actors' power: the (normalized) indegree group centrality,[4] the (normalized) outdegree group centrality, the average (normalized) indegree[5] and the average in-Bonacich power.[6] While the first two measures grasp the overall prestige and outreach of the coalition without considering the internal ties, the latter two also take into account the density of the coalition (but only for prestige purposes). In power terms, the first two measures assess only the power of the coalition in civil society, while the second attempt to offer a more nuanced picture considering also the power structure within the coalition.

Contextual data: network size and history

In both cities, there is a sub-group of Catholic organizations as well as a Leftist sub-group. However, there are many differences regarding the number of actors involved and their relative position (Table 8.1). While in Kielce non-affiliated organizations (also called third parties) are the most numerous sub-group, followed by the Catholic, in Turin the Leftist group is the widest. Moreover the Leftist group is very small in Kielce, while the Catholic is quite large in Turin.

The structure of information networks is depicted in Figure 8.1, where squares are organizations that fulfill the Catholic criteria and the black triangles are those fulfilling (post)Communist or Leftist criteria. At a first glance, it can be noted that in both countries some organizations are more active in information exchange than others. Moreover, the two coalitions can be clearly identified as can the presence of cross-cleavage ties.[7] Kielce shows a rather small network of thirty two nodes, while the Turin network is twice as big. Furthermore, Kielce has a better-defined core-periphery structure than Turin.[8]

Table 8.1 The information network: coalitions' size

	Kielce	Turin
Non-affiliated	56%	30%
Catholic	34%	28%
Leftist	9%	42%
N	32	60

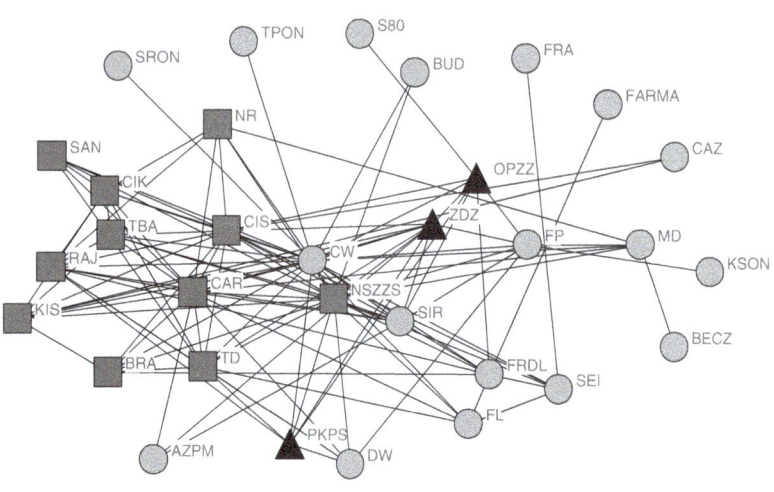

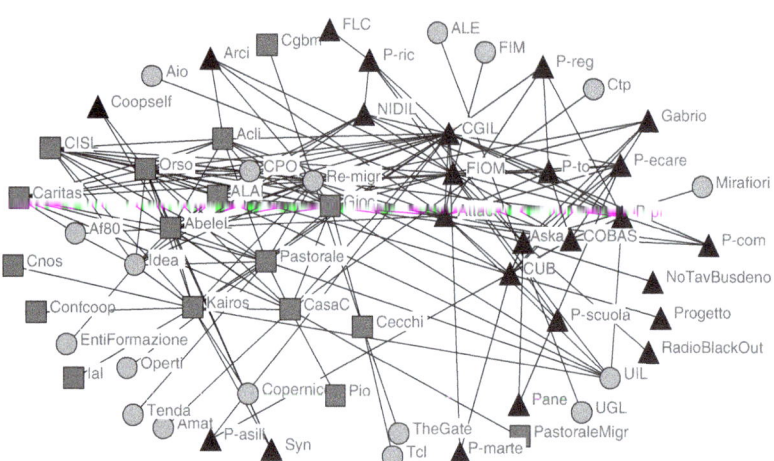

Figure 8.1 The information network, Kielce on the top and Turin on the bottom (shape by ideological affiliation)

Source: Network graphed with Netdraw (Borgatti 2002) position given by the scaling ordination (iterative metrics) procedure.

The origins of the Turin coalitions

It can be argued that Italian contemporary civil society has its origins in the 19th century, when civil initiatives linked to both the workers' socialist movement and the development of the Catholic Church. These initiatives gave place to modern political parties, trade unions, cooperatives, mutual benefit societies, charitable organizations and networks of community centers, poor people's shelters and social canteens. These ideological traditions strongly contribute to the creation of a set of social institutions (cooperatives, banks, associations) to fight the threat of the vanishing equilibrium between state and market. These two traditions, the Catholic rooted in the Veneto region, and the socialist in Emilia and Tuscany, had a strong influence on the overall political debate for, firstly, low polarization between capitalists and proletariats in the peripheral regions and secondly, the ideological cleavage between the two. As regards the first aspect, the two traditions, for a set of different reasons, trigger the growth of a sense of common aim (or brotherhood) between capitalist and proletariat in those peripheral areas where capitalism was far from being what we now acknowledge by this term. In relation to the second aspect, the clash between the two shared normative systems was fierce because of the strong anticlericalism of Italian socialism and the conservatism of the Catholic tradition. More importantly, the two opposing cultural traditions were both very distant from the liberal imprinting of the new country and opposing to its creation (Moro and Vannini 2006).

Once the nation building process was settled (to some extent) and electoral suffrage was implemented, the two cultural traditions already rooted in the civil society moved to the political sphere with the first mass parties: the socialist party (PSI-Partito Socialista Italiano, founded in 1892), the Christian democrat (DC-Democrazia Cristiana, first founded in 1919 and recreated in 1942), and the Communist party (PCI-Partito Comunista Italiano, founded in 1921). After the fascist parenthesis, which suppressed both political parties and independent organizations, the country was locked into a polarized party system (Sartori 1976), characterized by the presence of a post-fascist party (MSI-Movimento Sociale Italiano), a Communist party with a strong relationship with the Soviet Union (PCI), a centrist Christian Democratic party (DC), and many smaller parties (regionalist, socialist, liberal, etc.). Even though the number of parties, along with the strong polarization, created a highly fragmented party system, they did not have the same influence on civil society. There were also many factors stabilizing the system: the influence of "foreign powers" and the international bipolar system (Del Pero 2003; Gualtieri 2004); the anti-fascist context of the constitutional setting (Salvati 2003); and finally the "formal" exclusion of the Communist party from the government. The complex interplay of these factors (Salvati 2003), along with a strong fascist legacy in civil society, pushed the two major parties (DC and PCI) toward service provision and leisure activities. "The large numbers of Catholics and Leftists among the former Fascist masses [...] had to be governed and channeled within and through a democratic party network. At the end of the war, the main mass parties were aware of the urgency of this pedagogic task and promptly devoted themselves to its realization" (Salvati 2003: 557).

Hence DC and PCI, as well as playing a strong political role within the political sphere, were also the main actors in the societal sphere, via an increasing number of clearly identifiable flanking institutions (Ignazi and Ysmael 1998). The two parties were fundamentally aiming not only at recruiting members and seeking votes but also at promoting a unified framework of beliefs, behaviors, and understandings. "After the collapse of the state during the war as the symbol of national identity, the two main parties, Communist and Catholic, built up their respective influences by emphasizing the feeling of belonging to a large, integrated institution and to its protective network of relief organizations" (Salvati 2003: 562). However, there was a strong asymmetry in the so-called Italian *consociativismo* (Pizzorno 1993): Mutual recognition was to be found in the division between state control (granted to DC) and civil society occupation (by PCI).

Given this overall picture of the Italian civil society, some specifications are required for the city of Turin. The city is an interesting case as regards the so-called Italian *sub-culture* (political sub-cultures) given its specific industrial tradition. First of all, the city is a former capital of Italy (1861–1871), where most intellectuals where liberals; secondly, in the city there was a strong tradition of charitable Catholic institutions (such as Istituto Pio, the Saint Vincent organization) and educational institutions (the confraternity of Salesiani), and finally, it also represents the industrial heart of Italy with a strong Trade Unions and Communist Party. Communist mayors ran the city from 1945 to 1951, and the Communist party of Turin often played an important role in forging national elites. Due to these intertwined variables, the city represents an interesting case of the role of Catholic and Leftist affiliation. Indeed, while in some regions, such as Emilia Romagna, the role of Communist tradition is mostly a matter of lack of other traditions, in Turin there is the co-presence of both traditions without a clear predominance (Diamanti 2009).

Coalitions' origins in Kielce

The post-war development of Polish civil society organizations reveals its "mixed heritage" (Ekiert and Kubik 1999; Rose-Ackermann 2008; Leś 2000). This refers to two parallel processes taking place before the collapse of the communist regime in 1989. The first is the creation of quasi-nongovernmental organizations, almost fully dependent on the governing communist party. The second is the existence of the opposition movement of civil society initiatives attached to Catholic Church and the rise of Social Movement Solidarność in the early eighties.

Despite the fact that many organizations active since the early twenties were reactivated shortly after WWII, most of them were illegal until 1950. Many broadly acknowledged and active organizations like the Polish Scouts' Association (ZHP), the Polish YMCA, the Warsaw Charity Association, Polish Caritas and many others were abolished by the communist government. The most common practice was to close autonomous organizations followed either by the nationalization of their assets or by granting them to newly established organizations with a similar name under the full control of the ruling party. Similarly, groups of independent organizations active in similar policy fields were often forced to unite. In both cases, the communist party imposed the charter and the steering committee of newly established organizations. The registration of an organization was impossible unless support of the national regime was explicitly declared as its main aim. Moreover, it was often the ruling Workers' Party Steering Committee's initiative to register certain organizations in order to "transmit proper ideology" to certain social groups. This was, for example, the case of "the Polish Female League," whose aim was to "affirm the socialistic regime by women." Thus, all organizations established in the 1940s and 1950s were fully dependent on the state, and in many cases (the Polish Red Cross, Friends of Children Association, Polish Committee of Social Assistance) they experienced stagnation and regression in the subsequent period.

Simultaneously, there was a specific sphere of associational freedom within Catholic Church that had been part of the Polish tradition since the partition of the country and its occupation at the end of XVIII century. This attachment of autonomous and opposition civil activity to the institution of Catholic Church was also visible in the post-war period. In particular since 1956, the rise of associational practices under the auspices of the Church is noticeable as indicated by the establishment of "Clubs of Catholic Intelligentsia," political discussion clubs and parish charity activities. The further development of this trend in the

1970s is described as the rise of "second," "alternative," or "parallel" to society (as described by the official ideology) and the emergence of "ethos groups" within the civil society (Rymsza 2007: 26). Certain opposition organizations like the "Workers' Self-defense Committee" (KOR) and the "Human's and Citizen's Rights Defending Committee" were established. As presented by the classic analysis of Osa (2003), this was a time when ideological, political, and social foundations of Solidarność social movement were created. They were based on a dense network of informal contacts, which allowed to mobilize future support for diverse activities. This could explain why immediately after the establishment of Solidarność in the 1980, 54% of people working in the nationalized economy enrolled as its members.

The attachment of independent civil activity in Poland to the institution of Catholic Church became more evident in the period of Marshal Law (1982–1989). As scholars describe, the Catholic Church was a "shelter" for the opposition (above all the illegal Solidarność and "Independent Students' Association" structures) and a sphere where the "ideological war" against the communist regime took place. The Church, including its "Bishop's Help Committees," was the organization receiving the vast majority of financial support from the West during this period. Subsequently, at the end of the 1980s, financial support from the West increased significantly and took the form of providing economic as well as organizational and educational support to several civil society organizations.

Despite the widespread change in the functioning of Polish civil society organizations that has been taking place for over 20 years (which includes acting as a bolster of the economic change, responding to the neoliberal withdrawal of state's responsibilities, professionalization, Europeanization, etc.), these "dual origins" seem to be still relevant as a context of right-left divergences in the organizational dimension of Polish civil society. This includes firstly the specific role of Catholic Church, which, on the one hand, ensured the existence of the unique independent public sphere during the communist era and on the other maintained a bond between religious rituals and the idea of a free Polish nation. Pope John Paul II reinforced this connection. As Marody and Mandes (2007: 414) claim, "the XIX century figures of a 'romantic nationalism' in Poland" were thus invigorated. Moreover, the link between the Catholic Church and civil society resulted in the emergence of the "communities of the moral rightness" (Ost 1990 2007: 365; Linz and Stepan 1996), and the "ethical civil society," which means that acting for the sake of values rather than for solving social problems, is seen as a legitimization of a civil society organization.

Secondly, both contemporary private networks and the styles of functioning of civil society organizations reveal this "dual heritage." Many studies, including analyses of Solidarity structures, show the use of former opposition networks in creating contemporary civil society in Poland (Gliński 2006: 32). This was also explicitly expressed in Kielce, where our respondent from the Catholic coalition said: "we know each other very well since 1980 from 'the Bishop's Committees'." Consequently, the analyses of the organizational types of civil society organizations in Poland conducted by Gliński shows that a "nostalgic post-communist style," a post-communist "style of the 'converted'," as well as a "style of mature civic enclaves" based on dense organizational networks (represented, for example, by Caritas), are, among others, to be found in the Polish third sector.

Do birds of a feather flock together?

If the cooperation of Catholic and Leftist organizations in both cities is definitely not a coincidence, two questions emerge: To what extent do Catholic and (post)Communist organizations in Turin and Kielce exchange information with those sharing their normative system and political affiliation? We chose to investigate this problem by using two different approaches. In order to measure the preferences of relationships within the same "values world" (organization with analogous affiliation), different concepts can be deployed: the tendency towards homophily (the preference for organization of the same kind) and the presence of Simmelian ties (cliques) among similar organizations. While the first assess the tendency to be connected with similar actors, the second grasps the strength of these relationships.

As it is presented in Table 8.2 (first row), the homophily (without third parties) measured by HI is relatively high (close to -1) in both cities, whereas it is much stronger in Kielce because of the size of the Catholic world: The number of internal ties is greater than that of cross-cleavage ties. However, if we measure homophily only as regards the Catholic organizations (Table 8.2, second row), HI level turns out to be lower and similar in both cities (-0.34 for Turin and -30 in Kielce). Therefore, although Catholic organizations have a strong tendency toward homophily in Poland, given the presence of other important actors, they need to forge external ties as well (not toward the other coalition but toward third parties).

The third HI measure also takes into account third parties alongside the Catholic and Leftist organizations (Table 8.2, third row). Homophily

Table 8.2 Homophily index[9] in different information networks in Turin and Kielce

	Turin	Kielce
Homophily – Catholic and Leftist organizations without third parties	−0.59	−0.71
Homophily considering only the group of Catholic organizations	−0.34	−0.30
Homophily considering Catholic, Leftist and third parties organizations as a group	−0.16	−0.12

Source: Data imputed into UCINET (Borgatti et al. 2002), homophily analysis with two and three groups, respectively.

levels are much lower in this case because third parties tend not to be self-centered (they forge only limited internal ties and many external ties, towards either Catholic or Leftist organizations). Overall measures suggest that the division on the basis of ideological affiliation does not preclude third parties to be brokers – thus having the privileged position of bridging the two parts; however, there is a strong tendency (particularly in Kielce) not to have relationship with the other "ideological world." Meanwhile one affiliation per se (the Catholic) does not preclude cross-coalition linkages or the presence of relationships with third parties.

To what extent may this situation be regarded as significant and worth further analyses because the number of nodes (Catholic, Leftist, and non-affiliated) as well as the number of existing ties plays a major role in determining the actual level of HI index? For this reason, we also took into account the second homophily index – the so-called E-I index (Table 8.3). Its level is close to zero in Turin (−0.125) as in Kielce (−0.051). However, in both cities the value is below expected and it is also statistically different (which indicates the presence of homophily).[10] Indeed in Kielce, given the size of the three groups and the total amount of ties, the expected value is 0.149, while in Turin it is 0.334. Moreover, the strength of homophily in Turin is much higher than in Kielce (considering the difference between the actual and the expected value).

As stated above, it is important to look at the tendency toward homophily of each group separately. Assessing the E-I index of each group separately (Table 8.3, first column) helps to highlight features of the network that were overlooked by the general E-I index. In Turin, the

Table 8.3 E-I index in different information networks in Turin and Kielce

		E-I index with three groups	E-I index based on Catholic/ non-Catholic	E-I index based on Leftist/non-Leftist
Turin	Total	−0.125***	−0.307	−0.523***
	Expected value	0.334	−0.174	−0.011
	Other	0.672	−0.427	−0.580
	Catholic	−0.122	−0.122	/
	Leftist	−0.447	/	−0.447
Kielce	Total	−0.051***	−0.237	−0.661
	Expected value	0.149	−0.069	−0.649
	Other	0.056	−0.217	−0.810
	Catholic	−0.256	−0.256	/
	Leftist	0.538	/	0.538

Note: Level of significance: ***< .001; **< .01; *< .05.

index concerning the Leftist coalition is very low (−0.447) showing a strong tendency toward homophily, whereas it is much higher for the Catholic group (−0.122) of the same city. It is important to note that actors of both coalitions prefer to forge ties within the "ideological world" (negative values) rather than having external links. On the contrary, in Kielce the three Leftist actors show a clear tendency for heterophily (0.538). The Kielce Leftist actors are deeply embedded in the Catholic environment given the importance of the Catholic coalition in the societal sphere (see below).

Overall, the tendency toward homophily works at the aggregate level (first column of Table 8.3), while it is much weaker when considering other partitions (that is Catholic vs non-Catholic and Leftist vs non-Leftist). The reason for this behavior has to be traced back to the fact that third parties often play a brokerage role both in Kielce and in Turin. The major exception is the Leftist coalition in Turin that clearly sticks together, while third parties tend to affiliate with the Catholic coalition (the measure for "other" moves from a positive value in the first column to a strong negative value in the third). Even though single coalitions are not significant on their own, their composite behavior fully supports the homophily hypothesis. Overall, the classical adage "birds of a feather flock together" is confirmed in both Turin and Kielce.

However, despite the presence of homophily being suggested by the data collected on both cities, it is necessary to make some distinctions.

While in Kielce (post)Communist organizations have a positive E-I value (0.538) because they have linkage with the Catholic coalition, the same does not hold true in Turin. The Leftist coalition has a negative E-I value (−0.447), which is actually more negative than that of the Catholic coalition (−0.122). Secondly, the situation depicted by the HI and EI indices, along the overall distribution of the coalitions, suggests the presence of a hegemonic coalition in Kielce (the Catholic) and a bipolar situation in Turin. The Catholic coalition in Kielce has a strong tendency toward homophily, which is not counterbalanced by the third parties (which tend to be heterophilous). In Turin the situation appears to be more even. Both coalitions have a tendency toward internal ties, though the Leftist coalition has the stronger. Moreover, non-affiliated organizations tend to prefer the Catholic to the Leftist coalition. These data corroborate the idea that the societal landscape of Turin is inhabited by two coalitions which tend to be separated worlds (sub-cultures), while the Kielce civil society is strongly dependent on the Catholic Church in all its forms.

Figure 8.2 depicts the simmelian ties within the information networks in Turin and in Kielce. This figure allows comparison with the first (Figure 8.1): the same shape, color, size, and positions are kept; all ties have been deleted except the simmelian. Clearly, the Polish case reveals the existence of two coalitions, one formed by the organizations of the Catholic affiliation built around CIS, NSZZS, CAR, TBA, and CIK, and one consisting of post-Communist OPZZ and ZDZ plus FP as a third actor.

The situation in Turin is similar. There are five cliques in the Leftist field: four involving new-Leftist organizations and trade unions (P-ecare, Aska, and Cub; Cub, Aska, and Cobas; Cobas, Aska, and Fiom; Fiom, Atac, and P-to) and one among trade unions (CGIL, NIDIL, and FIOM).[11] There are also three cliques in the Catholic field (Gioc, Orso, and Acli; Gioc, Orso, and Alai; Gioc, Acli, and a third party – Re-migr). Nonetheless, there are also differences since in the Turin case two Leftist organizations (CGIL and NIDIL) forged bridges with the Catholic world, creating overlapping cliques between the two worlds. The cliques are among trade-unions (NIDIL, CGIL, and ALAI) and between the most important Italian trade union (CGIL) and two important Catholic organizations: Abele and Acli.

Overall, when considering the dimensions of homophily and simmelian ties, it is possible to observe that the ideological affiliation of the organization plays a significant role in shaping and clustering the Catholic and the Leftist worlds. However, the clustering is stronger

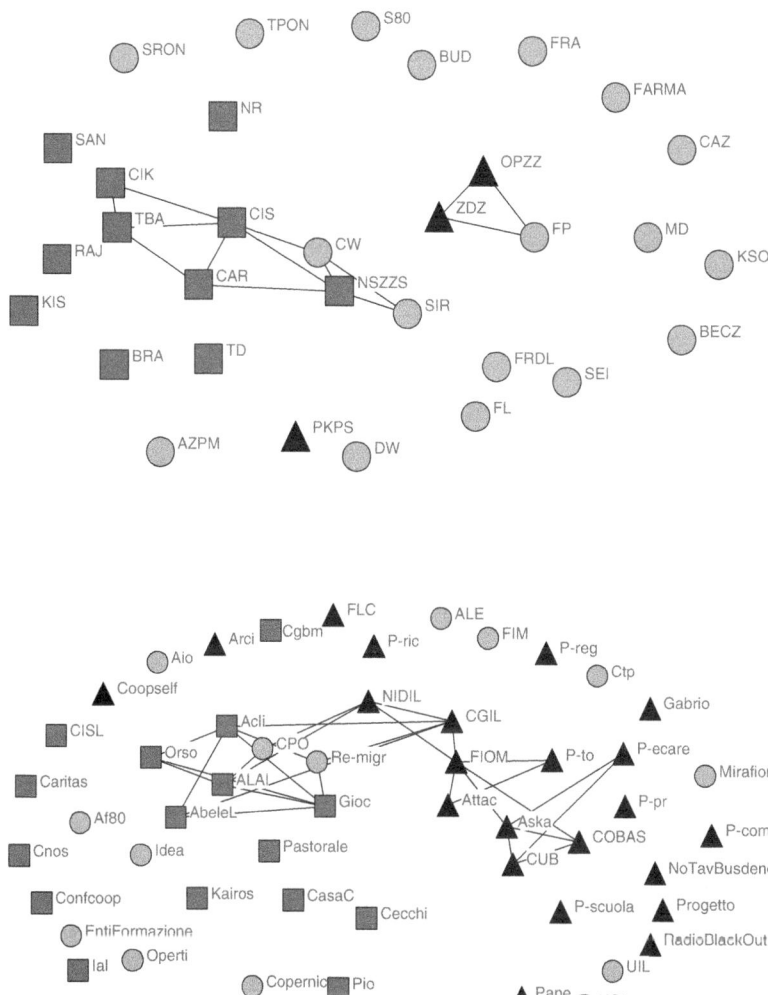

Figure 8.2 The information network – simmelian ties, Kielce on the top and Turin on the bottom (shape and color by ideological affiliation – square: the Catholic organization, triangle: the leftist organization)

Source: Network graphed with Netdraw (Borgatti 2002) position given by the scaling ordination (iterative metrics) procedure.

in Turin than in Kielce. This is because in Turin both cultures have a tendency toward internal ties and the Leftist coalition is a very strong driver (third column Table 8.2), while in Kielce the tendency is registered only among the Catholic organizations (it is also weak). Overall, the role of affiliation is higher in Turin and it is also supported by a dense network with many internal ties. Other than this, both networks are characterized by the presence of strong (simmelian) ties within the two coalitions. As presented, the divisions within the Polish network are vibrant – the simmelian ties are constrained by the two coalitions, while in Turin there are some intra-coalition ties, which happen to be strong simmelian ties.

The network power of two coalitions

So far we have been presenting data assessing the tendency that organizations have to forge ties with other actors sharing a similar ideological background. However, these tendencies could be marginal in the field of unemployment and precarity if the partners involved were marginal themselves. For this reason it is also important to assess the relative importance of actors involved in the homophily game. We therefore present here two measures that help to assess the coalitions' relative powers: the group average centrality and group centrality. While the former is the simple average of actors' centralities belonging to the group, the latter measures the impact of the coalition on the wider network.

As shown in Table 8.4 (first two columns for Kielce and for Turin) presenting group centralities, the two Catholic coalitions have more central positions compared to the Leftist ones (as well as to non-affiliated). Centrality measures are coherent in their ranking in Kielce but not in Turin. The Catholic coalition also has the highest outreach capacity: double the Leftist in Kielce and one point above the Leftist coalition in Turin. As regards its prestige, it is the most recognized coalition in Kielce but not in Turin. This finding is quite interesting because it is counterintuitive. On the one side, the non-affiliated organizations are linked to the Catholic coalition in Turin, while on the other it scores lower in this measure. The reason here has to be traced back to the direction of the tie: Third parties are often mentioned by the Catholic coalition (this increases both the outdegree of the Catholic actors and the homophily level of the Communist coalition), but Catholic organizations are recognized as a source of information by a smaller number of the Leftist organizations while Leftist organizations are recognized by the Catholic ones as source of information.

Table 8.4 Group centrality and group average centrality of different groups

	Kielce				Turin			
	Normalized group outdegree	Normalized group indegree	In-Bonacich Power**	Indegree**	Normalized group outdegree	Normalized group indegree	In-Bonacich Power**	Indegree*
Other	–	–	2.8	0.09	–	–	2.4	0.03
Catholic	0.524	0.429	6.89	0.22	0.488	0.209	8.2	0.09
Leftist	0.207	0.345	5.55	0.20	0.343	0.314	6.61	0.06

***< 0,001; **0.01; *< 0.05.

Source: Data imputed into UCINET (Borgatti et al. 2002), correlation on the three groups partition calculated with ANOVA algorithm 25000 permutations.

Considering internal (incoming) ties, that is exploiting average centralities (third and fourth columns), the ranking does not change: Leftist organizations are more central than the non-affiliated actors, but they score lower than the Catholic in both cities and both measures. Differences emerge in cross-national comparison: Italian organizations score higher in in-Bonacich power and lower in indegree centralities. All differences are statistically significant. This suggests that the Polish Catholic organizations have more ties (higher indegree), while Italian Catholic organizations tend to have less ties but to actors that are themselves central as well (as measured by in-Bonacich power) and more internal ties (they score lower in group centrality). This confirms the power structure in Kielce: Civil society is centered around the Catholic coalition (many ties) although many Catholic organizations are themselves peripheral. On the contrary, the Catholic coalition in Turin is more prone to recognize the Leftist coalition than vice versa and it has an enormous share of internal ties, which increase both the average indegree and in-Bonacich power. Moreover, even if the Catholic coalition is hegemonic in the Polish context, the Leftist organizations are very central (they score just lower than the Catholic) given that they are recognized as a partner by the most important Catholic organizations, while in Turin the Catholic organizations are clearly above the Leftist as regards social status, if self-acknowledgment within the coalition is also considered.

As regards the average centralities, more specifications are needed because three different partitions have been tested in both cities for both measures. Overall, the partition composed of three groups is the most significant with the best R-square (as presented in Table 8.4). This suggests that the centralities of the three groups are ranked in a similar way. For example, in Kielce the centralities of Catholic organizations are higher than those of the Communist ones, which are greater than those of third parties. Obviously, this does not mean that each Catholic organization has a greater indegree centrality than any Communist equivalent, but it means that centrality distribution is not random. In Kielce there is a strong[12] correlation between being central and belonging to the Catholic coalition (both measures), while belonging to the Leftist does not correlate with either indegree centrality or the in-Bonacich. Therefore, the most important aspect that explains centrality distribution is not the ideological background per se but the Catholic tradition, although Leftist organizations are better off than non-affiliated ones. Similarly, in Turin there is a statistical correlation between the partition with the three groups and centralities. However, in this network the effect is weaker (for the indegree) and it is a composed effect: both coalitions are needed. Indeed, while the partition Catholic/non-Catholic shows statistical significance, in Turin it is not correlated with centrality. Thus, while in Kielce the stronger driver of centralities is being Catholic, in Turin the driver is the overall composition.

Concluding remarks

Considering the issue of "who talks to whom" in a policy subsystem by analyzing the organization's ideological affiliation leads us to observe a significance of values shared by civil society organizations in information exchange networks. In Turin as well as in Kielce there is a tendency toward preferring similar partners – it is not surprising to see that both Catholic and Leftist organizations tend to communicate relatively more often with those deriving from the same "ideological world." However, the fact that in both localities the cliques occur almost only among actors sharing same values (two brokers in Turin are exceptions) suggests, as the Social Movement literature does, that the ideological affiliation of organizations plays a significant role in facilitating exchange among them. However, it turned out that an "ideological division" might mean something different in various networks. If only the Catholic and (post)Communist organizations are taken into account (without third parties), we can observe a higher clustering level in Kielce than in Turin. If third parties are included in the analysis, the clustering level is higher in Turin – the non-affiliated are more prone to exchange information rather than the Catholic coalition members. Still, taking into account the homophily level in networks subgroups we can see that there is a hegemonic position of the Catholic coalition in Kielce and bipolar network structure in Turin.

The higher homophily level within Catholic organizations' group in Kielce coexists with the relatively high network power of this group. This regards both the outreach capacity and the indicators of the group's prestige, whereas in Turin the latter does not occur (prestige measured by indegree is higher for the leftist coalition).

The differences between the two cities may be partially explained by the number of civil society organizations, general number of relationships, and the maturity of a policy subsystem. Indeed other findings of the YOUNEX research program show high discrepancy between Kielce and Turin in terms of CSOs specialization in youth unemployment and precarious policy – whereas in Turin actions in this field were relatively crucial for the researched organizations, in Kielce the interviewed organizations were almost all local organizations dealing with social problems (Theiss 2011). This could suggest that since a more vibrant civil society at the organizational level in Turin may well function with a high level of polarization, such ideological division needs to be overcome in order to share the insufficient organizational resources in Kielce.

The second and possibly complementary explanation refers to our research question on the role of both concurring ideological affiliations. It seems that some values count more in certain cultural contexts. This is particularly evident in Kielce, where being of Catholic origin might be an asset for an organization, which includes both social capital (social networks and contacts even from the "Solidarity" times (Osa 2003) and symbolic capital (representing as Linz and Stephan (1996) call it "a community of a moral rightness").

On the contrary, in Turin we observed that the affiliation of an organization does not translate to it being a member of a cluster or to it being central. This could be explained by the fact that the strong cleavage between Communists and anti-Communists of the fifties decreased its salience in Italy throughout the sixties and seventies because of the increasing dominance of the anti-Communist coalition. Moreover, in the so-called Italian *consociativismo* (Pizzorno 1993), the mutual recognition that was not possible at the political level (given the harsh ideological clash) was to be found in civil society. With the demise of the Communist ideology, the political and ideological cleavage became less relevant, while new actors without any prior shared ideological system appeared on the scene. Also, traditional Communist-related institutions, as for example the cultural club confederation ARCI, had to struggle to re-build their own identity (Bassoli and Pincella 2010), with a renewed willingness to bridge ideological differences.

The role of structural (related to the size and the composition of the network), as well as symbolic (related to the sense of certain values constructed in a public discourse), contextual factors in explaining the role of organizations' ideological affiliation in a policy network is a further research question that remains unanswered. The need for deeper research also refers to the consequences of structuring the political networks along shared values. In the social policy subsystem a powerful civil society organizations' coalition might significantly influence local social citizenship, both in its material and symbolic dimension. Other YOUNEX findings revealed the predominance of addressed charitable services in Kielce and the high level of diverse political activities in Turin, including political mobilization initiatives, which are almost absent in Kielce (Theiss 2011). Thus, the issue of "who talks to whom" might translate into a shared notion of who deserves what under which conditions.

Annex – The list of researched organizations

Kielce – Interviewed and mentioned organizations

AZPM   Świętokrzyskie Stowarzyszenie Na Rzecz Aktywizacji Zawodowej i Pomocy Młodzieży w Kielcach (vocational training center)

BECZ   Świetlica środowiskowa "Beczka" (integrational daycare for children)

BRA   Fundacja Gospodarcza św. Brata Alberta (hostel for homeless men)

BUD   Centrum Budzenia Inicjatyw Młodzieżowych "Budzik" (civic education centre)

CAR   Caritas Diecezji Kieleckiej CAR Rel. (Caritas Polska running about 20 places offering help: free medical center, used clothing storage, consultation center for the addicted)

CAZ   Świętokrzyskie Centrum Aktywizacji Zatrudnienia Kobiet (women's activitation center)

CIK   Centrum Interwencji Kryzysowej (Service Centre for abused women)

CIS   Centrum Integracji Społecznej w Kielcach (social integration center)

CW   Stowarzyszenie Centrum Wolontariatu (association – Network of Centres of Voluntary Work)

DW   Fundacja dla Dobra Wspólnego (civic organization offering, help to the unemployed)

FARMA   Fundacja Aktywizacji i Rozwoju Młodzieży FARMA (Youth activitation centre)

FL   Stowarzyszenie Świętokrzyski Fundusz Lokalny (a local fund mainly supporting youth's education)

FP   Stowarzyszenie Forum Pracodawców (employers' association)

FRDL   Fundacja Rozwoju Demokracji Lokalnej (fund, broad scope of activities to support civic society)

KIS   Klub Integracji Społecznej KIS (social integration center)

MD   Stowarzyszenie "Młodzi Demokraci" (youth's club of a liberal party "Platforma Obywatelska")

NR   Nadzieja Rodzinie (organization offering social assistance and training to families)

NSZZ   "Solidarność" Region Świętokrzyski (Trade union "Solidarity")

OPZZ	Ogólnopolskie Porozumienie Związków Zawodowych (Labor union)
PKPS	Polski Komitet Pomocy Społecznej (Polish Comitee of Social Assistance)
RAJ	Świętokrzyski Klub Abstynentów "Raj" (abstinents' association)
S80	Solidarność 80 (Labor union)
SAN	Stowarzyszenie "Arka Nadziei" (ecumenical self-help organization for the homeless and addicted people)
SEI	Stowarzyszenie Edukacja przez Internet (organization running e-learning projects)
SIR	Stowarzyszenie "Integracja i Rozwój" (services centre, mainly educational activity)
TBA	Towarzystwo Pomocy im. Św. Brata Alberta (St. Brother Albert's Aid Society – hostel for the homeless men)
TD	Towarzystwo Dobroczynności (charity of Catholic origin, helping the poor and the persons with disabilities)
ZDZ	Zakład Doskonalenia Zawodowego (vocational training center)

Turin – Interviewed and mentioned organizations

Abelel	Consorzio Sociale Abele Lavoro (A social purpose company, consortium of social cooperatives)
Acli	Associazioni Cattolica Lavoratori Italiani ("Christian Association of Italian Workers"' – Social Work Activities)
Af80	Formazione 80 (Association promoting adult education)
ALAI	Associazione Lavoratori Atipici Italiani – Confederazione Italiana Sindacati dei Lavoratori provincia di Torino (Catholic inspired Precarious worker union, part of CISL)
ALE	Associazione Lavoratori Emergenti – Unione Generale del Lavoro provincia di Torino (Catholic-inspired Precarious worker union, part of UIL)
Aska	CSOA – Askatasuna (Occupied social centre)
Attac	Attac Torino (Local branch of the international Attac network: www.attac.org)
CasaC	Fondazine Casa della Carita' Onlus ("House of charity foundation," catholic vocational training centre)
Cecchi	Centro giovanile Cecchi Point (Neighbourhood art and educational centre)
CGIL	Confederazione Generale Italiana del Lavoro (Post-Communist confederation of trade unions)

CISL	Confederazione Italiana Sindacati Lavoratori (Catholic confederation of trade unions)
COBAS	Confederazione dei Cobas della provincia di Torino (grassroot confederation of trade unions)
CPO	Centri Per l'Occupazione – Unione Italiana Lavoratori provincia di Torino (Leftist Precarious worker union, part of UIL)
CUB	Confederazione Unitaria di Base provincia di Torino (grassroot confederation of trade unions)
FIOM	Federazione Impiegati Operai Metallurgici – Confederazione Generale Lavoratori Italiani della Provincia di Torino (Post-Communist metalworkers union, part of CGIL)
Gabrio	CSOA Gabrio (Occupied social centre)
Gioc	Gioventù Operaia Cristiana ("Young Christian Workers" Association aiming at education, training and evangelization)
Idea	Associazione Idea Lavoro Onlus (Work guidance and vocational training association)
IDV	Italia dei valori ("Italy of Values," centrist, populist and anti-corruption party founded in 1998)
Kairos	Consorzio sociale Kairos (A social purpose company, consortium of social cooperatives)
LADX	La Destra
LN	Lega Nord per la indipendenza della Padania ("North League for the Independence of Padania," federalist and regionalist political party founded in 1991)
MODERATI	Moderati per il Piemonte ("Moderates for Piedmont," regional centrist political party active in Piedmont founded in 2006)
NIDIL	Nuove Identità del Lavoro – Confederazione Generale Italiana dei Lavoratori provincia di Torino (Post-Communist Precarious worker union, part of CGIL)
Orso	Cooperativa ORSO (Social cooperative working on active labor policies)
P-ecare	Collettivo Comdata Torino (Informal worker group of the Comdata enterprise)
P-pr	Comitato precario provincia di Torino (Precarious worker group of the Province of Turin)
P-ric	Rete Nazionale Ricercatori Precari nodo di Torino (Local branch of the National network of precarious researchers)

P-scuola	Autoconvocati Precari Scuola Torino (Turin precarious worker group of the Ministry of Education)
P-to	Torino Precaria Torino (Turin precarious worker group)
Pastorale	Pastorale del lavoro (Diocesan pastoral council on labor issues)
PD	Partito Democratico ("Democratic party," social-democratic political party founded in 2007, inheritor of both the PCI and partially DC)
PDCI	Partito dei Comunisti Italiani ("Party of Italian Communists," communist party founded in 1998)
PDL	Popolo delle libertà ("The People of Freedom," centre-right party founded in 2009)
RC	Partito della Rifondazione Comunista ("Communist Refoundation Party," communist party founded in 1991)
Re-migr	Associazione Animazione Interculturale ("Intecultural association for animation" association working on the issue of cultural mediation)
SD	Sinistra Democratica ("Democratic Left" was a democratic socialist political party founded in 2007 and dissolved in 2010)
UIL	Unione Italiana del Lavoro Lavoratori (Leftist confederation of trade unions)

Notes

1. Borgatti and Halgin suggest distinguishing "network theory" from "theory of networks." As they stress, the "network theory" is about the consequences of network variables, whereas the theory of networks refers to explanations of a networks' structure (Borgatti and Halgin 2011: 1).
2. The level of homophily is given by the percentage of external ties minus the percentage of internal ties. Its value "can range from 1 to −1 and can be seen as a measure of the extent a group chooses themselves a value of −1 showing homophily and a value of +1 showing heterophily" (Borgatti et al. 2002).
3. "Given a partition of a network into a number of mutually exclusive groups (different cultural heritage) then the E-I index is the number of ties external to the groups minus the number of ties that are internal to the group divided by the total number of ties" (Borgatti et al. 2002). Indeed, the only way to statistically assess if the level of homophily is above the random chance is to use a permutation test assessing the possibility of random ties against the actual network empirically mapped. However, the problem we have to face is that we are not using a natural partition (that is either you are A or B, you cannot be anything in between) but an ideological affiliation, which permeates the society but does not divide it into two mutually exclusive parts since we have third parties.

4. Given a network of N actors, a subset of node G (the group) and the subset of node V (those actors which mentioned at least one actor of G), the normalized indegree group centrality = V/N – G.

5. It is a percentage calculated as the number of incoming ties the actor over the maximum possible degree. Thus the group indegree is the average score of coalition members.

6. In-Bonacich power weights the incoming centrality of each node by the incoming centrality of its alters. Therefore it is not only a matter of receiving ties, but also to consider from whom they are coming.

7. For abbreviations see Annex 1; other features are presented in detail in Baglioni and Giugni and Bassoli and Cinalli (this volume).

8. See Bassoli and Cinalli in this volume for further details on the measure applied on the project network only. As regards the information network, Turin has Density matrix a core density of 0.36 (fitness equal to 0.506), Kielce 0.492 (fitness 0.528).

9. HI index ranges between −1 (maximal homophily) and +1 (maximal heterophily).

10. The test has been run using Ucinet (Borgatti et al. 2002) using the E-I test with 50 thousand permutations.

11. This clique is not among different trade unions but within the same confederation, since both FIOM and NIDIL are confederated of CGIL.

12. Using the Anova routine (Borgatti et al. 2002), it is possible to check the statistical significance of the distribution of one variable against another. The analysis of variance is based on a permutation test to generate the significance level so that standard assumptions on independence and random sampling are not required. In both cities the eigenvector centrality variance can be (partially) explained by ideological background of the involved associations.

References

Adam, S. and H. Kriesi (2007) "The Advocacy Coalition Framework: Innovations and Clarifications," in Sabatier, P. A. (ed.), *Theories of the Policy Process* (Boulder: Westview Press).

Bassoli, M. and M. Cinalli (forthcoming) "Political Participation of Local Publics in the Unemployment Field: A Comparison of Lyon and Turin," *Social Movement Studies*.

Bassoli, M. and C. Pincella (2010) "Reproducing Cultural Goods as a Collective Effort of Identity Building in Italy," in *ESA Research Network Sociology of Culture*, presented at the Midterm Conference: Culture and the Making of Worlds, ESA Research Network Sociology of Culture, Milano.

Biorcio, R. (2007) "Democrazia e populismo nella Seconda Repubblica," in Maraffi, M. (ed.), *Gli italiani e la politica* (Bologna: Il Mulino).

Borgatti, S. P. (2002) *NetDraw Software for Network Visualization* (Lexington, KY: Analytic Technologies).

Borgatti, S. P. and D. S. Halgin (2011) "'On Network Theory'," *Organization Science*, 22, 1168–1181.

Borgatti, S. P., M. G. Everett, and L.C Freeman (2002) *Ucinet for Windows: Software for Social Network Analysis* (Harvard, MA: Analytic Technologies).

Christopoulos, D. (2006) "Relational Attributes of Political Entrepreneurs: A Network Perspective," *Journal of European Public Policy*, 13, 757–778.

della Porta, D. and M. Diani (2006) *Social Movements: An Introduction* (Oxford: Blackwell).

Del Pero, M. (2003) "Containing Containment: Rethinking Italy's Experience during the Cold War," *Journal of Modern Italian Studies*, 8, 532–555.

Diamanti, I. (2009) *Mappe dell'Italia politica bianco, rosso, verde, azzurro ... e tricolore* (Bologna: Il Mulino).

Diani, M. and I. Bison (2004) "Organizations, Coalitions, and Movements," *Theory and Society*, 33, 281–309.

Ekiert, G. and J. Kubik (1999) *Rebellious Civil Society: Popular Protest and Democratic Consolidation in Poland* (Ann Arbor, MI: University of Michigan Press).

Everett, M. G. and S. P. Borgatti (2005) "Extending Centrality," in Carrington, P. J., J. Scott, and S. Wasserman (eds), *Models and Methods in Social Network Analysis* (Cambridge/New York: Cambridge University Press).

Freeman, L. C. (1978) "Centrality in Social Networks Conceptual Clarification," *Social Networks* 1, 215–239.

Gliński, P. (2006) *Style działań organizacji pozarządowych w Polsce: grupy interesu czy pożytku publicznego?* (Warsaw: IFiS PAN).

Gualtieri, R. (2004) "The Italian Political System and Détente (1963–1981)," *Journal of Modern Italian Studies*, 9, 428–449.

Ignazi, P. and C. Ysmal (1998) *The Organization of Political Parties in Southern Europe* (Westport: Praeger).

Knoke, K. and S. Yang (2008) *Social Network Analysis* (Los Angeles: Sage).

Krackhardt, K. (1998) "Simmelian Ties: Super Strong and Sticky," in Kramer, R. and M. Neale (eds), *Power and Influence in Organizations* (Thousand Oaks, CA: Sage).

Krackhardt, D. and R. N. Stern (1988) "Informal Networks and Organizational Crises: An Experimental Simulation," *Social Psychology Quarterly*, 51, 123–140.

Leś, E. (2000) *Od filantropii do pomocniczości: Studium porównawcze rozwoju i dzialalnosci organizacji spolecznych* (Warszawa: Dom Wydaw, ELIPSA).

Linz, J. J. and A. Stepan (1996) *Problems of Democratic Transition and Consolidation: Southern Europe, South America and Post-Communist Europe* (Baltimore/London: John's Hopkins University Press).

Marody, M. and S. Mandes (2007) "Religijność a tożsamość narodowa Polaków," in Marody, M. (ed.), *Wymiary życia społecznego: Polska na przełomie XX i XXI w.* (Warsaw: Scholar).

McPherson, M., L. Smith-Lovin, and J. M. Cook (2001) "Birds of a Feather: Homophily in Social Networks," *Annual Review of Sociology*, 27, 415–444.

Moro, G. and I. Vannini (2006) *Italian Civil Society Facing New Challenges* (CIVICUS Civil Society Index Report for Italy, Fondaca).

Oliver, P. and H. Johnston (2000) "What a Good Idea! Ideologies and Frames in Social Movement Research," *Mobilization*, 5, 37–54.

Osa, M. (2003) "Networks in Opposition: Linking Organizations through Activists in the Polish People's Republic," in Diani, M. and D. McAdam (eds), *Social Movements and Networks* (Oxford/New York: Oxford University Press).

Ost, D. (1990) *Solidarity and the Politics of Anti-Politics: Opposition and Reform in Poland since 1998* (Philadelphia: Temple University Press).

Ost, D. (2007) *Klęska "Solidarności": gniew i polityka w postkomunistycznej Europie* (Warszawa: Muza).

Pizzorno, A. (1993) *Le radici della politica assoluta e altri saggi* (Milano: Feltrinelli).

Rose-Ackerman, S. (2008) "The Voluntary Sector and Public Participation: The Case of Hungary," *Annals of Public and Cooperative Economics*, 79, 601–623.

Rymsza, M. (2007) "Polityka państwa wobec sektora obywatelskiego w Polsce w latach 1989–2007," in Rymsza, M., G. Markowski, and M. Dudkiewicz (eds), *Państwo a trzeci sektor* (Warsaw: ISP).

Sabatier, P. A. and C. Weible (2007) "The Advocacy Coalition Framework: Innovations and Clarifications," in Sabatier, P. A. (ed.), *Theories of the Policy Process* (Boulder: Westview Press).

Salvati, M. (2003) "Behind the Cold War: Rethinking the Left, the State and Civil Society in Italy (1940s–1970s)," *Journal of Modern Italian Studies*, 8, 556–577.

Sartori, G. (1976) *Parties and Party Systems: A Framework for Analysis* (Cambridge: Cambridge University Press).

Snow, D. (2004) "Framing Process, Ideology and Discursive Field," in Snow, D., S. H. Soule, and H. Kriesi (eds), *The Blackwell Companion to Social Movements* (Oxford: Blackwell).

Thatcher, M. (1998) "The Development of Policy Network Analyses: From Modest Origins to Overarching Frameworks," *Journal of Theoretical Politics*, 10, 389–416.

Theiss, M. (2011) "The National Context of Local Social Policy in the Field of Youth Unemployment Exclusion," paper presented at Conference of European Consortium for Political Research (ECPR), 26.07.2011, Reykjavík.

Zafonte, M. and P. A. Sabatier (1998) "Shared Beliefs and Imposed Interdependencies as Determinants of Ally Networks in Overlapping Subsystems," *Journal of Theoretical Politics*, 10, 473–505.

9
Mind the Gap: Local Civil Society Organizations and the European Union

Christian Lahusen

Introduction

Civil society has been an important issue to the European Union (EU) since the 1990s because European institutions are convinced that civil society organizations can solve pending societal problems, represent the needs and interests of constituencies with no voice in the policy-making process, and generally increase the quality of democratic governance across the European, national, and local levels. These arguments also apply to employment and labor market policies. When youth unemployment rates rose again in reaction to the 2008 economic crisis, social non-governmental organizations (NGOs) were recognized as important intermediate actors within this policy field. Their activities have been strongly welcomed by European institutions. In the European employment observatory review on youth employment measures from 2010, the European Commission identified civil society organizations (CSOs) as important actors and called "for a closer involvement of such organizations in both the design and implementation of youth policies" (European Commission 2011). Consequently, EU institutions have engaged in more structured forms of dialogue with CSOs (European Parliament 2008). For example, in 2005, the European Council of Ministers adopted a resolution on youth policies to establish structured dialogue among EU institutions, member states, and young people and their organizations (Council of the European Union 2005). The European Youth Forum is formally included as the EU institutions' primary partner. Since 2007, several rounds of debate have been launched, consisting of various consultations at the European and national levels. Priorities have been identified through cooperation with the Council of Youth Ministers and consecutive Presidencies of the Council (Council of the European Union 2011). Since early 2010, the thematic priority defined by the Spanish, Belgian, and Hungarian governments during their Presidency of the Council has been youth employment.

As a reaction to these developments, social science researchers have been paying more attention to the role of organized civil society at the EU level, documenting the gradual growth in this field, analyzing its involvement in European policy-making processes, and discussing its ability to increase the democratic quality of European policy-making and implementation (Smismans 2006; Kröger 2008; Ruzza and Bozzini 2008; della Porta and Caiani 2009; Kohler-Koch 2010; Liebert and Trenz 2010; Steffek and Hahn 2010; Kohler-Koch and Quittkat 2013). However, less evidence is available about the relationship between local civil societies and EU institutions. If civil society indeed plays an important role in solving problems related to youth unemployment, and if solutions are to be found at the local level too, then several questions must be answered. What relations do local CSOs maintain with the EU? Is the EU a reference point for local civil societies at all? Do local CSOs maintain contact with European institutions, or is there a gap between them despite their public claims?

Relevant studies tend to draw an inconclusive picture, although they do indicate a rather pronounced gap between European institutions and local civil societies. For instance, research on political participation and social capital has shown that civil society organizations are not necessarily successful in mediating between citizens and EU institutions. While members of local CSOs exhibit stronger identification with the EU, support for the EU is not higher (Maloney and van Deth 2008 and 2010). It is quite probable that the mediating effect varies across issues and types of organizations. European institutions prefer more conventional forms of interest aggregation and representation while maintaining greater distance from more contentious groups (Marks and McAdam 1999; Rucht 2001; Lahusen 2004; Balme and Chabanet 2008). Finally, local CSOs might recognize the importance of the EU yet be tied to the exigencies of their immediate contexts. Consequently, even European CSO federations are not necessarily able to secure the commitment of their grassroots constituencies (Lahusen and Jauß 2001; Petrova and Tarrow 2007; Tarrow 1998: 190–192; della Porta and Tarrow 2005).

In the following chapter, evidence on the relationship between local CSOs and European institutions will be presented for a specific organizational sector, namely, organizations dealing with youth unemployment-related problems. This focus on a specific sector of local civil society certainly limits the possibilities for generalizing conclusions. However, it has the immediate advantage of disentangling the heterogeneous groups of civil society organizations and concentrating on one organizational field in which the EU has expressed an explicit intention to pursue policy changes. Therefore, I will draw on the original data from the organizational survey for the research project on which this book is based (see Baglioni and Giugni in this volume). The subsequent analysis will examine the organizational relationships between local CSOs and EU institutions in the cities of Cologne, Geneva, Kielce, Lisbon, Lyons, and Turin. I will describe the quantity and quality of organizational contacts and relations that local CSOs maintain with the EU. These insights will help identify organizational links or gaps between the two levels. Moreover, I will try to explain the descriptive findings by isolating the organizational factors that promote or hinder local–European linkages. Before moving on to the empirical findings, I must discuss the guiding research assumptions and the data in more detail.

Theoretical assumptions and research hypotheses

This study of organizational relations between local civil societies and EU institutions is guided by a number of assumptions about their nature and the main influencing factors. I highlight four assumptions, two related to the demand and supply sides of organizational relations, and two centered on specific traits of those relations. These assumptions focus on different, partially conflicting explanatory factors that contribute to specific research hypotheses.

First, I propose considering the *supply side* and argue that formalized and comparatively bigger civil society organizations are the most likely to maintain contact with EU institutions because they have a greater need for funds, information, and influence in order to guarantee organizational maintenance and legitimize their work. Moreover, such organizations are also marked more strongly by internal differentiation along organizational functions, tasks, and targets, thus making it more probable that they will have developed specialized units devoted to EU relations. This assumption builds on early organizational theory (Merton 1957; Michels 1962; Etzioni 1964), which argued that organizations follow a self-reinforcing process of formalization and bureaucratization that has unintended effects on internal processes and external relations. Once created, organizations will begin to focus on their own requirements or organizational needs. Consequently, organizational maintenance becomes a core priority, sometimes to the detriment of that organization's initial mission. I therefore assume that civil society organizations will develop more strategic relations with their surrounding environments – the EU included – in order to guarantee their own maintenance, even if their goals do not necessarily include a European dimension or their missions involve critical stances toward the EU and its policies. This strategic orientation will be more pronounced among bigger CSOs with more formalized organizational structures because they will have developed stronger needs for funding, information, and support from public authorities such as European ones. Consequently, I propose my first hypothesis: The extent to which CSOs maintain contact with EU institutions depends on the size, formalization level, and internal differentiations of those organizations.

Second, with regard to the *demand side*, I assume that decisions taken by local CSOs with respect to their organizational contacts are shaped by institutionalized opportunities and assets at the European level, among others. The EU has committed itself to supporting civil society through funding, information, organizational support, and symbolic recognition. Moreover, the EU provides a series of opportunities for CSOs to participate in developing and implementing European policies in order to make European governance more effective. Research has demonstrated that these institutionalized assets and opportunities in the EU have encouraged the formation of a supranational field of European interest groups (Greenwood 2003; Bouwen 2004; Balme and Chabanet 2008). Additionally, scholars argue that the EU is a multi-level system that is open to public interest groups from the national and regional levels (Eising 2004; Klüver 2010; Woll and Jacquot 2010). Euro-groups in particular work as intermediaries or information brokers that help national or regional actors to access European funds, consultations, and legislative processes in addition to any related opportunities these actors might have at the national or local levels (Ruzza and Bozzini 2008). Following these observations, it seems plausible to maintain that the EU has established a growing demand for civil society participation that encourages local CSOs to also engage in social relations with EU institutions. This is true with respect to youth unemployment issues. However, given the fact that youth unemployment touches a number of areas such as labor relations and poverty, migration, gender, and disabilities, it is more useful to also distinguish among the various activity domains to which these CSOs are committed. I hypothesize that the EU's attraction should be particularly strong for agencies working in policy fields for which the EU has proper legislative competencies. Hence, the EU relations among local CSOs should vary considerably among policy fields. Organizations working on behalf of women, for instance, should be more involved with the EU compared to CSOs focusing on disabled people and migrants, and organizations operating in the fields of business and labor relations should be more active than CSOs dealing with poverty. These arguments allow formulating another research hypothesis: Local CSOs whose activity domains center on Europeanized policy fields will maintain more EU relations than those working in other areas.

Third, debates about the process of European integration tend to focus on the pronounced gap between the EU and the ordinary citizen, which has been criticized by academics (Neunreither 1995; Erikson and Fossum 2000) and European institutions alike (European Commission 2006). While civil societies have been heralded as a means of overcoming this gap (Smismans 2003), the distance between European institutions and local civil societies still prevails, as documented by previous research (Lahusen 2004; Smismans 2006; Petrova and Tarrow 2007; Steffek and Hahn 2010). This assumption is based on an insight stressed particularly by scholars devoted to the study of European multi-level governance (Marks et al. 1996; Bache and Flinders 2004). According to this concept, the EU covers several policy-making fields – European, national, regional, and local. These are interdependent; however, each level exhibits its own set of policy agendas, political actors, and working rules. The EU is thus an institutionalized arena that organizes and limits the access and participation of political actors from other policy levels (Marks and McAdam 1999; Balme and Chabanet 2008). Consequently, even if multi-level governance implies interdependence among the various policy fields, the participation of local policy actors depends on their readiness and ability to raise their voices in the European arena. In accordance with this argument, I propose the following hypothesis: Working relations with the EU are more diffused among CSOs with multi-level organizational structures and international scopes of action. Civil society organizations should have more difficulty in working with European institutions if their areas of operation are situated only at local levels. Their chances of engaging with EU institutions rise as soon as they acquire a multi-level structure that assures their access and presence at the EU level.

Fourth, it is plausible to assume that organizational relations with EU institutions depend not only on structure but also on the respective compatibility of their action repertoires and organizational routines. Scholarly writing describes the EU arena as a relatively closed policy domain dominated by conventional forms of interest intermediation and a technocratic style of political deliberation and policy-making.

Unconventional, contentious, or disruptive actors and activities remain alien to the institutionalized preferences associated with such deliberation (Marks and McAdam 1999; Rucht 2001; Lahusen 2004; Balme and Chabanet 2008). The policy research concepts of *goodness of fit* or *misfit* can be applied here (Börzel 1999; Héritier et al. 2001; Knill, Tosun, and Bauer 2009). In this case, I assume that the fit or misfit applies to organizational missions and action repertoires as well. That is, organizations will differ in their probability of maintaining relations with EU institutions based on whether their routines and activities fit the standard operating procedures of EU policy-making. Two hypotheses can be derived from this assumption. On the one hand, I expect that local CSOs devoted to disruptive and militant activities (e.g., sit-ins, rallies) would be less likely to relate to EU institutions than those concentrating on education, training, and conventional forms of interest representation. On the other, I intend to examine whether this misfit extends to politicization. The guiding assumption here is that CSOs devoted to political events should be less likely to work with the EU compared to those focusing on cultural, intellectual, educational, leisure, and sports activities.

Overall, these assumptions fuse into a specific profile of the CSOs I expect will maintain more extensive contact with EU institutions: The larger, more formalized CSOs with multi-level structures and more conventional behavior, which are working in the areas of women, business, or labor relations, will be strongly linked to EU institutions. Smaller, less formally organized groups with more contentious action repertoires and strong local biases will have little contact with EU institutions.

Data, methods and operationalization

The following empirical analysis must clarify whether these assumptions are correct. For this purpose, I will make use of the data gathered by the Younex research team, which has already been presented systematically in this book (see Baglioni and Giugni in this volume). The organizational sample consists of 161 civil society organizations dealing with youth unemployment issues from Cologne, Geneva, Kielce, Lisbon, Lyons, and Turin; the city of Karlstad was not included in this analysis.[1] This sample is certainly not representative of the local civil societies in the six cities under analysis. However, it is an approximate full-population survey in the specific issue field that interests us. For this reason, it seems justifiable to conduct exploratory data analyses to describe the quantity of EU relations and discuss their specific organizational traits.

This objective requires us first to operationalize the various assumptions and hypotheses identified above. EU relations (the dependent variable) will be measured by three items from the questionnaire: the affirmation that a given organization receives some funding from the EU, the confirmation that the CSO seeks contact with EU institutions, and the acknowledgment that it receives official information from those institutions. Moreover, for organizations seeking contact, the data include information about the quality of those contacts – the friendliness or hostility of the EU institutions toward them. These questions give us good indicators of the perceived interrelations (seeking and receiving) and of the important areas of operation (funds, consultations, information) at these organizations.

Moreover, I operationalized the assumptions and hypotheses indicated above along the following lines. First, the effect of organizational traits will be measured by three datasets: organizational size, by means of the number of full-time staff members and the annual budget; formality, by reference to the existence of an organizational constitution and formal positions (i.e., a board and elected officers); and internal differentiation, with regard to the existence of committees or working groups addressing specific issues.[2] Second, I propose analyzing the different opportunities and assets provided by the EU by looking at the issues to which CSOs are committed. I will assume that the EU's attraction is marked only within a few specific policy fields, probably those where the EU itself is more active (i.e., women, business, and labor relations). I will use a questionnaire item that asked organizations to list the sectors in which they had been active during the last 12 months. That list consisted of 29 activity domains ranging from poverty to health, education, or the environment.[3]

Third, I aim to check the potential effect of the EU's multi-level governance and the related need of CSOs to develop multi-level organizational structures by looking at two questions from the guidelines. Interviewees were asked to indicate whether their organizations were members of any regional, national, and/or international organizations, as well as whether their CSOs were active within any of several geographical areas ranging from local neighborhoods to the EU.[4] Finally, the assumption of misfit, or the incompatibility of actions, will be assessed by taking a look at the activities and events organized by local CSOs. I will assume that conventional forms of consultation and service delivery are the preferred options among EU institutions. Three sets of responses will be used. Organizational representatives specified the main actions their organizations used to reach their aims. Here,

I will focus on the following items: "mobilizing members through protest, demonstrations, and direct actions"; "interest representation and lobbying institutions"; and "political education of citizens and raising awareness," assuming that the likelihood of having EU relations is stronger among CSOs focusing on the latter and weaker among those committed to mobilizing members through more controversial actions. Respondents were also asked which kinds of activities they conducted specifically for unemployed and precariously employed people. For the purposes of this study, I will focus on two: sit-ins and rallies.[5] Finally, I want to check whether EU relations are mediated by the degree of politicization. Hence, I draw on information about the type and frequency of events put on by local CSOs. Two areas of work, political and cultural events, will be considered, and it will be assumed that organizations active in the former arena are less connected to the EU than the latter.[6]

European affairs among local civil society organizations

Table 9.1 summarizes my main findings with regard to the organizational relations between local CSOs and EU institutions, the most striking of which is that a minority of organizations confirmed any connections to the EU. One out of ten organizations said it receives funding from the EU, one out of five reported obtaining official information from the EU, and one out of four is seeking contact with EU institutions. A closer look at this last group shows that out of these 34 organizations, most tend to play an active role; however, almost every other respondent seeking contact reported experiencing hostility. It is interesting to note that social movement organizations are among the organizations that are not maintaining any contact to the EU, with the exception of one that did receive official information. However, it is necessary to keep in mind that 22.4% of all CSOs either could not or would not answer the questions regarding financial and contact information. Nearly one out of five cases did not address the question of official information either.

These findings can be best assessed when compared to the number of contacts these organizations have with national institutions, specifically national parliaments or governments. In general, the number of CSOs working with national institutions is higher than those dealing with the EU. In fact, 14.3% of local CSOs said they receive national funding (126 cases; 21.7% did not know), compared to 9.3% of those receiving EU funds. 32.2% acknowledged receipt of official information from their national parliaments or governments (46 out of 161 cases are

Table 9.1   Relations with EU institutions (by percentage)

	No %	Yes %	Don't know/ refuse %	Total N
Funding institution: European Union	68.2	9.4	22.4[a]	161
Does your organization receive official information from EU institutions?	81.4	18.6	–	129
Contacts with public authorities: EU institutions				
Our organization seeks contact[b]	53.2	24.5	22.3	139
The EU hardly listens to our organization although our organization does try to influence them.		*5.8*		
Sometimes receives our organization with hostility and other times is welcoming to us.		*4.3*		
Is friendly to our organization, but our organization initiates most of the contact.		*12.2*		
Frequently seeks the advice of our organization.		*2.2*		

[a] Most of those organizations were unable or unwilling to specify whether they had public funding, including grants from the EU.
[b] The questionnaire inquiry was formulated this way: "Does not seek any contact" for those not answering the statements in italics. To facilitate my analysis, I recoded the variable. Those not seeking contact are now coded as "no," those affirming any of the statements in italics were coded as "seeking contacts."

missing), and 56.8% noted that they seek contact from these institutions (22 cases are missing; 18 did not know how to answer), compared to 18.6% and 24.5% of those reporting contact with EU institutions. Hence, local CSOs are mainly linked to their immediate organizational environments, and institutional relations diminish as they move from the national to the European level.

Another observation that illustrates the distance between local civil society organizations from both national and EU levels is provided in Table 9.2, which summarizes the geographical areas of operation for the various organizations interviewed. The data demonstrate that the vast number of local CSOs – more than two-thirds – works at the city and regional levels. One out of three operates at the national level, and less

Table 9.2 Areas of activity (by percentage)

In which of these geographical areas is your organization/group active?	%	(N)	Total N (missing)
Only in the local neighborhood	9.9	(14)	142 (19)
In the city in general	69.1	(96)	139 (22)
In the wider region/province	70.0	(98)	140 (21)
Throughout the whole country	34.3	(48)	140 (21)
In other countries	17.0	(24)	141 (20)
At the European Union level	19.9	(28)	141 (20)

than 20% are active internationally. A closer inspection of the sample revealed that social movement organizations are strongly attached to the local level; out of the 12 organizations that responded, ten were active at the city level, seven at the regional, three at the national, and none at the European.

Broken down by country of origin, the data show that CSOs from Turin and Lyons, as well as some from Lisbon, are much more connected to the EU than the organizations from Polish and German cities. For instance, every other French organization and one out of four Italian CSOs reported receiving funds from EU institutions, while none of the groups from Kielce and Cologne did. Information about contact with the EU paints a similar picture. One out of three groups from Turin and Lyons seeks contacts, and two out of three CSOs from Lisbon do, but this is true only for one out of six in the Polish and German groups. One out of three Portuguese and French organizations receives official information from the EU, but this is only true for one or two organizations in the other countries. CSOs from Geneva do have some relations with the EU. Funding does not play the expected role, but four CSOs reported seeking contact and two said to receive information.

Overall, the findings corroborate the assumption of a marked gap between local civil societies and EU institutions, particularly among social movement organizations with a stronger focus on mobilization and collective protest. EU relations are more developed in Turin, Lyons, and Lisbon, and much less so among the other cities. This is probably due to the fact that the state and public spheres are less favorable to the sample organizations from these three cities in terms of state funding, public support, and political involvement, when compared, for instance, to Cologne. Local CSOs from these cities might be more interested in reaching out to the EU in search of institutional and financial support in order to circumvent potential obstacles at the local and national levels. This strategy of *externalization* is well documented for social movement organizations and political protesters (Imig and Tarrow 2001; Chabanet 2008; della Porta and Caiani 2009: 52). The lower intensity of EU relations among German CSOs conforms to the findings of previous research, which testifies to a pronounced integration of civil society organizations within the corporatist structures of the German welfare system (Salamon and Anheier 1998). The weak EU ties of CSOs in Kielce might be explained by Poland's recent accession to the EU.

Determining factors in EU relations

The distance between local civil society organizations and EU institutions requires explanation. Table 9.3 deals with the first assumption, namely the supply side and thus with the question of whether EU relations depend on the organizational traits of local CSOs, particularly their size, degree of formalization, and internal differentiation. Organizations may develop a stronger propensity to engage in contact with the EU as they grow and formalize, irrespective of their missions or positions toward EU policies. Organizational maintenance thus becomes the assumed driving force in local CSOs' EU relations. This assumption is largely corroborated by my findings in Table 9.3.

Table 9.3 shows that organization size in terms of staff and annual budget correlates mostly significantly with EU relations. The same is true for committees and work groups dealing with specific issues. CSOs with internal units are either more willing or better able to exchange

Table 9.3   Organizational traits (Cramer's V coefficients and number of cases)

Relations with the EU	EU funding		Receives official information		Contact with EU institutions	
	coeff.	N	coeff.	N	coeff.	N
Full-time staff	.204*	123	.271**	125	.343***	104
Annual operating budget	.248**	112	.167	113	.288**	94
Constitution	.123	123	.173**	129	.279***	106
Board	−.035	125	.127	129	.089	108
Leader/President	.221**	125	.190**	129	.266***	108
Treasurer	.051	123	.096	127	.060	107
Committees/Work groups	.137	125	.247***	129	.310***	108

$*p < .10; **p < .05; ***p < .01.$

views and information with the EU. With regard to formal positions, having a constitution and a designated leader or president makes a difference. However, not all formal positions are relevant (e.g., boards and treasurers, as well as positions not included in this table such as secretaries and spokespeople). The findings illustrate that organizational traits do not share the same relevancy across the board. In fact, EU funding is correlated significantly with budget, staff size, and the existence of a leader or president only. It seems as though formal leadership and working power play major roles when money is at stake. With a bigger budget, the likelihood increases that the organization will apply for and receive EU funding. However, it is necessary to keep in mind that almost one out of four CSOs proved unable or unwilling to state whether public funding had been received, and this may dilute the above findings.

The difference between receiving official information from the EU and seeking contact is mainly in the clarity and significance of the relationship. Organizational traits are more clearly associated with the CSOs' readiness to contact the EU than to their likelihood of being contacted by EU institutions. This could be because receiving information is a rather blurry process, given the fact that local CSOs might receive official EU information on the basis of their own contact efforts, via extended mailing lists, or by means of national and international memberships. Among other possibilities, it could be that EU institutions provide information to those organizations working in policy fields that are of particular importance to European policy initiatives regardless of the size or formality of the local CSOs involved.

Consequently, and following the second assumption we argue that EU relations with local CSOs might also be determined by the *demand side*, i.e., the EU's readiness to seek out the support of local CSOs. This institutional demand can be measured by distinguishing among various policy fields. Local CSOs working on issues where the EU has policy-making competency and has been developing policy initiatives might be more inclined toward contacting EU institutions or capitalizing on assets and opportunities provided by the EU. Table 9.4 shows the differences among a number of policy fields, along with targeted groups and constituencies. It disproves my second assumption because it shows that EU relations with local CSOs are not governed by either policy or issue fields. That is, it does not matter whether CSOs work on issues pertaining to women, disabled, or elderly people, or whether they focus on poverty, jobs, or consumer interests. Only CSOs working on two issues (business relations and youth) are particularly likely to seek contact with the EU, reflecting not only the prominence of market and business

Table 9.4   Policy fields (Cramer's V coefficients and number of cases)

Relations with the EU	EU funding (N = 125)	Receives official information (N = 129)	Contact with EU institutions (N = 108)
Target Groups			
Disabled	.094	.168**	.063
Pensioners, elderly	−.129	.144	−.078
Youth, students	.038	.109	.231**
Women	.132	.073	.105
Immigrants	.175*	.098	.143
Constituencies			
Business relations	.030	.094	.280**
Labor relations	−.012	.035	.072
Consumer's interests	−.053	.139	.141
precarity, unemployment	.088	.095	.058
Poverty	.060	.080	−.099

*$p < .10$; **$p < .05$; ***$p < .01$.

issues within European policies but also the visibility of EU initiatives targeting youth. Such efforts include the structured dialogue launched in 2005 among EU institutions, member states, and youth organizations (Council of the European Union 2005) or the flagship program Youth on the Move from 2010 (European Commission 2010).

However, this does not explain why organizations working on women's issues are not more clearly motivated to engage in EU relations, given the importance the EU has assigned to gender equality and mainstreaming. Almost all 29 issue fields included in the questionnaire proved to be causally unrelated to local organizations' propensity to seek EU funding and information. Hence, it does not matter whether local CSOs' fields are more or less Europeanized in terms of competency, opportunities, and assets. EU institutions are not necessarily the most convincing or appealing targets for local CSOs, even those working in fields where the EU claims to have a say and aims to arouse public debate and support. Other factors seem to play a much more important role in explaining EU relations.

A third reason that might increase the probability of local CSOs contacting the EU is provided by another organizational trait, namely, the multi-level structure of organizations. Earlier in this chapter, I argued that the EU is a multi-level system that involves local, national, and supranational arenas of political deliberation and policy-making, along with a full set of policy agendas, actors, and working rules. The EU is thus an institutional arena that requires CSOs to develop a complementary multi-level structure of organization in order to be able to participate in EU politics, communicate with EU institutions, and capitalize on the opportunities provided by the EU (Marks and McAdam 1999; Imig and Tarrow 2001; della Porta and Caiani 2009: 10–18). The findings presented in Table 9.5 show that this assumption is largely correct. Seeking contact and receiving information requires that local CSOs be present at the European level. Without a multi-level structure, the gap between local organizations and EU institutions prevails. The only exception to this rule is EU financing, which is statistically unrelated to the multi-level structure of affiliations and areas of operation. Being present at the EU level does not necessarily increase the likelihood of receiving European grants, nor does an absence exclude the possibility of being funded by the EU. Local CSOs can also participate in EU-financed programs organized by other public or non-state organizations.

With regard to the two other forms of EU relations, Table 9.5 illustrates that being present in other countries and at the EU level is a significant factor. Receiving official EU information is determined only by memberships in national and international federations, and a CSO's own geographical area of operation is not necessarily relevant. As mentioned before, local CSOs may well receive official information via their participation in national or international federations. The situation is different for the proactive contacts local CSOs pursue with the EU. Here, it seems essential to be individually represented or active at the international level.

Table 9.5 Organizational multi-level structures (Cramer's V coefficients and number of cases)

Relations with the EU	EU funding		Receives official information		Contact with EU institutions	
	coeff.	N	coeff.	N	coeff.	N
Membership						
Regional federation	.104	94	.111	108	.042	95
National federation	.150	96	.246***	110	.145	97
International federation	.101	96	.285***	110	.355***	97
Geographical area of operation						
Active in other countries	.100	111	.236**	111	.374***	98
Active at EU level	.089	111	.064	111	.274***	98

$*p < .10$; $**p < .05$; $***p < .01$.

Table 9.6 summarizes the findings with reference to the last hypothesis. It demonstrates that the types of events and activities conducted by local CSOs are associated with EU relations only partially. Following the argument introduced previously, I expected that the CSOs engaged in more political, contentious, and militant forms of action would be less likely to maintain EU relations, with regard to receiving funds and information as well as seeking contact with EU institutions. With reference to scholarly writing, I assumed that today's EU institutions were committed to a conventional and technocratic style of consultation and policy-making (Rucht 2001; Lahusen 2004; Balme and Chabanet 2008). CSOs with a more politicized and militant approach would therefore be less likely to be heard by or to approach the EU institutions, thus exposing a bilateral misfit between differing action repertoires and political approaches.

Table 9.6 illustrates that this assumption is only true in part, at least for local CSOs. Associations organizing events more frequently are among the group of organizations most strongly interrelated with EU institutions. This means that these organizations are generally more active within the public sphere, probably more visible, and more dependent on exchanging information with public authorities, the EU included.

Table 9.6   Events and action repertoires (Cramer's V coefficients and number of cases)

Relations with the EU	EU funding		Receives official information		Contact with EU institutions	
	coeff.	N	coeff.	N	coeff.	N
Events						
Frequency of all events (index)	.040	107	.232**	109	.451***	90
Culture, education, and leisure	.159*	119	.324***	122	.471***	102
Political events	−.274***	125	.119	129	.061	108
Main activities						
Mobilizing members	−.182**	124	.151*	129	.071	108
Interest representation/lobbying	−.179**	124	.170*	129	.075	108
Political education/awareness	−.055	124	.162*	129	.279***	108
Activities with jobless and precariously employed						
Sit-ins	−.044	116	.228***	126	−.021	105
Rallies	−.056	117	.065	128	.019	107

*p < .10; **p < .05; ***p < .01.3.

Two pieces of information seem to hint at the direction of a fit or misfit. Table 9.6 differentiates among activities and proves that CSOs organizing cultural, intellectual, educational, and sporting or leisure events are strongly and significantly connected to the EU institutions. This figure indicates that there is a stronger *fit* or compatibility between cultural activities and EU institutions. However, political events provide no reason to abstain from contacting the EU institutions. The same is true for action repertoires. The more moderate activities of political education and awareness raising are interrelated positively with EU contact. However, more aggressive forms of political interest aggregation and representation do not prohibit CSOs from exchanging information with EU institutions. The table also demonstrates that more militant behavior (mobilizing members, sit-ins) is a reason for receiving official information, even if the effect is weak. That is, activity and visibility seem to be more important than the specific types of action employed. In general, though, the correlations are rather feeble.

Hence, while there is a stronger fit, or affinity, between EU institutions and CSOs engaging in the realms of culture, education, and leisure, there is no significant misfit concerning political and controversial activities. This latter observation might be because political and militant activities do not necessarily imply hostility toward the EU. The picture changes, however, in the case of finances. When it comes to money, the misfit seems to emerge much more clearly. In fact, the findings reveal that CSOs with more militant behavior do receive less EU funding, although the correlation is not very strong. Moreover, activities directed only at the jobless and precariously employed do not interrelate with EU funding. Nevertheless, CSOs devoted to political events receive less EU funding, while those engaged in cultural, educational, intellectual, and leisure activities rely more often on this support. These differences might be due to the priorities of European funding schemes or the readiness of the respective CSOs. Again, the effect is moderate.

Discussion of findings

The data from the organizational survey show several patterns that govern the relations local CSOs in the six European cities under analysis maintain with the EU. Generally speaking, the data corroborate a rather extended gap between local CSOs and EU institutions. Only one out of four CSOs say they actively seek contact, one out of five receives official information, and only one out of ten gets funded by the EU. Moreover, the data highlight a series of beneficial conditions that raise the probability of CSOs bridging this gap. Differences emerged with regard to the type of relations the CSOs exhibited at the EU level. At approximately 25% of all CSOs, seeking contact was the most commonly stated form of interacting with the EU. This was the most proactive item in the survey and helped detect the main organizational features associated with EU affairs. Bigger CSOs with formalized structure and leadership and with specialized committees were tended to be more active in contacting the EU institutions. This was also the case among CSOs represented at the supranational level, for instance, as members of international federations. These findings illustrate that formal organization is an important factor affecting the likelihood of local civil society actors to engage in EU relations.

Issue fields and action repertoires matter less. However, some peculiarities must be noted. Organizations working in the areas of youth and business relations were more likely to communicate with the EU, and the same was true for those CSOs that were busily organizing a multiplicity of activities, primarily in the realms of culture, sports and leisure, and intellectual and educational events. This does not mean that organizations committed to political agendas and controversial behavior abstain from contacting EU institutions. The absence of significant correlations points to the fact that politicization and contentiousness is not necessarily a segregating factor; rather, these organizations are just as active in contacting the EU institutions as the average population. However, there is a bias toward linking EU relations to a cultural and educational mission. This finding demonstrates that the gap between local CSOs and EU institutions is smaller for less contentious areas of activity, where common agendas and interests seem to prevail.

The picture is less clear when focusing on official information from the EU. Generally speaking, the main findings summarized before apply here as well. The size, formalization, and internal differentiation of the organizations are as important in identifying the CSOs receiving official information as their multi-level structures. The intensity of activities and the commitment to organize cultural, educational, and leisure events was also positively correlated with EU relations. However, the data exposed smaller effects on a lower significance level. Most areas of activity had a positive effect on this item, even the more controversial and militant ones. Finally, being active at the EU level does not improve the chances that an organization will receive EU information. On the one hand, CSOs active at the EU level might still not be part of European policy deliberations. On the other, CSOs not active at the EU level might also receive official information. Indeed, whether a local CSO receives information depends not only on itself but also on the EU and other intermediaries. That is, CSOs not active at the EU might receive information through their memberships elsewhere, and the same could be true for smaller CSOs and for those committed to more contentious forms of action. Nonetheless, the patterns identified in this analysis still apply, even if in a more diluted manner.

With regard to the last link to the EU, funding, a couple of observations have to be made. The number of factors associated with EU funding was reduced markedly, and most of these correlations proved to be weaker and less significant. Only the size of the organization and the existence of a leader or president make any difference. The structure of an organization and its affiliations do not relate to EU funding. A decisive factor with regard to finances is the misfit between the activities of local CSOs and EU grants. The more CSOs engage in political events and protest-oriented forms of action, the less likely they are to receive EU funding. As soon as it comes to money, relations with the EU become more exclusive, thus segregating the more culturally focused and service-oriented organizations from the more controversial political groups.

These findings need to be taken with caution because the analyses involved a number of missing cases. However, with the required prudence, several patterns can be identified. Organizational traits are most closely interrelated with European affairs. In accordance with the first hypothesis, evidence corroborates the importance of organizational maintenance to EU relations. Moreover, the data also prove the third hypothesis to be true because organizations with a multi-level structure are more likely to communicate and exchange information with the EU institutions. The second hypothesis, the one related to the demand side, has been refuted. CSOs working on more Europeanized issues are not attracted more strongly toward the EU. There are almost no differences among the various fields, youth and business relations excluded. Finally, findings are mixed when referring to the fourth hypothesis about a misfit between the EU and local CSOs relating to organizational activities and action repertoires. The data prove that more active CSOs maintain EU relations more often. Additionally, there is a significant fit between the EU institutions and those organizations active in the areas of culture, sport, leisure, and education. The more controversial political groups are not necessarily excluded from information exchanges. However, funding seems to point in the direction of a misfit or segregation.

Conclusions

The findings presented so far provide further proof for the distance between local-level civil society organizations and the European arena. The fact that local CSOs tend to operate primarily on a local level is not very surprising, given the fact that these organizations are strongly rooted within local communities and that they are clearly committed to solving area problems and meeting the needs of the surrounding citizenry. They have developed organizational structures and action strategies to accomplish their missions in this specific context. It was to be expected that contact with national institutions would not play the same role as that with local public authorities. What is more surprising is the strongly reduced number of organizational relations with EU institutions, even though the CSOs interviewed in the organizational survey work in a field – youth unemployment and precarious work – to which those institutions are committed to bringing policy solutions.

The gap clearly contradicts the official EU rhetoric. In fact, EU institutions regularly tout the importance of civil societies and the need to involve CSOs more proactively to solve pressing societal problems and represent underserved minorities (Council of the European Union 2005; European Parliament 2008; European Commission 2011). However, my analysis shows that these claimed attempts are far from the reality. Moreover, I have found that only a specific group of local CSOs seems to engage in EU relations at all. This group consists of bigger and markedly formalized organizations that are already active at the local, national, and European levels alike, and which are clearly committed to organizing cultural, educational, and sport or leisure activities (e.g., concerts, exhibitions, lectures, debates, museum tours, courses, and competitions). On the contrary, smaller, less formalized CSOs more strongly restricted to local or regional areas of operation are quite distant from the EU. With regard to EU financing, militant and contentious groups tend to be more detached from EU institutions.

These observations illustrate the structural impediments that govern the relations between local CSOs and EU institutions. The EU has established its own political opportunity structure that could be conducive for civil society organizations seeking to secure their organizational maintenance, further their missions, and reach their goals (Marks and McAdam 1999; Imig and Tarrow 2001). These additional opportunities might even spur the Europeanization of local civil societies and the externalization or transnationalization of their work (Chabanet 2008; della Porta and

Caiani 2009; Ruzza and Bozzini 2008). However, the analysis conducted here demonstrates that this process is quite limited and most clearly tied to a certain type of civil society organization, namely, large, formalized CSOs active in the areas of culture, education, leisure, and sports.

At the same time, the EU's opportunity structure implies constraints and requirements that local CSOs reaching out to the supranational level need to meet: developing the necessary knowledge and skills, recruiting experienced staff, generating well-adapted working procedures, and maintaining offices or keeping regular contact with European federations (Rucht 2001; Lahusen 2004; della Porta and Caiani 2009). These requirements tend to marginalize or exclude civil society organizations, especially the smaller and less formalized actors. To a certain extent, these requirements seem to conflict with organizational needs and missions at the grassroots level (Imig and Tarrow 2001; Petrova and Tarrow 2007; Balme and Chabanet 2008).

The institutional structures and demands of the various arenas of organizational activity help to explain the apparent gap between local CSOs and EU institutions. However, the findings presented in this paper also show that this gap can be transcended. Formal organization is a core prerequisite for overcoming the institutionalized distance between the local and the European levels. The consolidation and formalization of an organization, the creation of specialized units or committees, and the hiring of full-time staff are, among other organizational decisions, important for building relations with EU institutions. Moreover, obtaining memberships in national and international federations bridges the distance between the local and European levels by establishing an organizational arrangement that mirrors the multi-level structure of the EU itself.

These prerequisites have various consequences. The implication is that constituencies, issues, and needs that are difficult to organize or that are only weakly organized (e.g., young people, poor people, unemployed, and migrants) will have fewer chances to reach out to the EU or receive its attention and support (Balme and Chabanet 2008; Chabanet and Faniel 2012; Jenkins 1983). They will be more frequently excluded from European politics and policy-making, deepening the democratic deficit and reducing the effectiveness of European governance (Sismans 2006; Kröger 2008; Steffek and Hahn 2010; Kohler-Koch and Quittkat 2013).

Formal organization seems to be a factor that is able to reduce the gap between local CSOs and EU institutions. However, this might entail non-intended consequences. According to classical organizational theory, formal organizations will tend to prioritize their own mainte-nance (Merton 1957; Etzioni 1964). EU relations become a functional prerequisite for securing organizational survival by allowing CSOs to raise the necessary funds, information, political support, or symbolic recognition. This does not mean that formal organizations will inevi-tably detach themselves from their initial missions, constituencies, programmatic positions, and action repertoires, but this is a general and realistic risk. Moreover, formal organization goes hand in hand with processes of standardization, bureaucratization, and professionalization (Michels 1962; McCarthy and Zald 1973; Staggenborg 1988). Hence, local civil societies raising voices at the EU level will need to use the speech of professionalized, standardized, and formalized ventures. More spontaneous, contentious, or innovative forms of collective association and activism will be ignored.

This selectivity is lamentable from a normative point of view because it deprives the EU of making important developments at the grassroots level. My findings have demonstrated that the EU does not necessarily discriminate proactively against the more overtly political and militant forms of interest aggregation and articulation. However, some tenden-cies are apparent when looking at EU funding and when comparing these organizations with the closer relationship between the EU and local CSOs working in cultural and educational fields.

Local civil societies might do without the support of the EU, if their ability to cultivate their roots within local communities and secure area support can be trusted. But is this true for the EU as well? Due to the apparent gap I corroborated in this chapter, the EU is not in a position to benefit from the input of local civil societies. This deficiency is cer-tainly not restricted to the institutions of the EU, but it is of particular importance there, given the fact that those institutions are farther away from the citizenry and thus more dependent on organized forms of intermediation. The EU does not contribute enough to transcend this gap. In times of crisis, the EU tends to fence itself off from local civil societies and the protest potential generated by the negative socio-economic and political developments. Under these conditions, political deliberations and policy-making at the EU level are grounded in the contributions from local civil societies only to a limited degree. They privilege formalized organizations and marginalize more spontane-ous and contentious groups, initiatives, and discourses. This situation is detaching the EU from the vibrant societal life at the local level. It is insulating the EU from contentious political conflicts, but it is also depriving it of social and political innovations.

Notes

1. The organizational survey for the overarching research project was also conducted in Karlstad, Sweden. This city will be excluded from our analysis because it has a very low number of civil society organizations dealing with youth unemployment. Moreover, these organizations' relations with the EU remain unclear in many cases. In fact, every other Swedish organization generated missing cases when asked about their contact with the EU

2. The variable *full-time staff* was recoded into three categories: no staff members, one to six staff members, and more than seven persons. The annual operating budget was recoded into three fractions: less than 50,000 Euros, 50,000–199,000 Euros, and more than 200,000 Euros. The variables measuring formality and international differentiations are binary (yes/no).

3. The respondents could choose from the following list of 29 items, answering either yes or no: poverty, health, disabled, pensioners/elderly, religious activities, education, sports, youth/students, culture/music/theater, peace/anti-militarism/conflict resolution, women, human rights, childcare/other children's services, politics, business relations, labor relations, job insecurity/precarity unemployment, consumers' interests, fair trade/ethical finances, family, employment/training, housing, crime, homosexuality, immigration, international cooperation, environment, alternative communication/media activism, and social integration.

4. All of these questions were coded as separate binary variables with yes/no answers.

5. These questions were also coded as separate binary variables (yes/no). Respondents were asked to answer this question for unemployed and precariously employed people separately. For my purposes, I constructed a combined binary variable that measured whether or not CSOs organized these kinds of activities for unemployed or precariously employed people.

6. The question was formulated as follows: "How frequently has your organization engaged in the following activities in the last two years?" The first variable to be tested used the responses to the following inquiry: "Organize targeted political events (lobbying, demonstrations, public meetings, strikes, etc.)." A binary variable was computed that discriminated between two groups of equal size: those that never organized political events and those committed to them in some way (from rarely to daily). For the opposite variable, I constructed an index on the basis of the following items: cultural events (concerts, exhibitions, performances), intellectual events (lectures, debates, conferences), educational activities (visits to museums, courses), and sports and leisure activities (competitions, fitness courses). I computed two equally sized groups of those who were conducting activities in this area rarely or regularly.

References

Bache, I. and M. Flinders (eds) (2004) *Multi-level Governance* (Oxford: Oxford University Press).

Balme, R. and D. Chabanet (2008) *European Governance and Democracy: Power and Protest in the EU* (Lanham, MD: Rowman and Littlefield).

Börzel, T. A. (1999) "Towards Convergence in Europe? Institutional Adaptation to Europeanization in Germany and Spain," *Journal of Common Market Studies*, 37, 573–596.

Bouwen, P. (2004) "Exchange Access Good for Access: A Comparative Study of Business Lobbying in the EU Institutions," *European Journal of Political Research*, 43, 337–369.

Chabanet, D. (2008) "When the Unemployed Challenge the European Union: The European Marches as a Mode of Externalization of Protest," *Mobilization*, 13, 311–322.

Chabanet, D. and J. Faniel (eds) (2012) *The Mobilization of the Unemployed in Europe: From Acquiescence to Protest?* (Houndmills: Palgrave).

Council of the European Union (2005) Resolution of the Council and of the Representatives of the Governments of the Member States, meeting within the Council, on addressing the concerns of young people in Europe – implementing the European Pact for Youth and promoting active citizenship. [2005/C 292/03].

Council of the European Union (2011) Draft Council Resolution of the Council and of the representatives of the Governments of the Member States, meeting within the Council on the structured dialogue with young people on youth employment, from 15 April 2011. [8664/11].

della Porta, D. and M. Caiani (2009) *Social Movements and Europeanization* (Oxford: Oxford University Press).

della Porta, D. and S. Tarrow (2005) *Transnational Protest and Global Activism* (Lanham, MD: Rowman & Littlefield).

Eising, R. (2004) "Multilevel Governance and Business Interests in the European Union," *Governance*, 17, 211–245.

Erikson, E. O. and J. E. Fossum (eds) (2000) *Democracy in the European Union: Integration through Deliberation?* (London: Routledge).

Etzioni, A. (1964) *Modern Organizations* (Englewood Cliffs, NJ: Prentice Hall).

European Commission (2006) White Paper on a European Communication Policy [COM(2006) 35 final].

European Commission (2010) Youth on the Move. An initiative to unleash the potential of young people to achieve smart, sustainable, and inclusive growth in the European Union. Brussels: Communication from the Commission to the European Parliament, the Council, the European Economic and Social Committee, and the Committee of the Regions [COM(2010) 477 final].

European Commission (2011) Community System of Documentation on Employment: Youth Employment Measures. European Employment Observatory Review 2010 [COM(2011) SYSDEM].

European Parliament (2008) European Parliament resolution of 13 January 2009 on the perspectives for developing civil dialogue under the Treaty of Lisbon [2008/2067(INI)].

Greenwood, J. (2003) *Interest Representation in the European Union* (Houndmills: Palgrave).

Héritier, A., D. Kerwer, C. Knill, D. Lehmkuhl, M. Teutsch, and A.-C. Douillet (eds) (2001) *Differential Europe: The European Union Impact on National Policymaking*. *Governance in Europe* (Lanham, MD: Rowman & Littlefield).

Imig, D. and S. Tarrow (2001) "Studying Contention in an Emerging Polity," in Imig, D. and S. Tarrow (eds), *Contentious Europeans: Protest and Politics in an Emerging Polity* (Lanham: Rowman & Littlefield).

Jenkins, J. C. (1983) "Resource Mobilization Theory and the Study of Social Movements," *Annual Review of Sociology*, 9, 527–553.

Klüver, H. (2010) "Europeanization of Lobbying Activities: When National Interest Groups Spill Over to the European Level," *Journal of European Integration*, 32, 175–191.

Knill, C., J. Tosun, and M.W. Bauer (2009) "Neglected Faces of Europeanization: The Differential Impact of the EU on the Dismantling and Expansion of Domestic Policies," *Public Administration*, 87, 519–537.

Kohler-Koch, B. (2010) "How to Put Matters Right – Assessing the Role of Civil Society in EU Accountability," *West European Politics*, 33, 1117–1141.

Kohler-Koch, B. and C. Quittkat (2013) *De-mystification of Participatory Democracy: EU-Governance and Civil Society* (Oxford: Oxford University Press).

Kröger, S. (2008) "Nothing but Consultation: The Place of Organised Civil Society in EU Policy-Making across Policies," *European Governance Papers* (EUROGOV), Nr. C-08-03.

Lahusen, C. (2004) "Joining the Cocktail-Circuit: Social Movement Organizations at the European Union," *Mobilization*, 9, 55–71.

Lahusen, C. and C. Jauß (2001) *Lobbying als Beruf: Interessengruppen in der Europäischen Union* (Baden-Baden: Nomos).

Liebert, U. and H.-J. Trenz (eds) (2010) *The New Politics of European Civil Society* (London: Routledge).

Maloney, W. A. and J. W. van Deth (2008) *Civil Society and Governance in Europe: From National to International Linkages* (Glos: Edward Elgar).

Maloney, W. A. and J. W. van Deth (2010) *Civil Society and Activism in Europe: Contextualizing Engagement and Political Orientations* (London: Routledge).

Marks, G. and D. McAdam (1999) "On the Relationship of Political Opportunities to the Form of Collective Action: The Case of the European Union," in della Porta, D., H. Kriesi, and D. Rucht (eds), *Social Movements in a Globalizing World* (London: Macmillan Press).

Marks, G., L. Hooghe, and K. Blank (1996) "European Integration from the 1980s: State-Centric vs Multi-level Governance," *Journal of Common Market Studies*, 34, 341–378.

McCarthy, J. D. and M. N. Zald (1973) *The Trend of Social Movements in America: Professionalization and Resource Mobilization* (Morristown, NJ: General Learning Corporation).

Merton, R. (1957) *Social Theory and Social Structure* (Glencoe, IL: The Free Press).

Michels, R. (1962) *Political Parties: A Sociological Study of the Oligarchical Tendencies of Modern Democracy* (New York: Free Press).

Neunreither, K. (1995) "Citizens and the Exercise of Power in the European Union: Towards a New Social Contract?" In Rosas, A. and E. Antola (eds), *A Citizens' Europe: In Search of a New Order* (London: Sage).

Petrova, T. and S. Tarrow (2007) "Transactional and Participatory Activism in the Emerging European Polity: The Puzzle of East Central Europe," *Comparative Political Studies*, 40, 74–94.

Rucht, D. (2001) "Lobbying or Protest: Strategies to Influence EU Environmental Policies," in Imig, D. and S. Tarrow (eds), *Contentious Europeans: Protest and Politics in an Integrating Europe* (Boulder, CO: Rowman & Littlefield).

Ruzza, C. and E. Bozzini (2008) "Organised Civil Society and European Governance: Routes of Contestation," *European Political Science*, 7, 296–303.

Salamon L. M. and H. K. Anheier (1998) "Social Origins of Civil Society: Explaining the Nonprofit Sector Cross-Nationally," *Voluntas*, 9, 213–248.

Smismans, S. (2003) "European Civil Society: Shaped by Discourses and Institutional Interests," *European Law Journal*, 9, 473–495.

Smismans, S. (ed.) (2006) *Civil Society and Legitimate European Governance* (Cheltenham: Elgar).

Staggenborg, S. (1988) "The Consequences of Professionalization and Formalization in the Pro-Choice Movement," *American Sociological Review*, 53, 585–605.

Steffek, J. and K. Hahn (eds) (2010) *Evaluating Transnational NGOs: Legitimacy, Accountability, Representation* (Basingstoke: Palgrave Macmillan).

Tarrow, S. (1998) *Power in Movement: Social Movements and Contentious Politics* (Cambridge: Cambridge University Press).

Woll, C. and S. Jacquot (2010) "Using Europe: Strategic Action in Multi-Level Politics," *Comparative European Politics*, 8, 110–126.

Civil Society, Unemployment, and Precarity in Europe: A Conclusion

Marco Giugni and Simone Baglioni

Civil society organizations play a crucial role in the inclusion of resource-poor and deprived people who are at risk of exclusion. Young unemployed people are one such group. In fact, civil society organizations are important for people in general, as they contribute to the vitality of democracy, for example, by creating social capital which, in turn, benefits norms of cooperation, solidarity, and reciprocity (Putnam 1993, 2000). However, the role they play for young unemployed people as well as precarious young workers is particularly important as these are among the most fragile sectors of European societies.

In this concluding chapter we would like to briefly summarize the main findings of the analyses presented in the chapters comprising this book. We shall do so by highlighting four key issues stemming from the previous analysis and discussions: (1) the place of civil society organizations within the multi-organizational field of unemployment and precarity; (2) their role with regard to helping unemployed and precariously employed young people cope with the problem of joblessness or underemployment, in particular by stressing their dual role in terms of service providers and political actors; (3) the importance of the broader context both for their survival and for functioning; and (4) the relations between the local, the national, and the European levels in which civil society organizations in this field may act.

The multi-organizational field of unemployment and precarity

There are multiple organizations active in the field of unemployment and precarity. Although only a minority of them focus upon young people, they provide a variety of ways in which unemployed and precariously employed young people may be supported. In this sense, we can speak of a multi-organizational field (Curtis and Zurcher 1973) of unemployment and precarity, meaning that "the total possible number of organizations with which the movement organization might establish specific links" (Klandermans 2013: 796). As the previous chapters demonstrate, these include civil society organizations – that is, organizations which emerge in the space delimited by the state on the one hand and by the market on the other (Wuthnow 1991), including social movement organizations – religious organizations, trade unions, political parties as well as (although only in some contexts) other organizational types such as social cooperatives, not for profit service centers, and for profit service centers. This book has addressed the multi-organizational field of unemployment and precarity essentially from two different yet interrelated angles: from the angle of organizational characteristics and attributes and from the angle of their networks of exchanges and collaborations.

Concerning the first aspect, civil society organizations feature different levels of resources and types of activities. This is clearly illustrated in Chapter 3 by Mota and Mourão, who reveal that organizations vary considerably in terms of their personal and financial resources. The authors find that smaller organizations depend heavily upon volunteers for their survival and for carrying out their activities: unable to hire paid staff, they must rely upon the will of people who can invest in the organization without being paid. Most interestingly, the authors show that resources and activities are mutually related. In their analysis, the main domain of activity is a good predictor of organizational resources and professionalization. This finding reflects what others have found more specifically in relation to social movement organizations (Kriesi 1996) and suggests that organizations which are interested in internal growth and structuring should pay greater attention to what they do. Specifically, we need to examine both the role of associations in providing a number of services to their stakeholders – in this case, unemployed and precariously employed young people – as examined in Chapter 2 by Hobbins, Eriksson, and Bacia and their political role as they advocate for more and better rights for these same young people, as analyzed in Chapter 1 by Baglioni, Lorenzini, and Mosca. Concerning the latter, a particularly interesting research avenue consists in looking at what may impact upon the degree of politicization of the organizations, an aspect addressed in Chapter 4 by Cinalli and Giugni.

Concerning the second aspect, the multi-organizational field of unemployment and precarity is not only composed of single and isolated associations but is above all comprised of the relations between them. We therefore devoted an entire section of the book to the analysis of organizational networks. Chapter 5 by Bassoli and Cinalli has provided a picture of the organizational networks in the seven cities included in the study. They reveal how networks may vary in terms of a number of criteria such as scope, heterogeneity, reciprocity, coreness, centralization, dispersion, and positioning. They also indicate that there is a strong connection between state policies and the relational nature of civil society organizations, in the sense that the former need to be appraised in terms of relational outcomes in this field. Similarly, the analyses in Chapter 5 by Bassoli and Cinalli, and in Chapter 6 by Lahusen and Grimmer, and in Chapter 7 by Bassoli, Cinalli, and Giugni, all demonstrate the internal functioning of organizational networks in terms of, respectively, cooperation, brokerage, and information, and how such patterns of exchange among associations vary across cities. Finally, one must not forget to analyze how local civil society organizations may or – more often than not – may not branch out to reach the national or even the EU level, as has been explained by Lahusen in Chapter 9.

Civil society organizations between service and policy

The various chapters in this book have revealed a number of ways in which civil society organizations can help unemployed and precariously employed young people mitigate the negative consequences of the lack of paid work or a precarious position in the labor market. At the most fundamental level, there are two different ways in which they do so, which have been outlined in the introductory chapter. On the one hand, civil society organizations active in the field of unemployment and precarity may focus their activities upon service provisions. This can range from advising unemployed people on finding a job to financial and moral support. On the other hand, some organizations are inclined to take a more political role and engage in policy-related activities such as political lobbying, representation, and mobilization. These two different orientations underscore two distinct patterns through which civil society organizations may seek the social and political inclusion of unemployed and precariously employed young people: a service-oriented pattern characterized by inclusion via service delivery and a policy-oriented pattern of inclusion via the direct actions of individuals.

This distinction has informed many of the chapters in this volume, some overtly and others in a more implicit fashion. Thus, Chapter 2 by Hobbins, Eriksson, and Bacia and Chapter 1 by Baglioni, Lorenzini, and Mosca have respectively dealt with the role played by service-oriented and policy-oriented civil society organizations. There we have learned, on the one hand, that the former can be grouped along four main clusters of strategies aimed at achieving the goals of improving social integration or alleviating the consequences of poverty: work or work-related activities, services directed at the welfare system, services directed at individual psychosocial counseling, and finally activities related to the political structure. Within this range of strategies, work-related activities and activities aimed at increasing employability have a prominent position. We have also learned, on the other hand, that the degree of politicization of civil society organizations varies and that both service-oriented and policy-oriented organizations may establish political collaborations or ties with local political institutions, although the latter of course are more inclined to engage in political activities than the former.

This distinction between service and policy orientations is not only reflected in the specific activities of civil society organizations in this field but also characterizes the relations between these organizations. As the analysis conducted on the cities of Cologne and Turin in Chapter 6 by Lahusen and Grimmer in particular has demonstrated, civil society organizations tend to cooperate with organizations that possess similar organizational traits. Thus, for example, one observes more collaboration between organizations that have a policy orientation or, even more narrowly, that are protest-oriented. Cooperation across different kinds of associations, in contrast, proves more difficult.

The presence of a service/policy divide among civil society organizations in the field of unemployment and precarity points to a rather fragmented organizational network, where little cooperation exists across this divide. Moreover, other sources of heterogeneity, in addition to the associations' general orientation, such as, for example, a different ideological stance, might further prevent them from working together. The comparison between Kielce and Turin made in Chapter 8 by Bassoli and Theiss is a good example of this, as they highlight the importance of the values shared by civil society organizations in information exchange networks. In this sense, a normative affiliation facilitates exchange among associations, thereby strengthening the internal cohesion of the organizational network.

More generally speaking, Chapter 5 by Bassoli and Cinalli shows to what extent the degree of fragmentation – or the degree of internal coherence – of organizational networks in this field varies across cities. Given such fragmentation, the existence of key actors may assist civil society organizations in cooperating. Specifically, the presence of different types of brokers among the organizations might favor communication and exchanges between them. Such brokers, as Chapter 7 by Bassoli, Cinalli, and Giugni indicates, might play the role of gatekeeping, representation, or coordination, therefore leading to an increased horizontal integration of the civil society sector as well as to a stronger vertical integration with the policy domain. These authors emphasize in particular the importance of gatekeeping for the nexus between political engagement and brokerage.

The importance of the context

Civil society organizations do not operate in a vacuum. On the contrary, they are embedded in a broader context – social, cultural, and political – that influences their characteristics and activities, both constraining and enabling them. Many of the chapters in this volume have highlighted how context has a strong impact not only on the attributes of civil society organizations but also on their networks of exchanges and relations. Indeed, this dimension is central throughout the book.

Social movement scholars have emphasized for some time the crucial role played by the political context in increasing or decreasing the prospects of citizens making use of their internal resources to form social movements (Tarrow 2011). The concept of the political opportunity structure (Eisinger 1973; see further Kriesi 2004 and Meyer 2004) is obviously associated with this idea. First used to capture certain features of the institutional context – such as the degree of openness or closedness of the political system, the structure of political alignments, and the capacity and propensity of elites to use repression (McAdam 1996) – this concept has more recently been refined so as to include issue-specific or domain-specific aspects (Berclaz and Giugni 2005; Giugni 2009).

This more specific approach has recently been applied to the field of unemployment politics. In a previous study (Giugni 2010) we demonstrated that public claims-making on unemployment is channeled in important ways by what we termed "welfare state regimes," that is, the ways in which the state deals with unemployment regulations as well as labor market regulations. Providing a varying mixture of both institutional and discursive opportunities for collective action in the field, these contextual aspects account for cross-national variations in the "contentious politics of unemployment," that is, the relationships between political institutional approaches to employment policy and political conflicts mobilized by collective actors over unemployment in the public domain.

This approach has also informed the research project on which this volume rests and therefore the volume itself. It has been applied most explicitly in Chapter 4 by Cinalli and Giugni, in which the authors reveal how the political context impacts upon the politicization of civil society organizations. Based on their own previous work (Cinalli and Giugni 2013), they examine in particular the impact of general and issue-specific opportunities on two aspects of politicization: the general engagement of associations in political activities and their use of protest activities. Their findings clearly point to the important role played by political opportunity structures – in other words, by the institutional context – for organizational positioning in the field of unemployment and precarity. Although the relationship between opportunity and politicization is sometimes a curvilinear rather than a linear one, this analysis suggests that we can hardly study civil society organizations in this field – but also in general, for that matter – without taking into account the fact that what they do is affected by where they are.

However the institutional context matters in many other ways as well, not only for the inclination of civil society organizations to engage politically. This is most evident in Chapter 1 by Baglioni, Lorenzini, and Mosca. Their analysis points to the crucial impact of specific political opportunity structures (in terms of unemployment regulations) on policy-oriented organizations. Their analysis also reveals that there is a functional differentiation of civil society organizations in the field which depends upon the degree of inclusiveness in terms of unemployment policies. In a similar fashion, Chapter 2 by Hobbins, Eriksson, and Bacia suggests that, at least to some extent, welfare regime models matter when accounting for the strategies implemented by organizations when they engage in service-oriented activities. Interestingly, this goes hand in hand with the observation that none of the various welfare regime models, such as those famously distinguished by Esping-Andersen (1990) in his seminal study, provide for the needs of the weakest groups in a sufficient fashion.

Furthermore, analyses in this volume have stressed the role of context, not only in the resources and activities of civil society organizations but also in the ways in which interactions take place between them. In other words, the context also impacts upon the organizational networks. In a sense, all of the chapters in the book's second part provide insights into this nexus in some way. This is certainly true for Chapter 5 by Bassoli and Cinalli. Their analysis finds that there is a strong relationship between the relational characteristics of the multi-organizational field of unemployment and the exogenous characteristics of the political context. Specifically, actors have more self-management and control in contexts of inclusive unemployment policies than in contexts characterized by an exclusive approach.

Nevertheless, the importance of context is also present – implicitly or explicitly – in the other chapters. Take, for example, the analysis in Chapter 6 by Lahusen and Grimmer, who find that the organizational structures of local civil societies are patterned by the societal environment in which they act as well as by the relations between civil society organizations and public authorities. The power structures of the local policy domain have a differentiating impact on network ties among civil society organizations, forcing associations to adopt either a cooperative or a more confrontational approach and pushing advocacy organizations into a minority position while expanding the range of actions for their more moderate and service-oriented counterparts.

Finally, beyond the institutional environment, the broader cultural context also plays an important role in this respect. Bassoli and Theiss, in Chapter 8, point to the impact of shared values – both in terms of leftist and catholic ideological orientations – on the exchange networks of civil society organizations in the field of unemployment and precarity. Specifically, they highlight the hegemonic position of the Catholic coalition in Kielce while a bipolar network structure can be observed in Turin. One explanation they suggest for this is that some values count more in certain cultural contexts. Thus, in the specific cases they studied, the Catholic tradition can be an asset for an organization in Kielce, while in Turin the decline of Communist ideology has diminished the impact of this political and ideological cleavage.

Civil society organizations dealing with unemployment and precarity: local, national and European

The study on which this book rests has been conducted at the local level. Accordingly, the mapping of the civil society organizations to be analyzed has been done within cities. A variety of reasons led us to opt for this level of analysis, not least the fact that this is the level at which organizations most often act and have a direct link to both their constituency and the people on whose behalf they work. This does not mean that our findings have relevance only at that level, although this is obviously the most crucial one. Both the national and supranational levels, as well as their connections with the local level, play an important role as well.

The national level is important, among other things, because it provides a second layer of context – in addition to the local context – which may constrain or enable civil society organizations in their everyday work. As discussed in the previous section, the structure, activities, and the networks of organizations are strongly dependent upon both the general (in terms of political structures and configurations) and the specific (in terms of welfare and unemployment regimes) features of the political opportunity structures that characterize a given country at the national level and a given city at the local level.

The European level is perhaps the most neglected aspect in studies of civil society organizations and their impact; this reflects the difficulty that civil society actors have experienced in properly engaging at the EU level (Balme et al. 2002; Balme and Chabanet 2008; Imig and Tarrow 2001) but also the highly selective and exclusive approach the EU institutions have adopted when opening their policy processes to civil society, not to mention a stronger interest among EU scholars in state or institutional actors (Wallace 2005). While this book has focused upon the local level and its connections with the national level, Chapter 9 by Lahusen has addressed the EU level. His analysis ruthlessly points to the endemic problems of the relations between EU institutions and local realities. In particular, the author has highlighted the distance that exists, due to structural obstacles, between the local level of civil society organizations and the European arena. As a result, local associations adapt to working in specific local contexts and entertain only limited relations with EU institutions. The author argues that some kind of formal organization is needed in order to overcome such an institutional distance characterized by a high degree of bureaucratization and where the weakest groups tend to be excluded from those places in which issues are discussed and decisions are taken. As Lahusen also points out, the negative – or perhaps perverse – effect of all of this is that, in the end, the EU does not really benefit from local civil society organizations, and that this is in spite of the often evoked rhetoric that these organizations are a crucial resource for the EU in terms of finding solutions to the increasingly alarming problem of youth unemployment and precarity.

This state of affairs might lead – or perhaps it has already led – to a situation in which there is a mismatch between discourse and practice. On the one hand, there is the discourse articulated by EU institutions, but also by national and local elites regarding the need to improve the situation of unemployed and precariously employed young people, in terms of their employability as well as their social and political inclusion – but also, at the collective level, in terms of social cohesion – and the crucial role to be played by civil society organizations in this process. On the other hand, such a discourse collides with the reality that little consideration is given to the work carried out by civil society organizations, or the marginalization of some of them – especially the most politicized groups – or indeed the poor level of dialogue between local associations and local, national, and especially EU-level policy-makers. Redressing this situation is the first step towards a more effective role that can be played by civil society organizations in the field of unemployment and precarity, but also towards a more effective, better informed and participative form of policy-making.

Future research and policy recommendations

This book leaves some questions open which therefore calls for further research in this field. One possible avenue for future research consists in trying to better understand exactly what makes civil society organizations effective in promoting the interests of unemployed and precariously employed young people – and indeed precarious workers and the unemployed in general – as well as helping their social and political integration. In this book we have explored two such avenues: by providing specific services or by advocating policy reforms that would benefit the unemployed and precarious workers. We have shown that both paths can have beneficial effects, under certain circumstances, and have tried to demonstrate how and when this occurs. However, much more needs to be done in this regard. Research conducted on the impact of voluntary associations on political participation, for example, has stressed the fact that the direction of causality is far from being clear and straightforward. In other words, the correlation between associational involvement and trust, found in a wealth of studies, could be due to a self-selection effect, those being more trustful being more likely to get involved in voluntary associations (Bekkers 2012; Sønderskov 2011). So, while these studies deal with the relationship between trust and associational involvement at the individual level, we need to spell out more effectively the mechanisms through which associations may or may not help unemployed and precariously employed young people to be more participative and better integrated, both socially and politically. The use of panel data is of course one way to grasp this.

A second avenue for future research also refers to causality in some way. In this book, although the relevant literature follows the same direction, we have looked at civil society organizations active in the field of unemployment and precarity, focusing on their impact upon the situation of unemployed and precariously employed young people. But what if we consider this the other way around? What is the impact of unemployed and precariously employed young people on civil society organizations? We should not only ask what civil society can give to certain social groups that are disadvantaged or at risk of exclusion but also what the latter have to offer to the former. In other words, we need to reverse the causal order from the outset, that is, from the research questions, then implement a design which allows us to address this aspect.

In this regard, a third avenue for future research lies in a deeper analysis of the contribution of civil society organizations as well as of unemployed and precariously employed young people toward policy formulation and implementation. While this varies greatly from one country to another, civil society organizations are often included in policy formulation – if only in a consultative role – and, especially, in implementation. In this sense, complex societies are often characterized by an ambivalent relationship between civil society organizations and policy actors, one in which the former may act both in a conflicting and in a cooperative mode (Giugni and Passy 1998). In a way, this book has confirmed this, insofar as service provision and policy advocacy represent these two sides of the coin. The task for future research is to spell out more clearly those processes which lead to civil society organizations and the social groups on whose behalf they act, having an impact upon policy-making.

References

Balme, R. and D. Chabanet (2008) *European Governance and Democracy. Power and Protest in the EU* (Lanham: Rowman and Littlefield).

Balme, R., D. Chabanet, and V. Wright (2002) *L'action collective en Europe* (Paris: Presses de la Fondation Nationale des Sciences Politiques).

Bekkers, R. (2012) "Trust and Volunteering: Selection or Causation? Evidence from a 4 Year Panel Study," *Political Behavior*, 34: 225–247.

Berclaz, J. and M. Giugni (2005) Specifying the Concept of Political Opportunity Structures," in Kousis, M. and C. Tilly (eds), *Economic and Political Contention in Comparative Perspective* (Boulder, CO: Paradigm).

Cinalli, M. and M. Giugni (2013) "New Challenges for the Welfare State: The Emergence of 'Youth Unemployment Regimes' in Europe?" *International Journal of Social Welfare*, 22: 290–299.

Curtis, R. L. and L. A. Zurcher (1973) "Stable Resources of Protest Movements: The Multi-Organizational Field," *Social Forces*, 52: 53–61.

Eisinger, P. K. (1973) "The Conditions of Protest Behavior in American Cities," *American Political Science Review*, 67: 11–28.

Esping-Andersen, G. (1990) *The Three Worlds of Welfare Capitalism* (Princeton, NJ: Princeton University Press).

Giugni, M. (2009) "Political Opportunities: From Tilly to Tilly," *Swiss Political Science Review*, 15: 361–368.

Giugni, M. (ed.) (2010) *The Contentious Politics of Unemployment in Europe: Welfare States and Political Opportunities* (Houndmills: Palgrave).

Giugni, M. and F. Passy (1998) "Contentious Politics in Complex Societies: New Social Movements between Conflict and Cooperation," pp. 81–107 in Giugni, M., D. McAdam, and C. Tilly (eds), *From Contention to Democracy* (Lanham, MD: Rowman and Littlefield).

Imig, D. and S. Tarrow (eds) (2001) *Contentious Europeans: Politics and Protest in a Composite Polity* (Lanham: Rowman and Littlefield).

Klandermans, B. (2013) "Multiorganizational Fields," in Snow D. A., D. della Porta, B. Klandermans, and D. McAdam (eds), *The Wiley-Blackwell Encyclopedia of Social and Political Movements* (Oxford: Blackwell).

Kriesi, H. (1996) "The Organizational Structure of News Social Movements in a Political Context," in McAdam, D., J. D. McCarthy, and M. N. Zald (eds), *Comparative Perspectives on Social Movements* (Cambridge: Cambridge University Press).

Kriesi, H. (2004) "Political Context and Opportunity," in Snow, D. A., S. Soule, and H. Kriesi (eds), *The Blackwell Companion to Social Movements* (Oxford: Blackwell).

McAdam, D. (1996) "Conceptual Origins, Current Problems, Future Directions," in McAdam, D., J. D. McCarthy, and M. N. Zald (eds), *Comparative Perspectives on Social Movements* (Cambridge: Cambridge University Press).

Meyer, D. S. (2004) "Protest and Political Opportunities," *Annual Review of Sociology*, 30: 125–45.

Putnam, R. D. (1993) *Making Democracy Work: Civic Traditions in Modern Italy* (Princeton, NJ: Princeton University Press).

Putnam, R. D. (2000) *Bowling Alone: The Collapse and Revival of American Community* (New York: Simon & Schuster).

Sønderskov, K. M. (2011) "Does Generalized Social Trust Lead to Associational Membership? Unravelling a Bowl of Well-Tossed Spaghetti," *European Sociological Review*, 27: 419–343.

Tarrow, S. (2011) *Power in Movement: Social Movements and Contentious Politics* (Cambridge: Cambridge University Press).

Wallace, W. (2005) "Post-Sovereign Governance: The EU as a Partial Polity," in Wallace, H., W. Wallace, and M. A. Pollack (eds) *Policy Making in the European Union*, 5th ed. (Oxford: Oxford University Press).

Wuthnow, R. (1991) *Between States and Markets: The Voluntary Sector in Comparative Perspective* (Princeton, NJ: Princeton University Press).

Index

Printed and bound by CPI Group (UK) Ltd, Croydon, CR0 4YY